DEATHS AND MARRIAGES
FROM
TARBORO, NORTH CAROLINA
NEWSPAPERS

1824-1865

By
Hugh Buckner Johnston
Wilson, North Carolina
1983

Please Direct All Correspondence and Book Orders to:
Southern Historical Press, Inc.
PO Box 1267
375 West Broad Street
Greenville, SC 29602-1267
or
southernhistoricalpress@gmail.com

ISBN #0-89308-558-8

Dedicated To My Father

HUGH BOLDEN JOHNSTON

(April 16, 1889--December 6, 1958)

A Worthy Son of Edgecombe County

TABLE OF CONTENTS

INTRODUCTION

The reader will note that I have used abbreviations in the text to indicate the identifications of the several newspapers utilized in the present compilation of <u>Death And Marriage Notices From Tarboro Newspapers, 1824-1865</u>, and it will undoubtedly be helpful if I present these names here in their full forms, since someone may feel a desire from time to time to refer to the original records in the microfilm collections at the North Carolina Department of Archives and History in Raleigh, North Carolina.

F. P.   The Free Press.
N. C.   The North Carolinian.
N. C. P.   The North Carolina Press.
N. C. F. P.   The North-Carolina Free Press.
P. S.   Political Synopsis.
S.   The Southerner.
T. M.   The Tarboro' Mercury.
T. P.   The Tarborough Press.
T. S.   The Tarboro' Scaevola.

I have endeavored to be thorough in my summarizations of the names, dates, and other facts of biographic interest, although in many instances these details were disappointingly brief. It will also be of interest that there were many references to persons who had died in other Counties and States than Edgecombe County itself. I have normally ignored the literary and sometimes poetic effusions that appeared from time to time in a formal Obituary submitted by an admiring friend or relative. (These may have interested a modern literary enthusiast or have had some sentimental value for an occasional direct descendant five or six generations removed.)

It is rather surprising to note what a sizeable percentage of the Death Notices pertained to children and even to infants. On the other hand, we could naturally anticipate the attention paid to the final departure of merchants, planters, public officials, ministers, and even of the few aged veterans left from the Revolutionary War. A number of individuals who would otherwise have vanished into impoverished obscurity were recognized in print because they were murdered or happened to suffer some other violent and newsworthy departure from earthly life.

In the category of Marriages, the newspaper notices often provided the name of the father of the bride, a valuable detail normally unavailable from the Marriage Bonds surviving from that period of County Records. There were also frequent geographic identifications of the bride or the groom with a County neighboring upon Edgecombe County, and sometimes even with another State to the north, south, or west of North Carolina. The Minister or Justice of the Peace who performed the ceremony was often called by name, and the former provided a persuasive identification of the probable religious affiliation of the bride's (and often of the groom's) family at that period of history.

  I shall leave to some specialist in the history of early North Carolina newspapers the presentation of a detailed discussion of the Editors and Publishers associated for varying periods of time with the nine publications involved in the present statistical compilation. However, I cannot conclude without recognizing the truly outstanding contributions made by the Howard family in their leadership in both the social and the literary advancement of the Edgecombe County area during the Ante- and Post-Bellum periods of its history.

Hugh Buckner JOHNSTON
Wilson, North Carolina
November 10, 1983

INDEX TO DEATH NOTICES
IN
TARBORO NEWSPAPERS
1824-1865

By
Hugh Buckner Johnston

Wilson, North Carolina
1983

Mrs. Penelope ABINGDON died at Tarboro on October 17, 1855, aged about sixty, leaving no immediate family. (S. October, 20, 1855)

John ABRAMS died at Tarboro on August 7, 1828, as a result of blows inflicted on him a week earlier by David Hattaway of Halifax County in "a drunken frolic." The Superior Court later found Hattaway guilty of manslaughter, fining him $10 and costs with sixty days in jail. (F. P. August 15, 1828)

Miss Lucretia ADAMS was raped and murdered in Pitt County on September 24, 1860, for which Bryan Grimes's slave Henry was tried in the Superior Court. (S. March 23, 1861, page 1, columns 1/2)

Lewewellen Carter ADKINS, son of William ADKINS, died of brain fever in Edgecombe County on January 24, 1863, aged eight years and five months. (S. January 31, 1863)

Alexander ALLEN of Johnston County "was shot in the abdomen by a woman of doubtful character, near Smithfield, on Saturday last. [July 17] The wound is supposed to be mortal." (S. July 24, 1858)

James E. ALLEN, son of John H. ALLEN of Tarboro, died at Gravel Hill, Virginia, on July 26, 1862, aged about 20. He was a member of Captain Foxhall's Confederate Guards and had been wounded by a shell on July 2, 1862. (S. August 9, 1862)

Mrs. Temperance ALSOBROOK, wife of William ALSOBROOK, died in Edgecombe County on November 30, 1826, aged 26 and leaving two children. (F. P. December 26, 1826)

General Vine ALLEN died at New Bern on July 10, 1829, in his fifty-first year. (F. P. July 24, 1829)

Erasmus G. ALSTON died in Halifax on August 29, 1834, of pistol wounds at the hands of Arthur McDaniel who had shot in self-defense. (T. F. P. September 5, 1834)

Gideon ALSTON died in Halifax County on November 10, 1831, in his sixty-fifth year. (N. C. F. P. November 22, 1831)

Gideon ALSTON, Jr., died in Warren County on March 27, 1828, leaving a wife and two small children. (F.P. April 11, 1828)

General John ALSTON died in Halifax County on April 2, 1831, in his fifty-seventh year. (N. C. F. P. April 12, 1831)

Hon. Willis ALSTON of Halifax County died on April 13, 1837, aged seventy-one, having served in the N. C. Legislature and in Congress. (T. P. May 6, 1837)

Barnes AMASON died in Stantonsburg on April 13, 1844, aged about twenty-eight years. (T. P. April 20, 1844)

Roderick AMASON died in Edgecombe County on December 30, 1844. (T. P. January 4, 1845)

Thomas AMASON died near Jameston, Alabama, on January 4, 1843, being formerly of Edgecombe County. (T. P. January 28, 1843)

Mrs. Thomas AMASON died "a few days since." (N. C. F. P. April 17, 1832)

Andrew ANDERSON probably died on the night of February 29, 1836. His body was found on March 7, "partly devoured by hogs." An inquest was held over his body on March 8, 1836. (T. P. March 12, 1836)

Dr. Athelston ANDERSON died in Nashville on August 17, 1826. (T. P. August 29, 1826)

Mrs. Martha ANDERSON, wife of William ANDERSON, died on July 5, 1833, aged about seventy years. (N. C. F. P. July 13, 1833)

Colonel Ruel ANDERSON died in Pitt County on Friday, September 13, 1839. (T. P. September 21, 1839)

William ANDERSON, "a Revolutionary soldier," died in Edgecombe County on October 22, 1834, aged eighty years. (T. F. P. November 7, 1834)

Mrs. Elizabeth H. ANDREWS, wife of the late Colonel John P. ANDREWS of Warren County, died near Kittrell's Springs in Granville County on February 28, 1864, in her fifty-third year. (S. March 19, 1864)

Jane ANDREWS, daughter of William J. ANDREWS, died "a few days since aged about three years. (T. P. November 28, 1840)

Mrs. Nancy ANDREWS, widow of Whitney ANDREWS, died in Edgecombe County
on June 26, 1860. She had been born on April 2, 1766. (S. July
21, 1860)

Col. Whitmel H. ANTHONY died in Halifax County on October 30, 1851, aged
about forty years. (T. P. November 8, 1851)

Mrs. Martha Ann ARMSTRONG, wife of Gray ARMSTRONG, died in Edgecombe
County on May 15, 1849. (T. P. May 19, 1849)

Walter Cadwallader ARMSTRONG, son of Dr. S. D. ARMSTRONG, was born on
September 6, 1847, and died on May 16, 1850, at Rocky Mount. (T. P.
May 25, 1850)

J. P. ARNOT died in Halifax "a few days since." (F. P. January 30, 1829)

Mrs. Elizabeth ARRINGTON, wife of Dr. Joseph ARRINGTON, died in Nash
County on July 23, 1827. (F. P. July 28, 1827)

Mrs. Elizabeth ARRINGTON, wife of Arthur ARRINGTON and daughter of the
late John A. Irvin of Edgecombe County, died in Nash County on
September 25, 1831, leaving an infant. (N. C. F. P. September 27,
1831)

John ARRINGTON, Esq., died in Nash County on April 27, 1844, in his
eighty-first year and leaving three children. (T. P. May 11, 1844)

Mrs. Maria ARRINGTON, wife of Richard ARRINGTON, Esq., died in Nash
County on July 31, 1826. (T. P. August 29, 1826)

Mrs. Martha S. ARRINGTON, wife of the late Dr. John ARRINGTON of Nash
County, died at Warrenton on January 30, 1848, in her forty-third
year. (T. P. February 19, 1848)

Mrs. Mourning ARRINGTON, wife of Joseph ARRINGTON of Nash County, died
"a few days since." (F. P. May 5, 1827)

Mourning R. ARRINGTON, only daughter of Carter ARRINGTON, died in Halifax County after being sick for nine days and in her seventeenth
year, leaving her parents and brothers. (T. S. May 15, 1837 and
June 2, 1837)

Peter ARRINGTON died in Nash County on September 13, 1852, aged forty-
eight years. (S. October 2, 1852)

Peter ARRINGTON, Sr., died in Nash County on July 3, 1837, in his seventieth year, leaving a wife and six children. (T. P. July 15, 1837)

Mrs. Rhoda ARRINGTON died in Halifax County in her sixty-fifth year,
leaving two children and several grandchildren, date of death not
stated. (S. September 10, 1853)

Richard ARRINGTON, eldest son of Crawford ARRINGTON of Nash County, died
on November 4, 1843, in his twenty-first year. (T. P. November 25,
1843)

Robert Ricks ARRINGTON, formerly of Nash County, died in his thirty-first
year recently in Twiggs County, Georgia. (T. P. April 15, 1846)

Mrs. Sue ARRINGTON, wife of S. P. ARRINGTON, Esq., died at the age of
nineteen at the home of her father, William Eaton, Jr., of Warrenton, on September 20, 1858. (S. September 25, 1858)

Aaron ATKINSON, son of Willie ATKINSON, died in Edgecombe County on
November 16, 1847. He appears to have been born on July 12, 1837.
(T. P. November 27, 1847)

Benashley ATKINSON died in Pitt County on October 1, 1839. Sharlon
Lodge, No. 78, scheduled a Masonic Funeral for Sunday, October 20,
at his residence at Bensboro' eight miles N. W. of Greenville on
the road to Tarboro. (T. P. October 12, 1839)

Mrs. B. P. ATKINSON, wife of Robert ATKINSON and daughter of William and
Elizabeth Biggs of Edgecombe County, was from Halifax County but
died in Hinds County, Mississippi, on May 26, 1854, aged twenty-
five years. (S. July 8, 1854)

Mrs. Esther ATKINSON, widow of the Rev. John A. ATKINSON, died at the
home of Mrs. Mary Ruffin of Edgecombe County on August 14, 1843.

(T. P. August 19, 1843)

Mrs. Mary A. ATKINSON, wife of Alvin ATKINSON, Esq., of Wilson County, was murdered on April 11, 1858, in lower Johnston County by a negro boy belonging to Lovitt Atkinson, Esq. According to the Wilson Ledger, she died "by a blow upon the head by an axe in the hands of said negro......The negro was arrested and lodged in jail." (S. May 1, 1858, and May 8, 1858)

Payton A. ATKINSON, "a wealthy planter" of Pitt County, died of dyspepsia on February 22, 1863, aged about forty years. (S. March 7, 1863)

Mrs. Rebecca B. ATKINSON, wife of Benashly ATKINSON and daughter of Peyton R. Tunstall, Esq., died in Pitt County on September 27, 1829, in her twenty-seventh year. (F. P. October 23, 1829)

Henry AUSTIN, Esq., died at Tarboro on February 11, 1845, aged seventy years, leaving a wife and four children. He had been merchant, magistrate, and Baptist. (T. P. February 15, 1845)

Mrs. Jannette AUSTIN, wife of Robert H. AUSTIN and daughter of William Jeffreys of Franklin County, died of consumption in Tarboro on August 30, 1850, leaving three children. (S. September 4, 1858)

Mrs. Lydia AUSTIN, widow of Henry AUSTIN, died on January 9, 1853, in her seventy-first year. (S. January 15, 1853)

John AVENT of Nash County was killed about October 8, 1859, in a hunting accident. (S. October 15, 1859)

Alexander AVERYT, Esq., died "lately" in Johnston County, in his ninety-fourth year, being one of the last three members of the Halifax Congress of 1776 that adopted the North Carolina Constitution. (N. C. F. P. March 20, 1832)

Barton BAGGETT of Robeson County was killed by lightning on April 1, 1829. (F. P. April 17, 1829)

Catharine W. BAKER, infant daughter of David G. BAKER, Esq., of Edgecombe County died on September 19, 1844. (T. P. September 21, 1844)

David Calhoun BAKER, youngest child of the late David G. BAKER, Esq., and Mrs. Catharine BAKER, died on October 27, 1845, aged four years and four months. (T. P. October 29, 1845)

David S. BAKER, Esq., of Edgecombe County died on September 25, 1844, aged thirty-one years, leaving a widow and five small children. (T. P. October 5, 1844)

Edwin D. BAKER, son of Dr. J. H. BAKER, died at Tarboro on June 11, 1862, aged nearly three years. (S. June 14, 1862)

Mrs. Julia BAKER, daughter of Henry Shurley and wife of William S. BAKER, Esq., died in Edgecombe County on May 1, 1845, leaving five children. (T. P. May 3, 1845)

Moses BAKER, Esq., died on July 22, 1857, aged about seventy-seven years. He was a successful farmer and had represented Edgecombe County in several sessions of the General Assembly. (S. July 25, 1857)

Mrs. Nancy BAKER died at an advanced age at the William P. Little home in Warren County, on September 25, 1828. (F. P. October 10, 1828)

William BAKER, son of Dr. William S. BAKER, died in Edgecombe County on April 3, 1849, aged about seven years. (T. P. April 7, 1849)

Dr. William L. BALFOUR was born in Edgecombe County on March 25, 1802, and went to Mississippi in his early youth. He studied medicine, settled in Madison County, and became quite wealthy. He was for many years a member of the Baptist Church, as well as President of the Board of Trustees of the Mississippi College at Clinton. He died at Clinton on May 8, 1857. (S. May 23, 1857)

Willis BALLINGER, son of William S. BALLINGER, was killed at Smithfield by an exploding steam-boiler on February 15, 1853. (S. February 19, 1853)

Mrs. Susannah BANDY died in Edgecombe County on September 24, 1842, at an advanced age. (T. P. October 1, 1842)

3

Ethington BARFIELD died in Edgecombe County on April 18, 1838. (T. P. April 21, 1838)

John BARFIELD died in Edgecombe County on February 15, 1847, aged about forty years. (T. P. February 20, 1847)

Theodore BARFIELD of Goldsboro was killed by a negao on March 9, 1856. (S. March 15, 1856)

William BARFIELD, a Constable for over thirty years, died "a few days since." (N. C. F. P. March 23, 1833)

J. J. BARKER died in Edgecombe County on April 19, 1850. (T. P. April 20, 1850)

Miss Elizabeth BARKSDALE died near Enfield on August 31, 1829. (F. P. September 11, 1829)

Thaddeus B. BARLOW, a native of Edgecombe County, died on October 11, 1858, at the home of his father near Edwards' Depot in Hinds County, Mississippi, of consumption in his twenty-third year. (S. November 6, 1858)

Mrs. Winifred BARLOW, wife of A. K. BARLOW, died near Edwards' Depot in Hinds County, Mississippi, on August 16, 1850, in her thirty-eighth year. She was born in Halifax County and lived in Edgecombe County until going to Hinds County in the Fall of 1848. Her first child had died in 1832, but she left three sons, the youngest about five weeks old. (T. P. September 7, 1850) On November 26, 1849, she had become a member of the M. E. Church.

Major Edwin BARNES died "in the prime of life" in Edgecombe County on September 30, 1843. (T. P. October 7, 1843)

Elias BARNES of Wilson County was killed by lightning on June 12, 1856. (S. June 21, 1856)

James BARNES, Post Master at Oak Grove in Edgecombe County, died on December 9, 1842. (T. P. December 17, 1842)

Joseph J. M. BARNES died near Cooksville, Noxubee County, Mississippi, on July 8, 1840, aged twenty-five years. (T. P. August 15, 1840)

Nathan J. BARNES, son of James G. and Rebecca BARNES, was in Sumter County, Alabama, by 1841, and died on December 27, 1849, on the South Prong of the Feather River in California. He was born on September 8, 1823. (T. P. April 27, 1850)

Reddick BARNES died "a few days since" in Edgecombe County, "a highly respected planter" aged about fifty-six years. (T. P. November 28, 1835)

William BARNES, Sr., died near Wilson on May 18, 1858, aged sixty-six years. (S. June 5, 1858)

Wright BARNES died at Norfolk on January 10, 1857, in his thirty-fifth year. "He had been afflicted with cancer just below the knee for several years, and had gone to Norfolk in hopes of getting relief, but in vain. He left a family to mourn his loss. (S. January 24, 1857)

Lemuel BARNHILL, formerly of Pitt County, died on September 17, 1854, aged thirty years, at Conwayboro, South Carolina. (S. September, 23, 1854)

Reddick BARRETT, died in Edgecombe County on July 5, 1828, aged fifty-six, leaving a wife and several children. (F. P. July 18, 1828)

Joseph BARRINGTON, "a soldier of the Revolution," died in Tarboro on July 19, 1836, in his ninetieth year. (T. P. July 23, 1836)

Mrs. Joseph BARRINGTON, a Revolutionary War Pensioner, died near Tarboro on January 18, 1861, aged about ninety years. (S. January 19, 1861)

Frank BARRON died in Edgecombe County on October 27, 1856, aged about thirty. (S. November 1, 1856)

Joseph W. BARRON, son of James BARRON, died in Edgecombe County on January 15, 1839, aged nearly twelve years. (T. P. December 21, 1839)

Thomas BARRON of Edgecombe County died in his cart between Sparta and home "a few days since," leaving a wife and two children. (T. P. April 4, 1835) (On April 11, 1828, he had married Elise MORGAN by Benjamin Sharpe, Esq.)

Solomon BARTLETT, a free mulatto of Edgecombe County, died on February 10, 1829, as the result of a beating on February 9 by the brothers Ezekiel and Redding Staton, "men of families and of respectable standing." (F. P. February 20, 1829)

Mrs. Elizabeth BASSETT, wife of Richard B. BASSETT, and daughter of Mr. Sellers of Alamance County, died near Tarboro on October 15, 1859. (S. October 22, 1859)

Mollie BASSETT, daughter of William A. and Chloe Ann BASSETT, died in Tarboro on July 16, 1860, aged thirteen months. (S. July 21, 1860)

Alfred L. BATTLE of Edgecombe County died on February 5, 1847. (T. P. February 13, 1847)

Col. Benjamin Dossey BATTLE died on October 8, 1857, in his forty-seventh year in Nash County, leaving a widow and four children. (S. October 17, 1857)

C. C. BATTLE, fourth son of the late Joel BATTLE of Edgecombe County, died on May 16, 1859, at his home in Brownsville, Tennessee. (S. May 28, 1859)

Eliza BATTLE was burned to death on March 1, 1858, about 2:00 a. m. "above Kemp's landing." (S. March 20, 1858)

Mrs. Frances C. BATTLE, wife of James L. BATTLE and daughter of the Rev. Jesse Powell of Halifax, died near Tarborough on August 15, 1854, leaving three small sons and two small daughters. She was born on May 26, 1822, and joined the Conocanary Baptist Church in October of 1840. (S. August 19, 1854. September 30, 1854)

Henry Clay BATTLE, eldest son of Col. Benjamin D. BATTLE, died at Rocky Mount on July 28, 1848, in his fifteenth year. (T. P. August 5, 1848)

Isaac L. BATTLE died "a few days since" in Marianna, Florida. He was from Edgecombe County. (T. P. January 20, 1844)

James M. BATTLE, son of James S. BATTLE of "Cool Spring" in Edgecombe County, died suddenly at Goldsboro on October 11, 1850, while on his way to Mississippi. (T. P. October 19, 1850)

James S. BATTLE, Esq., died at his son's residence in Nash County on July 18, 1854, aged sixty-eight years. There was a long Obituary. (S. July 22, 1854. On August 12, 1854, page 2, column 1, there appeared an Appreciation of said BATTLE by a member of the Falls of Tar River Baptist Church in behalf of said Church.)

James Thomson BATTLE, only son of Amos J. and Margaret BATTLE, died on July 30, 1836, of cholera. He had been born on July 14, 1836. (T. P. August 27, 1836)

Jethro D. BATTLE, son of Alfred L. BATTLE, died at Fort Johnston on February 6, 1847. (T. P. February 13, 1847)

Dr. Joel H. BATTLE of Everettsville in Wayne County died on November 22, 1858, in Chapel Hill at the home of his father the Hon. W. H. BATTLE. (S. December 4, 1858)

Joseph S. BATTLE of Edgecombe County was murdered by a hoe in the hands of slave Austin on July 12, 1847. (T. P. July 17, 1847)

Sally Harriet BATTLE, wife of James S. BATTLE of Nashville, died on July 16, 1840, in her thirty-sixth year, at the residence of Mr. Davis in Greensville County, Virginia, near the junction of the Petersburg and Greensville Rail Road. (T. P. July 25, 1840. Her Obituary appeared on August 29, 1840)

Benjamin BATTS of Edgecombe County died on April 18, 1860, of "disease of the heart," and was buried on April 19, with Masonic ceremonies by Concord Lodge, No. 58. "Mr. BATTS was highly esteemed and respected, and has left a large circle of relatives and friends to mourn his loss." (S. April 21, 1860)

John BATTS, aged about twenty-eight years, died in Edgecombe County on November 2, 1837. (T. S. November 3, 1837. T. P. November 11, 1837)

Richard BAXTER, Overseer on Cool Spring Plantation, was stabbed to death by a slave on January 22, 1834. (T. F. P. January 24, 1834)

Mary BEARD, wife of George BEARD and daughter of the late William Harrell Esq., died at Washington on November 2, 1831, in her twenty-second year. (N. C. F. P. November 8, 1831)

John BEDFORD of Edgecombe County died on August 4, 1843, from his stabbing by Henry Lane. (T. P. August 5, 1843)

Mrs. Emily BELCHER, wife of Robert BELCHER, died at Sparta on July 12, 1848. (T. P. July 15, 1848)

John BELCHER died in Edgecombe County on February 18, 1838, aged fifty-three years. (T. P. February 24, 1838)

Wilie BELCHER of Edgecombe County died on April 14, 1848. (T. P. April 15, 1848)

Miss Barthena BELL died in Edgecombe County on June 15, 1845. (T. P. June 18, 1845)

Benjamin BELL died in Greenville on August 2, 1839, in his fiftieth year. (T. P. August 10, 1839)

Bennett H. BELL lost his middle-two children when his home burned on January 31, 1828, but the oldest and youngest and their parents escaped. (F. P. February 8, 1828)

David BELL, son of the late David C. BELL, died in Tarboro on May 3, 1846, aged about four years. (T. P. May 6, 1846)

David C. BELL died at Tarboro on February 20, 1842, leaving a wife and one child. (T. P. February 26, 1842)

Mrs. Elizabeth BELL, wife of Colonel Bennett BELL, died at Pine Bluff, Arkansas, on September 26, 1854. (S. October 28, 1854)

Frederick BELL died in Edgecombe County "at an advanced age" on December 16, 1845. (T. P. December 17, 1845)

Mrs. Harriet BELL, wife of Captain J. J. BELL and daughter of the late Col. Thomas Aldridge, died at the age of forty-three in Tuscumbria, Alabama, on January 2, 1843. She was a Presbyterian. (T. P. January 28, 1843)

Jesse BELL of lower Halifax County shot himself to death on March 7, 1855, about fifteen minutes after the death of his mother, Mrs. Nancy BELL. He was about twenty-two years of age. (S. March 31, 1855)

Capt. Jonas J. BELL was born on January 12, 1790, in Edgecombe County and died on July 15, 1852, in Tuscumbia, Alabama. He had been a volunteer in the War of 1812 and went West in 1815. He was a member of the Old School Presbyterian Church and had been Post Master for ten years. He was a member of Washington Masonic Lodge, No. 36, which held appropriate ceremonies at his funeral. (S. August 7, 1852)

Joseph BELL, Clerk of the Edgecombe County Court, died on April 14, 1840, in his sixtieth year. (T. P. April 18, 1840)

Miss Linsey BELL died in Edgecombe County on October 4, 1850. (T. P. October 12, 1850)

Lorenzo D. BELL died in Edgecombe County on May 11, 1847, leaving a wife and one child. (T. P. May 15, 1847)

Mrs. Lydia BELL, wife of Benjamin BELL, died at Greenville on August 3, 1834. (T. F. P. August 22, 1834)

Marmaduke N. BELL died in Edgecombe County on February 22, 1830, aged forty-four years. (F. P. February 26, 1830)

Masillon BELL, son of the late David C. BELL, died in Tarboro on October 7, 1843, in his third year. (T. P. October 14, 1843)

Mrs. Nancy BELL died in Malifax County on March 7, 1855. (S. March 31,

1855)

Noah BELL of Edgecombe County died suddenly on October 8, 1849. (T. P. October 13, 1849)

Reason W. BELL, "an aged and respectable planter of this county," died on November 9, 1827. (F. P. November 17, 1827)

Mrs. Sally BELL, wife of Colonel Joseph BELL, died at Tarboro on November 21, 1833. (T. F. P. November 29, 1833)

Sally Ann BELL, niece of Charles W. Knight of Edgecombe County, died in Halifax County on March 22, 1837, aged about fifteen years. (T. P. April 1, 1837)

Mrs. Winnifred BELL died in Edgecombe County on December 27, 1837. (T. P. January 5, 1838)

Mrs. Elizabeth Jane BELLAMY, wife of Dr. Samuel BELLAMY and daughter of the late General William Groom of Lenoir County, died on May 11, 1837, at Rockcave Plantation in Marianna, Florida, aged eighteen years, followed by her only child Alexander BELLAMY on May 19. (T. S. June 30, 1837. T. P. June 24, 1837)

James H. BELLAMY, son of Dr. John F. BELLAMY, died in Nash County on September 23, 1843, aged about six years. (T. P. October 7, 1843)

Mrs. Elizabeth Jane BELLAMY, daughter of the late General William Croom of Lenoir County.

Dr. John F. BELLAMY died at "Belle Mont" in Nash County on January 14, 1846, aged fifty-two years, and leaving several children. He was a Methodist and had been a member of the Constitutional Convention. (T. P. April 22, 1846)

Mrs. Dr. John F. BELLAMY died in Nash County on March 7, 1832. (N. C. F. P. March 13, 1832)

Mrs. Mary BELLAMY, wife of the Rev. William BELLAMY, died in Nash County on September 22, 1836, aged about sixty-four years. (T. P. October 1, 1836)

Mary E. BELLAMY died in Nash County on June 18, 1838, being the only daughter of the Rev. William BELLAMY. (T. P. June 23, 1838)

Rev. William BELLAMY died in Nash County on October 4, 1846, aged about eighty years. He had been a Methodist minister for about fifty years. (T. P. October 21, 1846)

Elizabeth BENNETT, only daughter of Bryant BENNETT, Esq., of Hamilton, died on October 17, 1850, aged sixteen years. (T. P. October 26, 1850)

Mrs. Elizabeth BENNETT, widow of Elder Mark BENNETT, died in Edgecombe County on May 9, 1854, aged sixty-two years. (S. May 13, 1854)

Mrs. Emily B. BENNETT, wife of Charles E. BENNETT, died on February 2, 1861, aged twenty years and seven months. (S. February 9, 1861)

John N. BENNETT, Esq., attorney and son of the Rev. Philemon BENNETT, died at Wood's Hotel in Nashville on October 21, 1827. (F. P. November 10, 1827)

Mark BENNETT, son of the Rev. Mark BENNETT of Edgecombe County, died at Chapel Hill on November 11, 1851. He appears to have been born on May 14, 1833. (T. P. November 15, 1851)

Rev. Philemon BENNETT died at Battleboro "a few days since," aged about eighty years. His wife Teresa BENNETT died the next day, aged about sixty years. He had been "an efficient and prominent minister of the Kehukee Baptist Association" for some thirty years in the past, but "in consequence of irregularities in doctrine and conduct, he has not since been recognized as a member of that demonination." (T. P. November 8, 1851)

Mrs. Susannah BENNETT, wife of the Rev. Philemon BENNETT, "dropped dead" in Nash County on March 31, 1829, leaving a husband and seven children. (F. P. April 24, 1829)

Joseph W. BENSON, son of the late Thomas BENSON, died "recently" in Nash County, aged eleven years and eight months. (S. June 10, 1854)

Thomas BENSON of Edgecombe County died at Philadelphia "a few days since." (T. P. September 19, 1840)

Mrs. Elizabeth D. BERRY, wife of Lemuel D. BERRY and lately of Alabama, died on January 9, 1827. (F. P. January 16, 1827)

Mrs. Elizabeth BEST, wife of William BEST, died in Edgecombe County on April 16, 1848, aged about forty-three years and leaving twelve children. (T. P. April 22, 1848)

Thomas BEST died in Edgecombe County on March 11, 1838, aged twenty-two years. (T. P. March 17, 1838)

Daniel BIGGS, son of Elder Joseph BIGGS, died near Williamston on May 7, 1834, leaving a wife and seven children. He was for some years Clerk of the Baptist Church. (T. F. P. May 16, 1834)

Mrs. Eliza BIGGS, wife of William BIGGS and formerly of Edgecombe County, died in Shelby County, Tennessee, on July 17, 1855, aged fifty years. (S. August 18, 1855)

James BIGGS, formerly of Edgecombe County, died near Memphis on August 31, 1859, in his eighty-third year. He had been a Baptist for about fifty years. (S. October 22, 1859)

Joseph BIGGS, son of William BIGGS, died in Edgecombe County on February 21, 1848, aged about fifteen years. (T. P. February 26, 1848)

Joseph BIGGS, Sr., died at Williamston on May 31, 1844, of paralysis, in his seventy-eighth year. (T. P. June 15, 1844)

James BILBRY died in Edgecombe County on June 24, 1861, aged about eighty-two years. (S. June 29, 1861)

Nathaniel BILBRY, "a soldier of the Revolution," died in Edgecombe County "a few days since, at an advanced age." (T. P. April 30, 1836)

Edward BIRD died in Martin County on December 30, 1830, aged ninety-three years. (N. C. F. P. January 4, 1831)

Henry BLAND was shot accidentally by Mr. Brown and died on December 17, 1851, aged about fourteen years. (S. January 3, 1852)

Benjamin BLOUNT, Sr., died in Nashville on February 3, 1858, in his seventy-first year, leaving a wife and several children. He was a Baptist for thirty years. (T. P. February 17, 1838)

Mrs. Frances BLOUNT, wife of General Henry BLOUNT, died in Nash County on April 14, 1829. (F. P. May 1, 1829)

John Gray BLOUNT, Esq., a Revolutionary War Patriot, died at Washington on January 4, 1833, in his eighty-first year. (N. C. F. P. January 8, 1833)

Major John G. BLOUNT of Edgecombe County died at Raleigh on September 4, 1828. (F. P. September 12, 1828)

Major John G. BLOUNT died in Nashville on July 5, 1837. (T. P. July 15, 1837)

Dr. Thomas W. BLOUNT, according to a notice dated April 26, 1840, would have a Masonic Funeral at Nashville on May 10, 1840. (T. P. April 26, 1840)

George BODDIE, Esq., died in Nash County on January 12, 1843, in his seventy-third year, leaving a widow and a large family. He was a former member of the North Carolina Legislature. (T. P. January 14, 1843)

Mrs. Lucy BODDIE, widow of George BODDIE, Esq., of Nash County, died in April 1849 in her sixty-seventh year. (T. P. June 2, 1849)

Thomas BODDIE, late of Nash County, died on October 15, 1826, in Madison County, Alabama. (F. P. November 7, 1826)

Fannie Norman BOND, daughter of John and Nannie BOND, died at Richmond on September 3, 1862, having been born on October 2, 1859. "Her remains will be deposited in the cemetery at this place," i. e., in Tarboro. (S. September 6, 1862)

Henry BOND, son of Lewis BOND, died at Tarboro on October 15, 1831, in his third year. (N. C. F. P. October 18, 1831)

Lewis BOND died at Tarboro on October 22, 1858, aged sixty-three years, and was buried with Masonic ceremonies. (S. October 23, 1858)

Mrs. Lewis BOND died at Tarborough on December 25, 1832. (Her husband was at that time a cabinet maker who also sold associated hardware materials.) (N. C. F. P. January 1, 1833)

Lewis Allen BOND, only son of John M. and Nannie R. BOND, died in Tarboro on August 10, 1864. He was born on September 30, 1863. (S. August 27, 1864)

Margaret BOND, daughter of Lewis BOND, died on October 8, 1843, in her nineteenth year. (T. P. October 14, 1843)

Mrs. Margaret BOND died at Greenville on February 1, 1844, in her sixty-fourth year. She was a Baptist. (T. P. February 10, 1844)

Mrs. Mary E. BOND, a native of Edenton, died at Tarboro recently at the age of sixty, being the widow of Lewis BOND who died about four years earlier. She was a member of the Baptist Church. (S. January 17, 1863)

Wiley BOND died at David Lawrence's home in Greenville on January 31, 1857, in his fifty-eighth year. (S. February 7, 1857)

Mrs. Caroline BONNER, daughter of the late Major Etheldred Gray and wife of Charles C. BONNER of Beaufort, died at her mother's residence in Rocky Mount on January 4, 1852. (S. January 10, 1852)

James BOOTH died on September 29, 1829, aged about twenty-four years. (F. P. October 2, 1829)

Arnold BORDEN, Esq., a native of Fall River, Massachusetts, died at Goldsboro on March 7, 1845, in his forty-seventh year. "He was endowed with a fine intellect, was energetic, moral, and temperate." (T. P. March 22, 1845)

George Abbott BOWDITCH, son of Joseph H. BOWDITCH, died at Tarboro on June 5, 1855, aged four years and eight months. (S. June 9, 1855)

Bartholomew BOWERS, formerly of Edgecombe County, died recently in Hardiman County, Tennessee. (T. P. November 7, 1840) The issue of March 13, 1841, stated that he was still living.

Harriet BOWERS, sister of Mr. Bart. Bowers of Edgecombe County, died on September 6, 1827. (F. P. September 8, 1827)

James BOWERS died in Martin County on November 2, 1846, aged about thirty years. (T. P. November 4, 1846)

John BOWERS, Sr., died in Pitt County on October 17, 1832, aged eighty-four years. "He was a revolutionary soldier," for over fifty years a Magistrate, and for over twenty-five years County Chairman. (N. C. F. P. October 30, 1832)

Lewelling BOWERS died in Martin County on February 23, 1838, aged about sixty. (T. P. March 3, 1838)

James BOYD died at Warrenton five hours after being "thrown by his horse against a tree" on September 23, 1828, aged seventeen years and six months. (F. P. October 3, 1828)

Dr. Benjamin BOYKIN practiced medicine in Tarboro for twenty years before going to Sumter County, Alabama, about 1837. He became a successful planter and died on August 14, 1857, in Noxubee County, Mississippi, aged sixty years, leaving a wife and four children. He had married Martha A. "Patsey" Dancy, daughter of Edwin Dancy. (S. August 29, 1857. Also September 5, 1857, page 2, columns 3/4)

B. B. BOYKIN of Sumter County, Alabama, was killed by one of his slaves on May 21, 1859. (S. June 25, 1859)

Eugenia BOYKIN, daughter of Dr. Benjamin BOYKIN, died on February 18, 1835, aged about three years. (T. P. February 21, 1835)

Mary Louisa BOYKIN, eldest daughter of Dr. Benjamin BOYKIN, died of typhus fever in Sumter County, Alabama, on December 23, 1842, aged nineteen years. She was formerly of Tarboro. (T. P. January 14, 1843)

Sarah E. BOYKIN, daughter of Dr. Benjamin BOYKIN and wife Martha Dancy of Noxubee County, Mississippi, died at her aunt's home near Tarboro on March 12, 1857. (S. March 21, 1857)

James BOZMAN, Esq., died at Edenton on March 9, 1831. (N. C. F. P. March 22, 1831)

Mrs. Eliza BRADDY, wife of Solomon T. BRADDY, died in Edgecombe County on August 10, 1844, leaving two children. (T. P. August 17, 1844)

Isaac B. BRADDY died at Hamilton on October 8, 1853, aged forty-four years, leaving a wife and one child. (S. October 22, 1853)

Mrs. Sarah BRADDY died in Edgecombe County on May 13, 1838, aged about sixty-two years. She had been a Baptist for many years. She had set her clothes on fire because of her view "that if she was not burnt the whole world would be shortly." (T. P. May 19, 1838)

Solomon T. BRADDY died in Edgecombe County on December 1, 1846. (T. P. December 8, 1846)

Rev. Henry BRADFORD of the Methodist Protestant Church died near Enfield in his seventy-first year. (N. C. F. P. March 23, 1833) The date was March 14, 1833.

Burrel BRADLEY died in Edgecombe County on June 12, 1838. (T. P. June 16, 1838)

David BRADLEY was born on October 27, 1777, and died in Edgecombe County on March 23, 1852. He had been a member of the Baptist Church for about forty-five years. (S. May 1, 1852)

James BRADLEY died rather suddenly on November 29, 1836. (T. P. December 3, 1836)

Mrs. Martha Caroline BRADLEY, wife of Stephen BRADLEY, died in Edgecombe County on January 14, 1850, aged about twenty-eight years, and leaving three children. (T. P. January 26, 1850)

Mrs. Mary BRADLEY, wife of Elias BRADLEY and daughter of Willis Bradley, died on February 16, 1849, leaving four children. (T. P. February 24, 1849)

Mrs. Obedience BRADLEY, a widow formerly from Edgecombe County, died on on July 17, 1839, in New Albany, Indiana, aged forty-seven years. (T. P. August 10, 1839)

Richard BRADLEY, "formerly of Stantonsburg," son of Burrel BRADLEY, died on April 17, 1833, at New Albany, Indiana, leaving a wife and four children. (N. C. F. P. July 20, 1833)

Stephen BRADLEY, Sr., died in Edgecombe County on February 6, 1830, aged seventy-seven years. (F. P. February 12, 1830)

Willis W. BRADLEY, son of Stephen BRADLEY, died on December 23, 1841, aged about two years. (T. P. December 25, 1841)

John Hardy BRAGG, a native of Edgecombe County, grew up in Washington, and went to Alabama with his family in 1835. He retired from the mercantile business in January of 1848 and died on his plantation a few miles from Greensboro, leaving a wife and two small children. He was a Mason. (T. P. November 2, 1850) He died October 1, 1850.

John BRANCH, "a respectable citizen," died at the home of Samuel Branch of Halifax County on October 14, 1827. (F. P. October 20, 1827)

Major Joseph BRANCH, formerly of Enfield, died "Lately" in Williamson County, Tennessee. (F. P. July 14, 1827)

Alexander BRASWELL died in Tarboro on April 14, 1838. (T. P. April 21, 1838)

Jacob BRASWELL died "at an advanced age" on July 25, 1837. (T. P. July 29, 1837)

Thomas A. BRASWELL of Wilson drowned in Tar River on April 3, 1856. (S. April 5, 1856)

Joseph J. S. M. BRICKLE, Esq., died at Greenville on December 22, 1829, in his twenty-sixth year. (F. P. December 25, 1829)

Charles BRIDGERS, son of John BRIDGERS, Esq., died near Tarboro on January 2, 1850, aged seventeen months. (T. P. January 12, 1850)

Benjamin BRILEY, "an aged and highly esteemed citizen," died in Pitt County on April 11, 1853. (S. April 16, 1853)

Abram BRINKLEY, "a revolutionary soldier," died in Edgecombe County on July 16, 1838, aged about seventy-four years. "He was a native of Virginia, but many years past became a resident of this State." He left many children and grandchildren. (T. P. July 21, 1838)

Mrs. Mary BRITT died of pneumonia in Edgecombe County on September 27, 1856, in her eighty-fifth year. (S. October 4, 1856)

G. L. BROCKETT, a former Tarboro businessman, served in the 15th Virginia Cavalry Regiment, C. S. A., and was killed on December 13, 1862, at the Battle of Fredericksburg. (S. March 21, 1863)

Christopher W. BROOKS, "recently from Caswell county," died in Tarboro on October 4, 1846. (T. P. October 7, 1846)

Sherwood H. BROOM, shoemaker from near Greenville in Pitt County, was stabbed fatally at Milton by Henry Brewer on July 4, 1828. (F. P. July 25, 1828)

Susan BROOME, wife of James R. BROOME, died in Greene County on June 20, 1838, leaving a husband and three small children. (T. P. June 30, 1838)

Sergt. David L. BROWN of Company B., 44th North Carolina Regiment, died of typhoid fever in the Wilson Confederate Hospital on February 24, 1863, in his twenty-fifth year. (S. March 7, 1863)

Edder BROWN died near Strawberry Hill in Pitt County on January 23, 1832, aged twenty-eight, leaving a wife and one child. (N. C. F. P. February 7, 1832)

George BROWN died in Martin County on January 25, 1849, aged about forty. (T. P. February 3, 1849)

John I. BROWN of Pitt County died in a Confederate Hospital at Richmond on September 11, 1862, aged thirty-four. (S. September 20, 1862)

Samuel BROWN, Clerk of Nash County Court, died at Nashville of the cholera on June 8, 1844, in his forty-seventh year. He was a native of Stockbridge, Massachusetts, and had lived in Nashville for fifteen years. In 1833 he represented Nash County in the North Carolina Legislature. (T. P. June 15, 1844)

Mrs. Obedience BROWNRIGG, widow of George BROWNRIGG, died about January of 1840 at sixty-seven years of age. (T. P. February 1, 1840)

Battle BRYAN died in Edgecombe County on January 18, 1835, aged about thirty years, and leaving a wife and two children. (T. P. January 24, 1835)

Dempsey BRYAN died in Edgecombe County on January 19, 1847, "one of our most wealthy and highly esteemed planters," in his seventy-third year. (T. P. January 23, 1847)

Drew BRYAN died "at an advanced age" in Edgecombe County on February 4, 1843. (T. P. February 11, 1843)

James BRYAN died in Edgecombe County on February 9, 1833, aged sixty years. (N. C. F. P. March 5, 1833)

James R. BRYAN, son of the late Robert BRYAN, died in Nash County on November 25, 1851, in his eighteenth year. (T. P. December 6, 1851)

Jesse B. BRYAN, Esq., died near Washington on March 16, 1832, aged forty-one years. (N. C. F. P. April 10, 1832)

Pattie BRYAN, daughter of Henry and Lucy BRYAN, died in Edgecombe County on June 4, 1863. She was born on May 15, 1862. (S. June 13, 1863)

Mrs. Virginia BRYAN, wife of Bartholomew BRYAN, died in Edgecombe County on July 16, 1859, aged about sixty-five years. (S. July 23, 1859)

David BULLUCK died on April 20, 1834, in Edgecombe County, in his ninety-third year. (T. F. P. April 25, 1834. May 2, 1835, age corrected from seventy-five years)

Orren BULLUCK died of dropsy "a few days ago," aged about sixty-three years. (S. June 13, 1863)

Thomas J. BULLUCK died "a few days since." (T. P. July 11, 1840)

John BUMPASS died in Nash County on September 17, 1855, aged ninety-eight years. (S. September 29, 1855)

Nancy BUMPASS, widow of John BUMPASS, died in Nash County on September 18, 1855, aged ninety years. (S. September 29, 1855)

Bennett BUNN died of cholera morbus on May 13, 1849, on the Nash County side of Rocky Mount. (T. P. May 19, 1849)

Redmun BUNN, Sr., died on August 19, 1826, in his seventy-ninth year. He was a member of the Hillsboro Convention of 1787. (T. P. August 29, 1826)

Willie BUNN died in Nash County "a few days since, at an advanced age." (N. C. F. P. November 1, 1831)

Dempsey BURGESS, formerly of Halifax County, died on December 22, 1842, in Livingston County, Kentucky. (T. P. February 18, 1843)

Baker BURNETT died in Edgecombe County on June 5, 1849, aged about twenty-three years. (T. P. June 9, 1849)

Charles E. BURNETT, son of William BURNETT, died at Tarboro on March 30, 1860, aged about nineteen years. (S. April 7, 1860)

Hellen Victoria BURNETT died at Tarboro on June 30, 1844, being a daughter of William BURNETT. She was born on August 8, 1838. (T. P. July 6, 1844)

Virginia BURNETT, daughter of William BURNETT, died at Tarboro on September 18, 1856, aged about five years. (S. September 27, 1856)

Emily Washington BURNITT, wife of John T. BURNITT and daughter of John and Duanna Allison, died near Huntsville, Alabama, on January 26, 1841, aged seventeen years, leaving an infant of twelve days. (T. P. March 27, 1841)

Conway W. BURTON, a recent resident of Tarboro, died on December 25, 1856, aged about twenty-five years, at New Boston, Massachusetts. (S. January 3, 1857)

Gideon BYNUM died in Edgecombe County at the home of Jacob S. Barnes, Esq., on July 11, 1848, in his twenty-fifth year. (T. P. August 5, 1848)

Gen. John Gray BYNUM, a distinguished lawyer, died at Wilmington on October 17, 1857. (S. October 24, 1857)

Mrs. Maria BYNUM, wife of Jesse A. BYNUM, died at Halifax on September 15, 1836. (T. P. October 1, 1836)

Asa CAIN was stabbed fatally by Cordie Drew at Hutson Bell's farm on Deep Creek on June 27, 1829. (F. P. July 10, 1829)

Joseph CALHOUN, a Revolutionary Soldier, died at his residence in Dooley County, Georgia, on November 11, 1856, "at the advanced age of one hundred years and ten months. . . . a native of Edgecombe County, N. C." (S. January 10, 1857)

Orrin D. CALHOON died in Edgecombe County on November 2, 1845, aged about forty-seven years and leaving a wife. (T. P. November 2, 1845)

Jonathan CALLOWAY died near Hamilton in Martin County on February 3, 1842, as the result of a fight with Arthur S. Cotten. (T. P. February 19, 1842)

James A. CARGILL, Jr., of Waterbury, Connecticut, died on typhoid fever at Tarboro on October 15, 1854, aged about nineteen years. (S. October 21, 1854)

Mrs. Cornelia CARMER, wife of James W. CARMER, died at the Joseph Carmer home in Tarboro on June 9, 1864. (S. June 18, 1864) She was thirty-seven years of age.

Richard CARNEY died on January 7, 1835, aged about thirty-seven years, leaving a wife and four children. (T. P. January 9, 1835)

Mrs. Celia CARR died near Sparta on June 19, 1840, "at an advanced age."

Executor J. J. CARR announced the sale of her personal property at her residence on December 28, 1840. (T. P. June 20, 1840)

Elizabeth Jane CARR, widow of Jonas J. CARR and daughter of the late James Hilliard of Hilliardston in Nash County, died on December 25, 1840, aged thirty-two years and leaving four children, one only four hours old. Her funeral was conducted by the Reverend Seth Speight and she was buried at the residence of the late Mrs. Celia Carr. (January 2, 1841, Obituary in the T. P.)

James H. CARR, son of Jonas J. CARR of Sparta, died at Hilliardston on September 23, 1841, aged nine months. (T. P. October 2, 1841)

Jonas J. CARR died at 9: p. m. in Edgecombe County on May 16, 1843, in his thirty-ninth year, leaving three small children. His funeral sermon was preached by the Rev. Seth Speight of Greene County. (His obituary was in the T. P. May 27, 1843. See also issue of May 20, 1843)

Mary CARR, wife of John CARR, died in Pitt County on March 16, 1846, leaving a husband and five children. (T. P. March 25, 1846)

Elder Green CARROWAN, son of William CARROWAN of Hyde County, began to preach about 1806 and was active in the Kehukee Baptist Association. He was born on July 27, 1778, and died on January 31, 1832. He married 1st a daughter of Foster Jarvis of Swanquarter and had seven children. He married 2nd a daughter of Henry Carrow of Matt-amuskeet Lake and had nine children. (N. C. F. P. December 25, 1832, page 4, for his Biography)

Richard CARSON of Pitt County "committed suicide, under very peculiar circumstances" by hanging himself "at a neighborhood frolic" on the evening of January 19, 1839. (T. P. January 26, 1839)

Elder John J. CARTER was a native of Virginia and a minister of the M. E. Church. His parents had moved to Ohio after the Southampton Insurrection. He died on November 3, 1833, aged about twenty-six years, at the home of Geraldus Toole, Esq., of Edgecombe County. (N. C. F. P. November 8, 1833)

Aaron CHERRY died in Edgecombe County on November 15, 1858, aged about sixty years, from burns suffered by falling into the fireplace. (S. November 20, 1858)

Aaron CHERRY, "an aged and highly respected citizen," died in Edgecombe County on October 1, 1835. (T. P. October 10, 1835)

Mrs. Ann E. CHERRY, wife of William R. CHERRY, died in Edgecombe County on May 28, 1856. (He would marry Frances Savage on April 22, 1857.) (S. May 31, 1856)

Augustus Benson CHERRY, son of Thomas B. CHERRY, died in his third year at Tarboro on October 7, 1833. (T. F. P. October 11, 1833)

Cader CHERRY died on April 2, 1848, in Edgecombe County, leaving a wife and six children. (T. P. April 8, 1848)

Mrs. Elizabeth CHERRY died on January 14, 1841, aged sixty-eight years. (T. P. January 16, 1841)

Frederick J. CHERRY, a native of Tarboro, enlisted on June 14, 1861, in Company K, 2nd North Carolina Regiment, C. S. A., and was killed in the Battle of Fredericksburg (Chancellorsville) on May 3, 1863. (S. May 23, 1863)

Georgiana CHERRY, daughter of William R. CHERRY, Esq., and wife Eliza, died of diphtheria on September 17, 1862, aged about eight years. (S. September 20, 1862) It was stated later that she died on August 17, 1862, in her tenth year. (S. September 27, 1862)

Isham CHERRY, son of Kinchen CHERRY and aged about eighteen years, "was thrown from his horse while running a race on the road near Col. Joab P. Pitt's, in this county, and was killed instantaneously" on October 10, 1829. (F. P. October 16, 1829)

James P. CHERRY, son of Roderick CHERRY, died on July 17, 1827, leaving his parents, two brothers, and three sisters. He was born on April 4, 1810. (F. P. July 21, 1827)

Major Jesse M. CHERRY dropped dead of a heart attack near Greenville on
November 21, 1836. (T. P. November 26, 1836)

John CHERRY, storekeeper of Greenville, was killed by a pistol in the
hands of Dempsey Eason on May 27, 1830, who had been wounded already
by a load of buckshot fired by CHERRY. A long article was published
later from Greenville to justify further Eason's action. (F. P.
June 2, 1830. June 11, 1830)

Captain Kinchen CHERRY died in Edgecombe County on November 15, 1837,
aged fifty-four years, leaving a wife and three children. (T. S.
November 17, 1837. T. P. November 25, 1837)

Lawrence CHERRY, Esq., "for many years Chairman of the County Court,"
died in Martin County on November 1, 1846. (T. P. November 4, 1846)

Lemuel CHERRY died in his seventieth year near Washington on March 24,
1830. (F. P. April 9, 1830)

Lewis K. CHERRY, formerly of Edgecombe County, died "a short time since"
in Macon County, Georgia. (T. P. December 22, 1838)

Lloyd T. CHERRY, son of Erastus CHERRY, died in Edgecombe County on July
12, 1860, aged six months. (S. July 21, 1860)

Mrs. Polly CHERRY, widow of Cador CHERRY, died in Edgecombe County on
July 18, 1854. (S. July 22, 1854)

Roderick CHERRY, aged fifty-five years and "for many years a member of
our State Legislature," died in Pitt County on May 25, 1837. (T.
P. June 3, 1837) (T. S. June 2, 1837)

Samuel CHERRY of Edgecombe County died in his seventy-sixth year on
October 2, 1815. (P. S. October 5 and 9, 1815)

Sarah Elizabeth CHERRY, daughter of Thomas B. CHERRY, died in Edgecombe
County on October 31, 1840, aged about eight years. (T. P. November 7, 1840)

Theophilus CHERRY died in Edgecombe County on December 12, 1839. A
Masonic funeral would be conducted by Rev. William Hyman on April
19, 1840. (T. P. December 14, 1839, and March 31, 1840)

William B. CHERRY died "of congestive fever" in Pitt County on September
9, 1845, aged twenty-one years, leaving a mother, brother, and
sister. (T. P. September 17, 1845)

Bettie CHESHIRE, daughter of the Rev. Joseph Blount CHESHIRE, died at
Tarboro on March 25, 1858, aged about fourteen months. (S. March
27, 1858)

John CHESHIRE, son of the Reverend J. B. CHESHIRE, died at Tarboro on
February 22, 1856, aged fourteen months. (S. March 1, 1856)

Mary Parker CHESHIRE, daughter of the Rev. Joseph B. CHESHIRE, died at
Tarboro on October 7, 1846, aged about thirteen months. (T. P.
October 14, 1846)

Christopher CLACK, confectioner, died at Halifax on October 30, 1827.
(F. P. November 17, 1827)

Mrs. Arabella CLARK died at the home of her son H. T. CLARK near Tarboro
on March 28, 1860, in her seventy-ninth year. (S. March 31, 1860)

David CLARK, "a wealthy and extensive Roanoke Planter," died at Scotland
Neck "a few days since . . . at an advanced age." (F. P. October
2, 1829)

Major James W. CLARK died at Tarboro on December 13, 1843, in his sixty-
fifth year. He was a native of Bertie County. (T. P. December 16,
1843)

Mrs. Louisa CLARK, wife of David CLARK, died at Scotland Neck on January
4, 1828. (F. P. January 18, 1828)

Mary CLARK, daughter of Colonel H. T. CLARK, died near Tarboro on January
11, 1857, aged about 4 years. (S. January 17, 1857)

Henry Blount CLARKE, son of Thomas SMITH (sic) died on October 13, 1834,
aged three years and three months. (T. F. P. October 24, 1834)

James F. CLARK of Beaufort County died at the home of Mrs. Powell near

Tarboro "at an advanced age" on May 20, 1862. (S. May 24, 1862)

Edward COBB died in Edgecombe County on March 29, 1836, in his forty-fourth year, leaving a wife and seven children. (T. P. April 9, 1836)

Florass COBB, eldest son of Gray and Martha COBB of Edgecombe County, died of scarlet fever on March 7, 1863, aged four years and one month. (S. April 4, 1863)

Gray COBB, son of Gray and Martha COBB, died of scarlet fever in Edgecombe County on March 14, 1863, aged one year and six months. (S. April 4, 1863)

James L. COBB, Post Master of Falkland in Pitt County, died on August 3, 1858. (S. September 25, 1858)

Corporal Job COBB of Company I, 15th North Carolina Regiment, C. S. A., was killed at the age of twenty-three near Richmond at Malvern Hill while charging an enemy battery. (S. July 26, 1862) He was killed on July 1, 1862.

John COBB died on May 19, 1837, aged about fifty-five years. (T. P. May 27, 1837)

Miss Mary E. COBB, aged about forty-eight years, died at the home of C. E. Neal in Tarboro. She was a member of the Primitive Baptist Church. (S. March 26, 1859) She died on March 23, 1859.

Orman COBB of Edgecombe County died on November 19, 1831, leaving a wife and four small children. (N. C. F. P. November 22, 1831)

Stephen COBB was born on November 2, 1768, and was "a consistent Baptist." He died in Pitt County on October 20, 1853. (S. October 29, 1853)

Mrs. Susan COBB, wife of Amariah B. COBB and daughter of the late Charles Wilkinson, died in Edgecombe County on July 19, 1860, aged about thirty years, about eight days after the birth of a son who died. (S. July 21, 1860)

William COBB of Edgecombe County died in Edgecombe County "a few days since" in his eighty-third year. (T. P. May 14, 1836)

Benjamin COFFIELD, "a soldier of the Revolution" and a Baptist, died in Edgecombe County on July 23, 1838, aged about seventy-five years and having outlived four sons and three daughters, each daughter having left a child. (T. P. July 28, 1838. August 4, 1838)

Mrs. Elizabeth COFFIELD, wife of Major Benjamin COFFIELD, died on January 28, 1832, in her sixty-ninth year. She was a member of the Baptist Church about forty years and had been married nearly fifty-two years. Seven of her eight children grew up, but all had died, and she was survived by her husband and three grandchildren. (N. C. F. P. February 7, 1832)

John COFFIELD, son of Benjamin COFFIELD, died on January 16, 1830. He was given a Masonic funeral. (F. P. January 29, 1830 and March 12, 1830) The funeral sermon was preached by the Rev. Joshua Lawrence at his father's home on March 28, 1830, for Concord Lodge, No. 58.

Dr. P. A. R. C. COHOON'S wife died at Tarboro on December 21, 1840. (T. P. January 2, 1841) On February 18, 1841, he married Mrs. Martha Sutton, daughter of Michael Hearn, by the Rev. Samuel Pearce. (T. P. February 20, 1841)

Phoebe COLEMAN, widow of Robert COLEMAN, petitioned in August Court 1839 for her dower; heirs Charles Coleman and William Coleman "are not residents of this State." (T. P. September 14, 1839)

Shadrach COLLINS died in Edgecombe County on November 14, 1814. (P. S. November 17, 1814)

Mrs. Eliza CONIGLAND, wife of Edward CONIGLAND, Esq., died at "White Hall" in Halifax County on January 14, 1852. (S. January 31, 1852)

Elder Blount COOPER, a native of Martin County, died in Edgecombe County on January 25, 1854, aged about forty-eight years, and "for many years the highly esteemed pastor of the Primitive Baptist Church in this place." (S. January 28, 1854. Obituary on February 4, 1854, page 2, columns 2/3)

Capt. George COOPER died in Nash County on October 12, 1845, in his sixty-first year. (T. P. October 29, 1845)

Jesse COOPER died in Martin County on May 2, 1859, in his eighty-third year, being a former member of the Legislature. (S. May 7, 1859)

Littleberry COSWAY died in Edgecombe County on June 7, 1863, aged about seventy-four years. (S. June 13, 1863)

Alexander S. COTTEN died in Edgecombe County on February 12, 1834. (T. F. P. February 14, 1834)

Mrs. Emily COTTEN, wife of John L. COTTEN and daughter of the late James Savage, died on November 7, 1837. (T. P. November 25, 1837)

Godwin COTTEN died in Tarboro on January 31, 1837, aged about thirty-eight years. (T. P. February 4, 1837)

John W. COTTEN died at Tarboro on May 16, 1845, aged about thirty-three years. He had just returned after a residence of several years in Tallahassee, Florida, and left a mother, wife, and three children. (T. P. May 24, 1845)

Martha Wilkins COTTEN, widow of the late Alexander S. COTTEN, died in Edgecombe County on January 30, 1837. (T. P. February 4, 1837)

Mrs. Mary COTTEN, wife of Andrew COTTEN, died in Edgecombe County on August 18, 1847. (T. P. August 21, 1847)

Randolph COTTEN died at Tarboro on July 20, 1852, in his eighty-fourth year. (S. July 24, 1852)

Spencer D. COTTEN, merchant of Tarboro, died on September 28, 1837, at Hot Springs, Virginia, in his fifty-ninth year, leaving a wife and two children. (T. P. October 7, 1837. T. S. October 6, 1847)

Mrs. Spencer D. COTTEN, formerly of Tarboro and for ten years a resident of Raleigh, died on December 6, 1855, at the residence of her son F. R. Cotten in Tallahassee, Florida. (S. December 22, 1855)

Captain Whitmel COTTEN died at Scotland Neck on March 29, 1831. (N. C. F. P. April 12, 1831)

Mrs. Eurydice COUNCIL died in Edgecombe County on September 2, 1828. She had been born on August 20, 1727. (F. P. September 5, 1828)

James B. COX, infant son of William R. COX, Esq., died in Raleigh on October 25, 1860. (S. November 3, 1860)

Olivia C. COX, infant daughter of William R. and P. B. COX, died on November 28, 1858, at the A. G. Payne residence in Nashville, Tennessee. (S. December 11, 1858)

Thomas COX died at Scotland Neck "a few days since." (T. P. February 20, 1836)

Robert Freeman CRENSHAW, son of Dr. William M. CRENSHAW from Wake County, died in Tarboro on October 7, 1847. He was born on March 31, 1842. (T. P. October 9, 1847)

Jesse CRISP, Sr., died in Edgecombe County on July 27, 1831, in his seventy-first year. (N. C. F. P. August 2, 1831)

Theophilus CRISP of Edgecombe County died of pleurisy on December 5, 1859, aged about thirty-eight years. (S. December 17, 1859)

William CROCKAT died at Tarboro on February 27, in his seventy-sixth year. He was a native of Dumfries, Scotland. (S. February 28, 1852)

Joel CROCKER of Johnston County drowned in Little River near Waynesboro on February 22, 1856. (S. March 8, 1856)

Mrs. Elizabeth CROMWELL died in Edgecombe County on January 11, 1840. (T. P. January 18, 1840)

Epenetus CROMWELL, Esq., "the late popular Proprietor of the Edgecombe House in Tarboro," died suddenly of apoplexy on February 2, 1861, aged forty-three years. (S. February 9, 1861)

Berrien CROMWELL, son of Patrick CROMWELL of Sumter County, Alabama, but formerly of Edgecombe County, lost his wife and one child who were burned to death on a steamboat "above Kemp's landing about 2:00 a.

m." on Monday, March 1, 1858. (S. March 20, 1858)

Mrs. Jane Eliza CROMWELL, wife of Epentus CROMWELL from Edgecombe County died of typhoid fever near Lagrange, Tennessee, on October 14, 1853, aged about thirty-five years. (S. November 5, 1853)

Newsom CROMWELL died on March 5, 1837, leaving a wife and one child. His Masonic funeral was held on April 16, 1837. (T. P. March 11, 1837, and April 1, 1837)

Sally Ann CROMWELL, wife of Elisha CROMWELL and a daughter of Coffield King, died on January 21, 1845, leaving a daughter three weeks old. (T. P. January 25, 1845)

Benjamin CROWELL of Halifax County died on April 23, 1828. (F. P. May 2, 1828)

William CROWELL died in Halifax County on August 23, 1826, in his thirtieth year, leaving a wife and three children. (T. P. September 12, 1826)

Eli CUTCHIN died in Edgecombe County on August 22, 1856. (S. September 6, 1856)

Mrs. Harriet CUTCHIN died in Edgecombe County on May 22, 1852. (S. May 29, 1852)

Henry DAFFIN, son of Joshua DAFFIN, died "a few days since" from a dose of laudanum taken by mistake for paregoric. (T. P. May 16, 1835)

Theophilus J. DAFFIN, formerly of Tarboro, died at New Orleans of yellow fever on September 13, 1853, aged about twenty-seven years. (S. October 8, 1853)

Michael DALEY was stabbed to death at Battleboro by R. S. "Sam" Taylor on May 25, 1860. (S. June 2, 1860)

Cornelia V. DANCY, wife of John S. DANCY, died at Tarboro on November 8, 1844, in her twentieth year. She was the eldest daughter of James S. Battle. (T. P. November 16, 1844)

Edwin Reid DANCY, son of Colonel Francis L. DANCY of Pilatke, Florida, died near Tarboro at the residence of his aunt, Mrs. Foxhall, on December 26, 1853, aged fifteen years. (S. January 7, 1854) (Obituary January 21, 1854)

Mrs. Elizabeth Mason DANCY, widow of the late Francis DANCY, died at "Dancy" in St. Mary's Parish, Louisiana, on April 4, 1859, aged about seventy-seven years. She was a native of Virginia and had formerly lived with her husband in north Alabama. (S. April 30, 1859)

Francis L. DANCY, Esq., died at Tarboro on June 19, 1848, in his seventy-third year. He graduated in 1801 from U. N. C. and was a longtime Edgecombe County solicitor. (T. P. June 24, 1848)

Francis Little DANCY, son of William F. and Mary E. DANCY, was born on January 24, 1859, and died on July 4, 1859. (S. July 9, 1859)

James DANCY died in the Tarboro jail on August 2, 1853, after killing William A. Taylor in a knife fight. (S. August 6, 1853)

John DANCY, son of the late William DANCY of Tarboro, died on September 29, 1844. (T. P. October 5, 1844)

Mrs. Lucy DANCY, widow of William DANCY, died on April 14, 1858, aged about seventy-four years. (April 17, 1858)

Martha C. DANCY, wife of William F. DANCY, Esq., and daughter of Gen. Wyatt Moye of Aberdeen, Mississippi, died at Tarboro on August 14, 1852, in her twenty-third year, about two years after arriving there as a bride. (S. August 21, 1852)

Lt. R. F. "Frank" DANCY was killed "by a piece of shell . . . . striking him on the left breast just over the heart" at the Battle of Ocean Pond in Florida on February 20, 1864. (S. March 19, 1864)

William DANCY died in Edgecombe County on September 16, 1840, aged about sixty-six years. (T. P. September 19, 1840)

Benjamin T. DANIEL died at Stantonsburg on June 4, 1857, aged about forty years. (S. June 13, 1857)

Delha DANIEL, daughter of Rev. John H. DANIEL, died in Edgecombe County
on October 10, 1846, aged about three years. (T. P. October 14,
1846)

James DANIEL of Warren County froze to death on January 17, 1853. He
had gone deer-hunting with some friends and was found at his stand
"sitting upon the ground with his chin resting upon the back of his
left hand." (S. January 29, 1853)

James N. DANIEL, son of Rev. John H. DANIEL, died in Edgecombe County
on August 15, 1859, aged about twenty-one years. (S. August 20,
1859)

Mrs. Jane DANIEL, wife of James P. DANIEL, late of Edgecombe County,
died "recently" in Pitt County leaving one child. (T. P. February
1, 1845)

Jethro DANIEL of Nash County was killed on August 26, 1847, by a blow
from _____ Ritter, an Overseer on the Wilmington & Raleigh Rail
Road. "The difficulty originated from Mr. Ritter whipping a negro
hired from Mr. DANIEL. Mr. Ritter has not yet been taken." (T. P.
August 28, 1847)

Dr. John J. DANIEL died in Edgecombe County on April 14, 1839, aged about
thirty. (T. P. April 20, 1839)

Josephine DANIEL, only daughter of the Hon. J. J. DANIEL, died at Halifax "a few days since." (F. P. November 28, 1828)

Justus Andrew Jackson DANIEL, son of John H. DANIEL, died on November
14, 1834, aged two months. (T. F. P. November 21, 1834)

Justus J. DANIEL died near Stantonsburg in Wilson County on May 16, 1859,
aged about fifty-five years, leaving a wife and seven children.
(S. May 21, 1859)

Laura DANIEL, daughter of Rev. John H. DANIEL, died in Edgecombe County
on October 27, 1848, aged about three years. (T. P. November 4,
1848)

Mrs. Lydia DANIEL, wife of Justus G. DANIEL of Greene County, died on
January 20, 1845, leaving two children. (T. P. February 1, 1845)

Mrs. Maria DANIEL, wife of the Hon. J. J. DANIEL of the N. C. Supreme
Court, died at Halifax on February 28, 1836. (T. P. March 5, 1836)

Mrs. Martha E. DANIEL of Halifax died on July 30, 1831. She was the
wife of John R. J. DANIEL, Esq. (N. C. F. P. August 9, 1831)

Meniza Elizabeth DANIEL, daughter of the Rev. John H. DANIEL, died in
Edgecombe County on July 7, 1853, aged about four years and four
months. (S. July 9, 1853)

Mrs. Sally Ann DANIEL, wife of Dr. John J. DANIEL, died on July 13, 1833,
in her twentieth year. Her infant daughter died on July 17, aged
fourteen days. (N. C. F. P. July 20, 1833)

William DANIEL, Sr., died in Martin County on February 5, 1832, in his
eightieth and sixth year. He had been a Baptist for nearly thirty
years. (N. C. F. P. February 28, 1832)

William S. DANIEL, son of John H. and Meniza DANIEL, died at Stantonsburg of typhoid fever on December 17, 1849, aged twenty-one years
and twelve days. (T. P. December 22, 1849)

Clemmons DARDEN, formerly of Tarboro, died at Sumter County, Alabama, on
December 11, 1841, at the residence of Dr. Benjamin Boykin. (T. P.
January 8, 1842)

Miles DARDEN was born in 1798 in North Carolina and was a Baptist. He
moved to Henderson County, Tennessee, where he died on January 23,
1857, weighing just over 1,000 pounds. (S. August 22, 1857, page
1, columns 1/2)

George DAVENPORT of Halifax "was shot through the body" and killed by
Winfield D. Staton in "a personal encounter" on March 30, 1863.
(S. April 4, 1863)

Mrs. Charlotte DAVID died "at an advanced age" in Edgecombe County on

June 16, 1845. (T. P. June 18, 1845)

Colonel Durham DAVIS died in Williamston on July 18, 1829. (F. P. July 31, 1829)

John DAVIS of Wayne County hanged himself on October 27, 1850. (T. P. November 2, 1850)

Mary Elizabeth DAVIS, daughter of James DAVIS, died in Greenville on August 22, 1845, in her tenth year. An acrostic poem spelled her name and was signed by the initials S. A. J. (T. P. September 3, 1845)

Matthew DAVIS died in Warren County on December 28, 1827, in his seventy-ninth year. He was "a soldier of the revolution." (F. P. January 27, 1827)

Miss Prudence DAVIS, a native of Greenville, died in Wilson on April 28, 1860, aged seventy years. (S. May 5, 1860)

John Henry DAWSON of Halifax County died on June 10, 1846. (T. P. June 17, 1846)

David DAY, "an old and respectable farmer," died in Halifax County on September 16, 1829. (F. P. October 2, 1829)

John DAY, son of John DAY, died at Tarboro on August 16, 1839, aged about three years. (T. P. August 24, 1839)

Mrs. Peggy DAY died at Tarboro on January 31, 1842. (T. P. February 5, 1842) (She had married John DAY on February 11, 1832.)

DEBERRY (refer to Berry).

Alice Ann DICKEN, daughter of William DICKEN, died in Nash County on October 7, 1843, in her eighth year. (T. P. October 21, 1843)

Benjamin DICKEN died in Edgecombe County on August 22, 1851, aged about fifty-four years. (T. P. August 30, 1851)

Dr. Christopher L. DICKEN died in Edgecombe County on November 19, 1859, aged forty-six years. (S. November 19, 1859)

Mrs. Elizabeth F. DICKEN, wife of Lewis B. K. DICKEN, Esq., died in Halifax County on October 5, 1842. (T. P. October 15, 1842)

Dr. Ephraim DICKEN died at Tarboro on November 20, 1845, aged about forty-seven years, after twenty-five years of residence there. (T. P. November 26, 1845)

Henry DICKEN of Edgecombe County died on April 26, 1845, in his forty-fifth year, after about two months of marriage. (T. P. May 3, 1845)

L. B. K. DICKEN, Esq., died in Halifax County on November 30, 1847, aged about forty-seven years. (T. P. December 11, 1847)

Mrs. Lucy DICKEN, wife of William DICKEN, died in Nash County on June 9, 1848, aged about thirty-five years and leaving five children. (T. P. June 10, 1848)

Lucy DICKEN, daughter of William DICKEN, died in Nash County on June 29, 1848, aged about four months. (T. P. July 1, 1848)

Dr. Richard H. DICKEN, Post Master of Roseneath, died at the home of Mrs. Mary Powell of Halifax County on September 24, 1826, aged thirty years. (F. P. October 3, 1826)

Benjamin A. DICKENS, Esq., a native of Halifax County, died at Marianna, Florida, on January 23, 1857, in his thirty-fourth year. (S. February 7, 1857)

Mrs. Elizabeth DIXON died at the Thomas Howenton residence in Edgecombe County on January 26, 1853, aged eighty-three years. Her funeral was preached by Rev. John F. Speight. (S. March 19, 1853)

William DOGGETT, Sr., died in Halifax County on June 25, 1835. (T. P. July 4, 1835)

J. B. DONAPOE of Nash County died recently "by shooting himself with a gun." (T. P. January 27, 1849)

Eliza DONLOP, eldest daughter of William Thomas and formerly of Franklin County, married David DONLOP on July 24, and died on August 7, 1834, in Maringo County, Alabama. (T. F. P. September 5, 1834)

Mrs. Margaret DONNELL, wife of the Hon. John R. DONNELL and only daughter of the late Governor Speight, died in New Bern on September 3, 1831, in her thirty-second year. (N. C. F. P. September 13, 1831)

Frederick DORTCH, son of the late William DORTCH, died in Nash County on April 7, 1833, in his nineteenth year, having "commenced the study of medicine." (N. C. F. P. July 20, 1833)

Isaac DORTCH died in Tennessee on January 28, 1849, in his eighty-fifth year. He was a native of Nash County, father-in-law of the Post Master General, and a resident of Tennessee for fifty-three years. (T. P. February 24, 1849)

Mrs. Jane DORTCH, wife of D. L. J. DORTCH, died of consumption at Stantonsburg on August 14, 1849, in her twenty-seventh year. (T. P. August 25, 1849)

Dr. Lewis J. DORTCH died at Stantonsburg on October 28, 1854, aged about thirty-six years. (S. November 4, 1854)

William Cary DOWD, son of the Rev. P. W. DOWD of Wake County, and grandson of the late Henry Austin of Tarboro, died at Christiansburg, Virginia, on June 30, 1860, and was buried on July 3 in the Episcopal Churchyard at Tarboro. He graduated from U. N. C. in 1858. (S. July 7, 1860)

Richmond DOZIER died in Edgecombe County on November 18, 1854, in his eightieth year, leaving a widow and two sons. He was of "the Messrs Dozier, merchants of Tarboro," and had been a Methodist for fifty years. (S. December 2, 1854)

Samuel DOZIER died on August 11, 1834, in his twentieth year. (T. F. P. August 22, 1834)

Charles Carroll DRAKE, son of Dr. Joseph A. DRAKE, died at Nashville on July 10, 1836, aged six weeks. (T. P. July 23, 1836)

Capt. Francis DRAKE died in Nash County on July 25, 1838, in his fifty-sixth year, leaving a wife and eight children. (T. P. August 18, 1838)

Green W. DRAKE of Alabama but formerly of Nash County died on June 3, 1838, in his thirty-first year, leaving a wife and four children. "He moved from his native home last fall, in search of a more fruitful soil." (T. P. August 18, 1838)

Major John H. DRAKE'S wife died at Nashville on February 9, 1840, "at an advanced age." (T. P. February 15, 1840)

Dr. John Richard DRAKE, formerly of Nash County, died at Auburn, Alabama, on March 7, 1859. (S. May 7, 1859)

Mrs. Mary DRAKE died in Edgecombe County on August 14, 1863. She had been born on October 18, 1779. (S. August 28, 1863)

Dr. Nicholas J. DRAKE died at the home of his father Major John H. DRAKE in Nash County on January 15, 1831. (N. C. F. P. February 1, 1831)

Rev. Q. A. DRAKE died in Nash County on November 29, 1859. He was a Baptist minister. (S. December 10, 1859)

William DRAKE died in Edgecombe County on March 7, 1827, aged seventy-seven years. (F. P. March 17, 1827)

William DRAKE, Esq., died on July 8, 1838, in his sixty-first year. (T. P. August 18, 1838)

William Franklin DRAKE, youngest son of Dr. John H. DRAKE, died at Nashville on April 21, 1842. (T. P. May 7, 1842)

William DRAUGHON of Edgecombe County was killed by lightning on May 30, 1846, aged about thirty and leaving a wife and three children. (T. P. June 3, 1846) (He had married Susan Lyon on October 29, 1836.)

Thomas DREW died in Edgecombe County on December 2, 1860, aged about thirty-eight years. (S. December 15, 1860)

Elizabeth DUDLEY, wife of Governor Edward DUDLEY, died at Raleigh on

October 14, 1840. (T. P. October 24, 1840)

Mrs. Evaline DUGGON, daughter of Asa and Nancy DANIEL, died at Stantonsburg on May 18, 1845, in her twenty-fifth year, leaving a husband and three children. (T. P. June 4, 1845)

Mrs. Ann DUNN, wife of Dr. Lemon S. DUNN, died on June 30, 1848. (T. P. July 1, 1848)

Jacob DUNN died in Edgecombe County on January 20, 1848. (T. P. January 22, 1848)

Lamon DUNN died of palsy in Edgecombe County "at an advanced age" on January 26, 1842. (T. P. January 29, 1842)

Allen DUPREE died in Edgecombe County on November 28, 1845, aged about twenty-five, leaving a wife and one child. (T. P. December 3, 1845) (He had married Mary Thigpen on August 12, 1843.)

Mrs. Amanda DUPREE, wife of Lewis DUPREE of Edgecombe County, died on June 17, 1843, leaving an infant aged nine weeks. (T. P. June 24, 1843)

Mrs. Ann DUPREE, wife of Rev. Thomas DUPREE, died in Pitt County on August 8, 1843, in her sixty-ninth year. They had been married on July 5, 1792. (T. P. August 19, 1843)

Mrs. Priscilla DUPREE, wife of Willis DUPREE, died in Edgecombe County on August 26, 1843. (T. P. September 2, 1843)

Lieut. R. W. DUPREE of Pitt County fell at the Battle of Bristow Station on October 14, 1863. A half-column was devoted to his memory. (S. November 21, 1863)

Willis DUPREE died in Edgecombe County on January 11, 1849. (T. P. January 13, 1849)

Sally Ann Jannette EAGLES, daughter of R. T. EAGLES, died on December 16, 1843, aged four years and nine months. (T. P. January 6, 1844)

Bennett B. EASON, formerly of Edgecombe County, died near Bainbridge in Franklin County, Alabama, on December 2, 1826, in his twenty-eighth year. (F. P. December 5, 1826)

George EASON, formerly of Edgecombe County, was murdered in Montgomery County, Alabama, on March 26, 1860, by a man named Peace. His parents then resided in Martin County. (S. July 14, 1860)

Jesse EASON, a convicted murderer, was executed in Camden County on June 3, 1831. (N. C. F. P. June 21, 1831)

Rebecca Harriet EASON, daughter of Captain Jonathan T. EASON, died on December 29, 1839, aged four or five years. (T. P. January 4, 1840)

Theophilus EASON, Esq., died on January 23, 1845, leaving a wife and a large family. (T. P. February 1, 1845)

Vesta EASON, oldest daughter of Jonathan T. EASON, died in Edgecombe County on October 20, 1841. (T. P. October 23, 1841)

Col. Charles EDMONDS died in Halifax County on April 10, 1828. (F. P. April 18, 1828)

Mrs. Ann B. EDMONDSON died at Greenwood in Halifax County on September 12, 1859, aged fifty-two years. (S. October 8, 1859)

Mrs. Elizabeth EDMONDSON, wife of John EDMONDSON and daughter of the late Kinchen Cobb, died in Pitt County on November 27, 1842, leaving two children. (T. P. January 21, 1843)

Tillitha EDMONDSON died in Edgecombe County on April 5, 1842, aged twenty-two years and survived by mother, brother, father-in-law, and three half-brothers and sisters. "The day of her death had been selected for her marriage to a worthy young man." (T. P. April 9, 1842)

Telitha EDMONDSON died in Edgecombe County on July 7, 1853, aged about twelve years. (S. July 9, 1853)

Rufus W. EDMONDSON, Esq., of Edgecombe County, married in Wake County on October 16, 1845, Caroline Wilder, daughter of Col. Hillory

Wilder. (T. P. October 29, 1845)

David B. EDWARDS, son of James G. EDWARDS formerly of Edgecombe County, died in White County, Arkansas, on November 4, 1859, in his twenty-fourth year. (S. February 18, 1860)

Edwin EDWARDS of Nash County was a suicide in late July of 1843. (T. P. August 12, 1843)

Mrs. Elizabeth EDWARDS, wife of Bryant EDWARDS, died on September 16, 1843, aged about fifty-nine years. (T. P. September 30, 1843)

Gray EDWARDS died in Edgecombe County on January 18, 1848. (T. P. January 22, 1848)

Jane EDWARDS, wife of William J. EDWARDS and daughter of Bythal HOWELL, died in Edgecombe County on April 11, 1858, aged about twenty-two years and leaving an infant about a fortnight old. (S. April 17, 1858)

Margaret EDWARDS, daughter of Bryant EDWARDS, died on September 9, 1843, aged about eighteen years. (T. P. September 16, 1843)

Mrs. Tabitha EDWARDS, wife of M. P. EDWARDS of Edgecombe County, died on July 25, 1859, aged about thirty-five years, leaving six children, "the youngest of whom was only a few hours old." (S. July 30, 1859)

Mrs. Dorothy EELBECK died near Halifax at the home of M. T. Ponton, Esq., on October 8, 1827, aged about eighty years. (F. P. October 13, 1827)

Urias ELKS of Pitt County died on July 22, 1852, aged ninety years and leaving two brothers and a sister aged respectively ninety-two, eighty-nine, and eighty-six years. He had been for forty years a member of the Baptist Church. (S. August 21, 1852)

Mrs. James ELLINOR died in Edgecombe County on January 15, 1844. (T. P. January 27, 1844)

Mrs. James ELLINOR died on January 19, 1845. (T. P. January 25, 1845)

James ELLINOR died in Edgecombe County on January 26, 1845. (T. P. February 1, 1845)

James ELLINOR'S Masonic Feneral was announced for October 26, 1845, by Secretary Weldon S. Hunter of Concord Lodge, No. 58, "at the residence of Patrick McDowell." (T. P. October 8, 1845)

Josiah ELLINOR'S wife died in Edgecombe County on June 27, 1840. (T. P. July 4, 1840)

Mrs. Nancy Pender ELLINOR died on August 14, 1831, aged seventeen years. (N. C. F. P. August 23, 1831) (She had been bonded on March 8, 1831, to marry Joseph Ellinor.)

Elijah ELLIOTT died in Edgecombe County on February 10, 1855, aged about sixty-four years. (S. February 17, 1855)

Mrs. Margaret ELLIOTT, wife of Elijah ELLIOTT, died at Tarboro on August 23, 1844. (T. P. August 24, 1844)

Elisha ELLIS died in Edgecombe County on November 2, 1843, "at an advanced age." (T. P. November 11, 1843)

Francis R. ELY, a native of North Carolina, died on January 4, 1858, at Marianna, Florida, being "one of the most wealthy, prominent and useful citizens of that place." (S. January 16, 1858)

Richard EPPS, son of Richard EPPS of Halifax, died on September 22, 1827. (F. P. September 29, 1827)

Richard EPPES, Clerk of the Halifax County Court, died "a few days since." (F. P. November 10, 1827)

Eliza ETHERIDGE, wife of Lewis ETHERIDGE, died at Tarboro on January 9, 1836, leaving an infant of three months. (T. P. January 16, 1836)

Capt. Jos. W. EURE died in Halifax County on June 19, 1828. (F. P. July 4, 1828)

Stephen EURE of Halifax County died "a few days since." (F. P. April 25, 1828)

Mrs. Edith EVERITT, a Baptist aged about seventy years, died in Martin County on July 23, 1836. (T. P. July 30, 1836)

Capt. James EXUM died in Northampton County on July 27, 1827. (F. P. August 11, 1827)

John EXUM died in Edgecombe County on May 28, 1838, aged about forty years. (T. P. June 9, 1838)

John EXUM, Esq., of Wayne County, died on September 4, 1850. He had been for some years a State Senator. (T. P. September 14, 1850)

Mrs. Mary EXUM died in Edgecombe County on February 18, 1856, aged about eighty-two years. (S. February 23, 1856)

Matthew EXUM died in Edgecombe County on October 13, 1854, of typhoid fever, aged about thirty years. (S. October 14, 1854)

Pherebe FAIRCLOTH, aged eighteen or nineteen years, hanged herself at the residence of her brother-in-law Samuel Reason of Edgecombe County, a few days since "at noon while the family were at dinner." (N. C. F. P. January 4, 1831)

Susan FAIRCLOTH, wife of William FAIRCLOTH, died near Speight's Bridge in Greene County on October 28, 1854, aged near fifty-six years, leaving a husband, three sons, and two daughters. She had lived in Edgecombe County until a few years before her death. (S. November 4, 1854)

Mrs. Jerusha FARMER died on February 16, 1832, in her seventy-sixth year. She had been a Baptist for fifty-seven years. (N. C. F. P. February 21, 1832)

Moses FARMER died in Edgecombe County on November 23, 1844, in his fifty-fourth year, leaving a wife and seven children. (T. P. November 30, 1844)

Willie Rountree FARMER, son of Col. J. W. and Obedience FARMER, was born on August 10, 1851, and died on October 2, 1852. (S. October 9, 1852)

William FARRELL was run over by a train near Everittsville on July 2 and died on July 6, 1860. (S. July 14, 1860)

Duncan FERGUSON, Esq., died at Rocky Mount on July 29, 1852. A resolution of respect was made on August 14 by Secretary D. W. Barnes of Mt. Lebanon Masonic Lodge, No. 117, of Wilson; and they announced on September 18 that a Masonic funeral would be held on October 1 "at his late residence at Rocky Mount" by the Reverend Lowe. (S. July 31, 1852, and August 28, 1852)

Laura Jane FERGUSON, daughter of Duncan and Martha FERGUSON, died at Rocky Mount Depot on June 7, 1848, aged two years and eight months. (T. P. June 17, 1848)

Robert F. FLEMING, son of Jesse L. FLEMING of Halifax County, fell on his head from a rail fence at the residence of Willis Fleming of Edgecombe County and was killed on January 12, 1851. (T. P. January 25, 1851)

Hardy FLOWERS, Esq., "for many years a member of the General Assembly," died a few days since at an advanced age. (T. P. November 5, 1836)

William FOLK died in Edgecombe County on June 29, 1860, aged ninety-seven years, having been regarded for several years past as "the oldest inhabitant" of the County. (S. July 7, 1860)

Mary Elizabeth FORBES, daughter of Peter and Catharine FORBES, died in Edgecombe County on January 25, 1852, aged nine months. (S. January 31, 1852)

Mrs. Henry FORD died in Edgecombe County on February 13, 1834. (T. F. P. February 28, 1834)

John FORD was "found dead in the road, Cause, liquor, some days since." (S. December 4, 1852)

Nelson FORD died at Tarboro on February 11, 1829, having been "for several years past a stage driver between this place and Halifax." (F. P. February 20, 1829)

Rix FORD, formerly of Edgecombe County and a volunteer in the Mexican War, died in Beaufort County on September 8, 1855, "from a stroke or strokes inflicted upon him on the 4th of August, by John Ross, Senior, of Durham's Creek. Ross, it is thought, may attempt to make his way South." (S. September 22, 1855)

Agesilaus S. FOREMAN of St. Bride's Parish, Norfolk County, Virginia, died at Tarboro on January 29, 1840, leaving a wife and child. (T. P. February 1, 1840, and February 15, 1840)

Camillus L. FOREMAN, son of the late A. S. FOREMAN, died at Tarboro on January 7, 1841, aged twenty-one months. (T. P. January 9, 1841. Obituary February 6, 1841)

Mrs. Eliza FOREMAN, widow of Josiah FOREMAN and daughter of Allen Jones, died recently in Edgecombe County. (S. July 31, 1858)

Ivey FOREMAN, Esq., of Pitt County died on August 31, 1832. (N. C. F. P. September 11, 1832)

William FOREMAN of Pitt County dropped dead suddenly "while walking in his corn field" on August 9, 1836, leaving a wife and two children. (T. P. August 13, 1836)

Hilliard FORT died in Halifax County on January 28, 1827, being "a wealthy and respectable planter" and a Mason. (F. P. February 3, 1827)

Jacob G. FORT'S Masonic funeral sermon was announced by Mount Moriah Lodge, No. 93, for November 9, 1828, at the home of Mrs. Elizabeth Cotten, with the Rev. Joshua Lawrence officiating. (F. P. October 24, 1828)

Ricks FORT died near Enfield on August 25, 1828. (F. P. August 29, 1828)

Thomas FOSTER, a gunsmith living near Enfield, was frozen to death on the night of February 11, 1835, "within a few hundred yards of his dwelling." (T. P. February 21, 1835)

Exum FOUNTAIN, aged about twenty-five years and unmarried, "kept a small groggery on the Halifax road, near Maj. L. R. Cherry's," and was struck by his own axe on the night of May 14, 1857. His mother found him the next day, but he died without recovering consciousness on May 16, 1857. Subsequently, "Negro Jin, the property of Willie Bradley, has been arrested and committed to jail to take his trial at the next Superior Court, charged with the homicide." (S. May 23, 1857; May 30, 1857)

Mrs. Sarah M. C. FOUNTAIN, daughter of Edward POWER, died in Edgecombe County on September 2, 1838, aged thirty-seven years and seven months, leaving "an aged father" and six children. (T. P. September 8, 1838)

Lt. Frank D. FOXHALL of Company A, 33rd North Carolina Regiment, C. S. A. and former Sheriff of Edgecombe County, died near Richmond on June 27, 1862, in his twenty-ninth year. (S. July 5, 1862 and July 19, 1862)

Henry FOXHALL died of pneumonia in Edgecombe County on January 31, 1849, aged about thirty years. (T. P. February 3, 1849)

Mrs. Martha FOXHALL, widow of Robert FOXHALL, died in Edgecombe County on the night of December 2, 1855, aged about seventy years. (S. December 8, 1855)

Martha FOXHALL, daughter of William FOXHALL, died in Edgecombe County on April 6, 1832. (N. C. F. P. April 10, 1832)

Mary Ann FOXHALL, daughter of William FOXHALL, died on May 8, 1834, in her twenty-third year. (T. F. P. May 16, 1834)

Robert FOXHALL died in Edgecombe County on January 21, 1842, leaving a wife and four children. (T. P. January 29, 1842)

William FOXHALL died near Tarboro on January 4, 1841. (T. P. January 9, 1841)

Mrs. Susannah FRANCIS of Edgecombe County died on August 19, 1827, in her one hundred and fifteenth year. (F. P. August 25, 1827)

24

Henry FREEAR died on August 31, 1829, aged about twenty-three years, at the home of M. T. Ponton, Esq., near Halifax. (F. P. September 11, 1829)

James FREEAR died at Halifax on January 18, 1829. (F. P. January 30, 1829)

Josiah FREEMAN died in Edgecombe County on April 30, 1839, aged sixty-eight years. (T. P. May 4, 1839)

Josiah FREEMAN of Edgecombe County died on July 15, 1843, leaving a wife and one child. (T. P. July 22, 1843)

Lavinia FREEMAN died in Edgecombe County on September 9, 1846, in her thirtieth year. (T. P. September 16, 1846)

Benjamin FULFORD was a native of Pitt County and served in Company B., North Carolina Volunteers, and died in Petersburg on August 20, 1848, aged twenty-one years. (T. P. September 2, 1848)

Peter FULLER, mail carrier between Louisburg and Rocky Mount, was found dead in his buggy on Monday of last week [September 15, 1856]---- cause unknown." (S. September 27, 1856)

Mrs. Mary FUTRAL, wife of Thomas FUTRAL, died in Greene County on February 13, 1835, in her thirty-second year. (T. P. February 28, 1835)

William GAITHER of Halifax County died on August 5, 1860, as the result of an accidental shot from his own hand at Enfield. His parents and two sisters resided near Tarboro. (S. August 11, 1860)

Dr. John A. GALLAGHER, recently of Washington, died in Wilson on July 30, 1862. "He was attending to the hospital in that town, and while operating on a deceased patient, he pricked his finger with a dissecting needle, which ultimately caused his death after intense suffering. He was about 30 years of age, and has left a wife and one child to mourn their sudden bereavement." (S. August 2, 1862)

Edward GARDNER, Sr., was killed at Greenville on July 29, 1836, by the accidental discharge of a cannon. He was "an aged and respectable citizen." (T. P. August 6, 1836)

William GARDNER'S administrator James Barron auctioned on November 7, 1837, at the dwelling house the household goods, farming utensils, shop tools, hogs, horses, cattle, slaves, etc. (T. S. November 3, 1837)

Mrs. Abigail GARRETT, widow of James GARRETT, died on February 6, 1834, aged about fifty years. (T. F. P. February 7, 1834)

Mrs. Elizabeth GARRETT, widow of John GARRETT, died in Edgecombe County on March 13, 1864, aged seventy-one years. (S. April 16, 1864)

Fanny GARRETT, wife of Stephen GARRETT, was murdered a month or two before September 30, 1842. (T. P. October 8, 1842)

John GARRETT of Tyancokey in Edgecombe County died on November 11, 1853, aged about sixty years, leaving a large family. He had been "crushed with the falling of some timber which he was erecting for a Cotton Screw." (S. November 12, 1853. Obituary on November 19, 1853)

Joseph GARRETT died near Plymouth on July 4, 1835, aged sixty-six years, leaving a widow and "a numerous family of children." (T. P. July 18, 1835)

Mary Delah GARRETT, late of Edgecombe County, died in Marengo County, Alabama, not long before this announcement. (T. P. October 22, 1836)

Mrs. Nancy GARRETT, daughter of John MERCER and Wife of Dr. J. J. GARRETT, died in Edgecombe County on October 29, 1849, aged about twenty years, and leaving a daughter about ten days old. (T. P. November 3, 1849)

Mrs. Susan GARRETT, wife of James J. GARRETT and daughter of Jesse C. KNIGHT, died in Edgecombe County on April 10, 1832, leaving an infant a few days old. (N. C. F. P. April 17, 1832)

Mrs. Susan GARRETT, wife of John GARRETT, died on January 6, 1836, leaving six children. "the youngest but a few days old." (T. P. January 16, 1836)

Ichabod GARRIS, overseer at the Goldsboro Poor House, was stabbed to death by inmate William Lane about February 26, 1852. (S. March 6, 1852)

Mrs. Julia GATLIN, widow of Thomas D. GATLIN, died at Tarboro on April 28, 1855, in her forty-eighth year, and leaving two sons and two daughters. She had been born on May 21, 1807, and joined the Tarboro Primitive Baptist Church on October 4, 1832. (S. May 5, 1855, and May 12, 1855) (Thomas GATLIN had married Julia Pender on or about June 18, 1829)

Captain Thomas D. GATLIN died on November 14, 1837, in Edgecombe County after falling from his horse and striking his head against a tree, when a stirrup broke. He was aged about thirty-three years and left a wife and four small children. The accident occurred on November 11, 1837, near the James Bridger home. The Concord Masonic Lodge, No. 58, held funeral rites on April 15, 1838, with preaching by the Rev. Joshua Lawrence. (T. S. November 17, 1837. T. P. November 18, 1837) (T. P. March 17, 1838)

Thomas Hall GATLIN, son of Thomas D. GATLIN, died at Tarboro on November 3, 1832, aged eight months and seven days. (N. C. F. P. November 6, 1832)

Ely GAY died in Edgecombe County on March 14, 1850. (T. P. April 6, 1850)

Mrs. Frances GAY, widow of Ely GAY, died in Edgecombe County on September 21, 1851, in her fifty-fourth year. (T. P. October 4, 1851)

William GAY died in Pitt County on January 23, 1827. (F. P. January 27, 1827)

William GAY from near Rocky Mount was killed when struck by a train on January 23, 1856. (S. January 26, 1856)

Jos. GEE, son of Colonel Neville GEE, died "a short time since" in Halifax County. (F. P. September 11, 1829)

Colonel Nevill GEE, "an old and respectable planter," died in Halifax County "a few days since." (F. P. September 29, 1827)

Mrs. Elizabeth GEORGE died in Edgecombe County on September 1, 1837. (T. P. September 9, 1837) She was sixty-seven or older and the mother of James GEORGE, lately Representative from Edgecombe County. She had belonged to the Baptist Church over twenty years. (T. S. September 8, 1837)

Richard GILLIAM of Virginia was killed instantly when the boiler of the steam mill of Willie Walston and J. H. Paine "about three miles from Sparta, burst with awful and fatal effect" on October 24, 1859. (S. October 29, 1859)

Dr. Peter I. GOELET died in Greenville on April 26, 1839. (T. P. May 4, 1839)

Major Etheldred GRAY of Edgecombe County died on March 24, 1846, aged about fifty, and leaving a wife and six children. (T. P. April 1, 1846) Concord Masonic Lodge, No. 58, scheduled a Masonic Funeral for him "at his late residence at Rocky Mount" on July 26, 1846, with the Rev. Mr. Barclay preaching. (T. P. June 10, 1846)

Henry GRAY, overseer of Marmaduke Battle, died suddenly on March 7, 1835. (T. P. March 14, 1835)

John GREGORY was stabbed through the heart at Enfield by William Collins on July 16, 1842. (T. P. July 23, 1842)

Mrs. Mary GREGORY died at Tarboro on August 5, 1858, in her ninetieth year. For over fifty years she had been the Proprietress of the Gregory Hotel in Tarboro and had accumulated a large property. She left one son, three grandsons, and one granddaughter, "children of the late Joseph R. Lloyd." (S. August 7, 1858)

Pattie GRIFFIN, daughter of James H. and Mary E. GRIFFIN, died at the home of her uncle Kenneth Thigpen on October 5, 1862, aged four years. (S. October 18, 1862)

Mrs. Telitha GRIMES, widow of William GRIMES, died in Edgecombe County on September 29, 1855, aged about seventy-five years. (S. October 6, 1855)

William GRIMES died in Edgecombe County on November 3, 1850, survived by his widow of eighty years, after about sixty years of marriage. (T.P. November 9, 1850)

Captain William A. GRIMMER died at Tarboro on May 30, 1857, in his thirty-eighth year, of typhoid fever, leaving a wife and three children. (S. June 6, 1857)

John W. GRIST, son of Allen GRIST, died at Washington on October 7, 1860, having been fatally wounded on October 4 by G. A. and Charles H. Latham who then fled, as the result of a political quarrel extending back to August. (S. October 13, 1860)

Mrs. Susan W. GUION, wife of Isaac D. GUION, died in Edgecombe County on July 16, 1828, aged about twenty-seven years. She was a daughter of the late Starling WALLER, Esq. (F. P. August 14, 1829)

Weeks P. HADLEY died at Tarboro on August 13, 1838, in his forty-second year. (T. P. August 18, 1838)

Mrs. Weeks P. HADLEY died at Tarboro on March 15, 1832. (N. C. F. P. March 20, 1832)

James H. HAILE died in Halifax on November 16, 1826. (F. P. December 12, 1826)

Dr. Thomas H. HALL, late State Senator and Member of Congress, died on June 23, 1853, aged about eighty years. (S. June 25, 1853)

Dr. B. F. HALSEY died in Tarboro on May 6, 1863, aged about forty-three years, of consumption. (S. May 16, 1863)

Edward G. HAMMOND, formerly of Edgecombe County, died in Caddo Parish, Louisiana, "recently" at the age of fifty-one years. (S. August 14, 1852)

Walter HANRAHAN died in Greenville on January 1, 1845, aged about eighty years. He was "a wealthy and highly respected citizen." (T. P. January 4, 1845)

Bythal HARDY died on August 10, 1827, aged about twenty-two years. (F. P. August 25, 1827)

Miss Priscilla HARE, aged about ninety, was fatally injured on August 9, 1850, "in an attempt to take a child from a buggy in which was an unruly horse." (T. P. August 17, 1850)

Franklin G. HARGRAVE died in Lexington, North Carolina, on October 14, 1845, aged about thirty-one years. (T. P. October 29, 1845)

John HARGRAVE, son-in-law of Theophilus Parker of Edgecombe County, died at Lexington on October 7, 1841, leaving a wife and two small children. (T. P. October 16, 1841)

Britton HARPER of Deep Creek in Edgecombe County died on December 26, 1829, after having been struck on the head by a stick wielded by James Bilbry on December 22. (F. P. January 1, 1830)

James HARPER, Esq., of Greene County, member-elect to the House of Commons, died "very recently." (T. P. September 7, 1844)

James R. HARPER died in Edgecombe County of typhoid fever on October 19, 1857, aged about twenty-five years. (S. October 24, 1857)

Mrs. Lizina HARRELL, widow of Christopher HARRELL, died in Edgecombe County on August 10, 1862, aged seventy-eight years. (S. August 16, 1862)

Allen HARRIS died in Edgecombe County on June 11, 1864, aged about fifty years. (S. June 18, 1864)

Bettie HARRIS, daughter of Spencer HARRIS, died near Falkland on August 22, 1858, in her nineteenth year. (S. August 28, 1858)

Mrs. Elizabeth HARRIS died in Edgecombe County on January 24, 1828, aged seventy-nine years. (F. P. February 1, 1828)

James HARRIS drowned in Tar River on May 31, 1850, leaving a wife and three children. (T. P. June 1, 1850) (In the Edgecombe County Census of 1850, Nancy Harris was listed with children Lucy, Jane, and James Harris.)

John HARRIS died suddenly in Edgecombe County on June 26, 1828. (F. P. July 18, 1828)

James HARRISS died in Halifax County on October 5, 1828. (F. P. October 24, 1828)

Henry E. HARRISON, son of Charles HARRISON, died in Edgecombe County on January 7, 1845. He was born on January 24, 1835. (T. P. January 25, 1845)

James B. HARRISON, only child of Richard HARRISON of Edgecombe County, died on October 16, 1826, aged twenty-two years. (F. P. October 24, 1826)

John W. HARRISON, Clerk of the Northampton County Court, died at the home of the Rev. John Weaver on October 14, 1830. (N. C. F. P. October 26, 1830)

Richard HARRISON, Esq., of Edgecombe County died on May 19, 1856. He had been born on January 30, 1768, in St. Mary's, Maryland. His large estate would be heired by descendants of his two sisters. (S. May 24, 1856)

William H. HARRISON died near Heningsville in Southampton County, Virginia on February 22, 1843, in his forty-first year, leaving a wife and three small children. (T. P. March 25, 1843)

Spencer L. HART, former Sheriff of Edgecombe County, died on June 19, 1853, aged seventy-eight years. (S. June 25, 1853)

Wilson S. HART of Halifax County died "a few days since" in Wilcox County, Alabama. (F. P. January 9, 1827)

Mary HASSELL, wife of Elder C. B. HASSELL of Williamston, died on June 29, 1846, at Louisburg, aged thirty-five years, leaving four children plus an infant born on June 21, 1846. (T. P. July 8, 1846)

Mary Bonner HATTON, daughter of James K. and Polly Ann HATTON, died at Tarboro on August 10, 1862, aged about nineteen months. (S. August 16, 1862)

Elza HAWKINS'S funeral was to be preached by the Rev. William Hyman on September 15, 1837. (T. P. September 2, 1837)

Colonel Philemon HAWKINS was born on December 3, 1753, and died on January 28, 1833, at Pleasant Hill in Warren County, being "the last of the signers of the Constitution of this State, in 1776." (N. C. F. P. February 12, 1833)

Sherwood HAYWOOD, Esq., died at Raleigh on October 5, 1829, in his sixty-eighth year. He owned a plantation in Edgecombe County and was Agent for the Bank of New Bern. (F. P. October 16, 1829)

William Henry HAYWOOD, Jr., died in Raleigh on October 7, 1852, in his fifty-first year. (S. October 16, 1852)

Edward HEARN, son of L. H. HEARN from Edgecombe County, was accidentally shot to death on March 14, 1854, aged twelve years and six months, in Jackson County, Florida. (S. April 15, 1854)

L. H. HEARN, formerly of Edgecombe County, died on May 7, 1854, in Jackson County, Florida, leaving a family. (S. May 20, 1854)

Mrs. Martha HEARN, wife of Michael HEARN and daughter of the late Edward HALL of Tarboro, died "recently" in Jacksonville, Florida, whither she had moved about five years ago. She was in her sixty-first year. (T. P. June 24, 1848)

Michael HEARN, formerly of Tarboro, died at Jacksonville, Florida, on October 28, 1854, aged about seventy-five years. He was a Mason and for many years Clerk of the Edgecombe County Court. (S. November 4, 1854)

Dr. William HENDERSON died at Williamston on August 17, 1838, leaving a wife and seven children. (T. P. September 1, 1838)

Joseph HENLEY of Franklin County was killed in Virginia on August 23, 1828, by the wheels of a wagon passing over his head. (F. P. August 29, 1828)

Dennis HEWELL was frozen to death "a few days since" in Pitt County. (T. P. January 21, 1846)

James Henry HICKS, son of Seth S. HICKS, died in Edgecombe County on June 30, 1860. (S. July 7, 1860) He was about four months old.

Solomon HICKS died of typhoid fever in Tarboro on September 30, 1856, aged about twenty-six years. (S. October 4, 1856)

Mrs. Adeline HIGGS, wife of Jacob HIGGS, died in Halifax County on March 11, 1858, aged about forty-years, leaving nine children, "the youngest about a fortnight old." (S. March 13, 1858)

Emily Ann HIGGS, daughter of the late Willie HIGGS, Esq., died in Halifax County at the Jacob Higgs residence on September 9, 1843, in her seventeenth year. (T. P. September 16, 1843)

Mrs. Sarah HIGGS died in Halifax County on April 1, 1837. (T. P. April 8, 1837)

John HILL was shot to death by William S. Powell of Halifax County in a quarrel over a slave on the night of December 23, 1829. (F. P. January 15, 1830)

Webb HILL of Wayne County died in his bed at Mrs. Griswold's Hotel on February 16, 1853. (S. March 5, 1853)

Carter HILLIARD died in Nash County on January 15, 1828, leaving a wife and seven children. (F. P. February 1, 1828)

James HILLIARD died at Hilliardston on July 6, 1832, being "a wealthy and respectable farmer." (N. C. F. P. July 17, 1832)

Dr. John T. HILLIARD died in Halifax County at the residence of his brother-in-law Isaac Hilliard on September 9, 1836, aged thirty-four years. He was a graduate of the Medical College of Philadelphia. (T. P. October 1, 1836)

Mrs. Mary HILLIARD, wife of James C. HILLIARD, Esq., and daughter of Mrs. Mary RUFFIN of Edgecombe County, died in Nash County on January 11, 1844, leaving a husband and four children. (T. P. January 13, 1844)

Jesse HILLMAN, a good Baptist, died in Halifax County on September 15, 1826. (T. P. September 19, 1826)

Benjamin R. HINES, Esq., died in Edgecombe County on July 5, 1841. (T. P. July 10, 1841)

Mrs. Caroline HINES, widow of the late Hon. Richard HINES, of Edgecombe County died at Raleigh on January 18, 1855. (S. February 3, 1855)

John E. HINES died in Edgecombe County on April 23, 1855, aged about sixty-two years and leaving two children. (S. April 28, 1855)

Mrs. Nancy HINES, wife of Richard HINES, Esq., died in Edgecombe County on February 17, 1830. (F. P. February 19, 1830)

Colonel Peter HINES died in Edgecombe County on April 1, 1850, aged about eighty years. (T. P. April 6, 1850)

Mrs. Sarah HINES, wife of Peter R. HINES and daughter of Edmund D. MACNAIR, died at the residence of Mrs. Tompkins in Nash County on October 28, 1837. (T. S. November 3, 1837. T. P. November 4, 1837)

Colonel William H. HINES died near Town Creek on December 21, 1824, aged about thirty-five years and leaving a wife and three children. He was a Methodist, Odd Fellow, Son of Temperance, and an esteemed Mason. (S. December 24, 1853. S. January 21, 1854)

Eli HODGE died in Edgecombe County on June 11, 1853, aged about twenty-three years. (S. June 18, 1853)

Richard HOLLAND died of typhoid fever at Tarboro on September 27, 1856 aged about twenty-three years. (October 4, 1856)

Thomas HOLLAND of Onslow County was murdered by his brother James HOLLAND on April 5, 1828, the latter having then fled from the County. (F. P. May 9, 1828)

General Gabriel HOLMES died in Sampson County on September 26, 1829, in his sixty-first year. He was educated in Law at Cambridge, Massachusetts, Governor of North Carolina 1821-1823, several times representative of Sampson County in the General Assembly, and at the time of his death was about to begin another term in Congress from the Fifth Congressional District. (F. P. October 16, 1829)

Benjamin L. HOPKINS died in Nash County on November 27, 1859, aged about sixty years. (S. December 3, 1859)

Colonel Daniel HOPKINS died in Edgecombe County on May 30, 1846. (T. P. June 3, 1846)

Frederick HOPKIBS died in Edgecombe County on October 18, 1850. (T. P. October 26, 1850)

George W. HOPKINS died in Edgecombe County "a few days since," aged about twenty-one years. (T. P. May 19, 1838)

Jarrett HOPKINS of Edgecombe County died on June 6, 1846. (T. P. June 10, 1846)

John HOPKINS, son of Frederick HOPKINS, died in Edgecombe County on May 29, 1835, aged thirty years. (T. P. June 6, 1835)

Dr. Thomas HOPKINS died in Edgecombe County on September 29, 1846. (T. P. September 30, 1846)

Dr. Thomas C. HOPKINS had died in Edgecombe County in September of 1846. (S. September 24, 1859) The article dealt with the "Legal Delays and Difficulties" involved in the prolonged settlement of his estate.

Van Buren HOPKINS died on September 16, 1859, aged about twenty-one years and unmarried, some time after having been struck in the head by an axe. (S. September 17, 1859) In July of 1859 he had been struck in Pitt County by twelve-years-old John Coggins who was acquitted on trial for the "absence of motive and imbecility of mind." (S. March 17, 1860)

Captain William D. HOPKINS died on March 10, 1841. (T. P. March 13,1841)

Jacob HORN died on the morning of September 22, 1826, in his eightieth year, in Edgecombe now[Wilson] County, having survived his wife Milicent for about six years. They had been married for about forty-eight years. "Reader," stated his Obituary, "few persons have lived and died like Jacob and Melicent HORN." (F. P. October 3, 1826)

Catharine HORNE, daughter of J. Lawrence HORNE of Edgecombe County, died "a few days since" at the Castalia Female Institute, aged about eleven years. (S. October 8, 1853)

Duke William HORNE died on Oak Hill in Marianna, Florida, on November 4, 1857, leaving a wife and children. He was a native of North Carolina (Edgecombe County) and a member of the Baptist Church at Orange Hill. He "came to this county from North Carolina, at an early date, and has resided in this and the adjoining county of Washington ever since." (S. November 21, 1857)

Eliza Jane HORNE, wife of John R. HORNE, died in Edgecombe County on December 9, 1839. (T. P. December 21, 1839)

Josiah HORNE, son of Joshua L. and Mary E. HORNE, died at Rocky Mount on September 3, 1848, in his thirteenth year. (T. P. September 9,1848)

Dr. Josiah R. HORNE of Edgecombe County died recently in Sumter County, Alabama. (T. P. November 7, 1840)

Elizabeth HOSKINS, infant daughter of R. T. HOSKINS, died at Tarboro on September 2, 1859. (S. September 3, 1859)

Thomas Owen HOSKINS, son of Richard H. HOSKINS, died at Tarboro on June 7, 1856, aged about four months. (S. June 14, 1856)

Mrs. Ann HOWARD died "A few days past on Ocracoke Island, . . . at the advanced age of 115 years." (T. P. November 6, 1841)

Corporal Calvin W. HOWARD, son of Wilson and Elizabeth HOWARD, died at

Richmond of typhoid fever on July 12, 1862, aged about twenty-two years, and a member of "The Edgecombe Rifles," Company G, 13th Regiment of North Carolina Volunteers. (S. July 26, 1862)

Frank HOWARD, son of Editor George HOWARD, died on July 28, 1854, in his fifth year. (S. August 5, 1854)

George HOWARD, one of the proprietors of this newspaper, died on March 25, 1863, in his sixty-sixth year. He had been in Tarboro about thirty-eight years and was Post Master. He was succeeded by his son William HOWARD. (S. April 4, 1863)

Margaret Adora HOWARD, daughter of Robert and Sarah HOWARD of Edgecombe County, was born on May 16, 1861, and died on June 21, 1861. (S. June 29, 1861)

Margaret M. HOWARD, daughter of George HOWARD, was born on February 4, 1845, and died on December 19, 1849, at Tarboro. (F. P. December 22, 1849)

Thomas HOWARD died at Tarboro on December 28, 1829. (F. P. January 1, 1830)

Thomas HOWARD died on August 15, 1834, aged twenty years. (T. F. P. August 22, 1834)

William HOWARD, son of Thomas HOWARD of Tarboro, died on January 1, 1830, aged seven years. (F. P. January 8, 1830)

Willie R. HOWARD, tavern keeper of Tarboro, died of intemperance and apoplexy on August 2, 1828. (F. P. August 8, 1828) Secretary Henry Horn of Joseph Warren Masonic Lodge, No. 92, of Stantonsburg, advertised his funeral rites at the Old Church in Tarborough on December 14, 1828. (F. P. December 12, 1828)

Wilson HOWARD died in Edgecombe County on November 4, 1840, aged nearly eighty-seven years. "He was a Revolutionary soldier, and was in two hard fought field battles. He continued a firm friend to republican principles until his death, was a respected citizen, and was a member of the Baptist church upwards of thirty years." (T. P. November 14, 1840) His will was probated in the County Court on November 23, 1840, naming as heirs William Howard, Jr., Peter E. and Mary Knight, Arthur B. and Sally Hyman, Joseph and Edney Howard, Willoughby Howard (a non-resident), and James and Charlotte Howard (non-residents). (T. P. January 9, 1841)

Anna HOWELL, daughter of the late James D. HOWELL, died at Rocky Mount on August 31, 1862, of typhoid fever, at the age of fourteen years. (S. September 6, 1862)

Augustin HOWELL died in Edgecombe County on November 5, 1859, aged about thirty-five years, leaving a wife and seven children. (S. November 12, 1859)

Augustus HOWELL died in Edgecombe County on November 5, 1859, aged about fourteen years. (T. M. November 9, 1859)

Baker HOWELL, son of William B. HOWELL of Tarboro, died on June 15, 1852. He was born on November 30, 1849. (S. June 19, 1852)

Eli HOWELL, Esq., of Edgecombe County died on October 14, 1831, aged forty or fifty years. (N. C. F. P. October 18, 1831)

Mrs. Eliza HOWELL, daughter of Jesse COOPER, Esq., and wife of William B. HOWELL, died near Tarboro on January 6, 1854. Her father lived in Martin County. (S. January 7, 1854)

Green B. HOWELL of Edgecombe County fell off the steamer WILLIAM GASTON on the night of November 30, 1850, and his body was recovered near Brunswick, Georgia, on December 5, and he was buried there. He was on his way from Tallahassee, Florida, to the home of his father Britton HOWELL of Edgecombe County. (T. P. January 4, 1851)

John HOWELL died in Edgecombe County on July 31, 1847, aged between seventy and eighty years. (T. P. August 7, 1847)

William J. HOWELL, son of William B. HOWELL, died at Tarboro on June 17, 1856, in his twenty-first year. (S. June 21, 1856)

Henry HOWINGTON died in Edgecombe County on October 15, 1844, aged fourteen years. (T. P. October 19, 1844)

James R. HOYLE died at Greenville in Pitt County on January 17, 1841.
(T. P. January 23, 1841)

Dr. Benjamin B. HUNTER, formerly of Tarboro, died in Nashville on March
20, 1827, aged thirty-eight years. (F. P. March 24, 1827)

Charles G. HUNTER, Esq., from "near this place," lost his mother of
about ninety-six years "a short time since" in Louisiana. (S.
March 11, 1854)

Rev. James HUNTER died near Enfield on December 4, 1831, leaving a widow
and several sons and daughters. He was a Methodist minister for
about forty years. (N. C. F. P. December 27, 1831)

Weldon Jackson HUNTER, child of Weldon S. HUNTER of Edgecombe County,
died on May 17, 1848, aged about eighteen months. (T. P. May 20,
1848)

Mrs. Absila HURSEY, wife of Thomas HURSEY, died at Rocky Mount on July
5, 1848. (T. P. July 8, 1848)

Jesse M. HURSEY died at Tarboro on November 2, 1849, aged about forty-
two years. (T. P. November 3, 1849)

Emeliza HUSSEY, daughter of Thomas C. HUSSEY, died at Tarboro on July
17, 1854. (S. July 22, 1854)

Mrs. Emeliza HUSSEY, wife of Thomas C. HUSSEY, died at Tarboro on August
7, 1854. Her infant of a week died on August 9, 1854. (S. August
12, 1854)

Jesse HYATT, son of Jesse B. HYATT, died at Tarboro on May 17, 1855,
aged about eighteen months. (S. May 19, 1855)

Jesse Joab HYATT, son of Jesse B. HYATT, died at Tarboro on March 26,
1857, aged thirteen months and three days. (S. April 4, 1857)

Mrs. Margaret HYATT, wife of Jesse B. HYATT, died at Tarboro on December
31, 1848. (T. P. January 6, 1849)

Mary Jane Elizabeth HYATT, daughter of Jesse B. HYATT, died at Tarboro
on October 27, 1855. She was born on January 19, 1855. (S. November 3, 1855)

Mrs. Frances HYMAN, wife of Elder William HYMAN, died in Edgecombe County
on March 1, 1856, aged about eighty-two years. (S. March 8, 1856)

Henry HYMAN "of the firm of Austin, Hyman & Co.," died near Tarboro on
December 27, 1856, aged about fifty years. (S. January 3, 1857)

Hugh HYMAN died in Martin County on July 4, 1844, in his seventy-ninth
year. He had been married for sixty-three years, had sixteen
children, and "never had a corpse in his house until his death."
(T. P. August 3, 1844)

Joseph W. HYMAN died in Edgecombe County on March 24, 1862, of the
measles, and aged about twenty years. (S. March 29, 1862)

Kenneth HYMAN died on September 26, 1834, aged forty-six years. (T. F.
P. October 10, 1834)

Kenneth HYMAN, son of Theophilus HYMAN, died in Edgecombe County "a
short time since," aged about two years. (S. September 2, 1854)

Martha HYMAN, daughter of the late Ely PORTER and Wife of Henry HYMAN,
died in Edgecombe County on January 11, 1846, leaving three children. (T. P. January 14, 1846)

Mrs. Sally HYMAN died on August 19, 1832, aged eighty-two years. (N. C.
F. P. August 28, 1832)

Mrs. Sarah HYMAN, wife of Arthur B. HYMAN, died in Edgecombe County on
October 23, 1859. She had been born on March 2, 1807. (S. November 12, 1859. T. M. November 9, 1859)

Theophilus HYMAN, formerly of Tarboro, died on April 11, 1841, at the
John W. Cotten residence near Tallahassee, Florida. (T. P. May 1,
1841)

John A. IRVIN, "a respectable farmer" and "himself and wife considerably advanced in years," died near Tarboro on May 2, 1829, followed by his wife Sarah IRVIN on May 6, 1829. (F. P. May 7 [8], 1829)

Benjamin M. JACKSON, Esq., died in Tarboro on November 1, 1860, aged about seventy-eight years. (S. November 3, 1860)

James JACKSON of Edgecombe County died on March 14, 1861, aged about seventy years. (S. March 16, 1861)

William JAMES died in Edgecombe County on January 19, 1848. (T. P. January 22, 1848)

Mrs. Brittania JENKINS, wife of Robertson JENKINS, died in Pitt County on September 15, 1845. (T. P. September 17, 1845)

Mrs. Elizabeth JENKINS, wife of Joab JENKINS and daughter of the late Richard CARNEY, died in Edgecombe County on October 14, 1858, aged about twenty-five years, and leaving three small children. (S. October 23, 1858)

Mrs. Frances JENKINS died in Pitt County on August 27, 1830, aged one hundred and eight years. Her husband had been nearly a hundred when he died "a few years since." (N. C. F. P. August 31, 1830)

Harmon JENKINS died in Pitt County on October 17, 1827, aged about twenty-seven years and leaving a wife and two small children. (F. P. October 20, 1827)

Henry JENKINS of Edgecombe County lost his wife on August 2, 1856, while she was visiting the home of her father Jesse STANSELL in Pitt County. (S. August 9, 1856)

Mrs. Joseph F. JENKINS, daughter of Colonel Daniel HOPKINS, died in Edgecombe County on July 22, 1837. (T. S. July 28, 1837)

Mary Frances JENKINS, daughter of John JENKINS, died at Tarboro on January 17, 1841, aged about three years. (T. P. January 23, 1841)

Mrs. Marina JENKINS, wife of James F. JENKINS and daughter of Colonel Daniel HOPKINS, died on July 22, 1837, aged about twenty-three years, leaving a husband and three children. (T. P. July 29, 1837)

Mrs. Mildred JENKINS, wife of James F. JENKINS, died in Edgecombe County on October 19, 1843. (T. P. October 21, 1843)

Mrs. Ridley JENKINS, wife of Joseph D. JENKINS, died on February 25, 1848, leaving three children. (T. P. March 4, 1848)

Colonel William A. JENKINS of Warren County died in Halifax on November 10, 1869. (N. C. November 12, 1869)

Charles JEROLD was murdered at New Hope in Wayne County on October 22, 1853, by Arthur Sasser and Bryant Johnston. (S. November 5, 1853)

Henry JOHNSON died of typhoid fever in Edgecombe County on July 8, 1854, in his thirty-second year, leaving a wife and three children. A Masonic Funeral was ordered for August 27 by the Concord Lodge, with preaching by the Rev. Mr. Daniel. (S. July 15, 1854)

Joseph A. JOHNSON of Edgecombe County enlisted about April 18, 1861, in Company A, 1st Regiment of North Carolina Volunteers, and fought in the Battle of Bethel. He died of typhoid pneumonia on July 23, 1861, in the Yorktown Hospital. (S. August 3, 1861)

Lawrence JOHNSON, Clerk of the Martin County Court, died at Williamston on November 21, 1858, leaving a wife and four children. (S. December 4, 1858)

Mrs. Nancy JOHNSON died in Edgecombe County on February 5, 1852. She had been born on January 6, 1745. (S. February 14, 1852)

Nancy JOHNSON, wife of Joseph J. JOHNSON, died in Edgecombe County on May 12, 1859, aged about forty-five years. (S. May 28, 1859)

Purvis JOHNSON of Austin County, Texas, lost his wife Mary EDMONDSON, daughter of John Edmondson and formerly of Edgecombe County, on September 15, 1851. She was about fifty-four years of age and a member of the Missionary Baptist Church. (Raleigh Register, November 22, 1851)

Robert A. JOHNSON died of consumption in Arkansas on February 25, 1860, aged about fifty years, leaving a wife and eight children. He had left his native Edgecombe County in January. (S. March 17, 1860)

General Robert R. JOHNSON died at Deep Creek in Warren County on March 19, 1827, in his forty-ninth year. (F. P. March 31, 1827)

William JOHNSON died near Stantonsburg in Wilson County on October 17, 1858. (S. November 6, 1858)

Aaron JOHNSTON died in Edgecombe County on February 14, 1847, aged about sixty years. (T. P. February 20, 1847)

Mrs. Catharine JOHNSTON died in Edgecombe County on May 29, 1842, "at an advanced age." She had been born on May 16, 1754. She was the widow of Amos JOHNSTON, Esq., and had been a "pious member of the Baptist church for the last sixty years of her life." (T. P. June 4, 1842, and June 11, 1842)

Mrs. Charlotte JOHNSTON, wife of Joseph J. JOHNSTON, died in Edgecombe County on February 14, 1847. (T. P. February 20, 1847)

Mrs. Emily JOHNSTON, widow of Henry JOHNSTON, died on August 9, 1841, leaving three small children. (T. P. August 14, 1841)

Mrs. Harriet JOHNSTON, wife of Henry JOHNSTON, merchant tailor of Tarboro, died on July 20, 1827. (F. P. July 28, 1827)

Henry JOHNSTON died at Tarboro on July 1, 1839, leaving a wife and two small children. He was a member of the Baptist Church. (T. P. July 6, 1839)

James Ward JOHNSTON, son of Henry JOHNSTON, died at Tarboro on May 30, 1836. (T. P. June 4, 1836)

Colonel Jonas JOHNSTON took part in several expeditions against the British and Tories during the Revolutionary War, fighting under Colonel Caswell at the Battle of Stono and dying on his way home after that battle. "Col. JOHNSTON was robust in person, active, capable of bearing much fatigue, vigilant and brave as an officer, and high-minded and honorable as a man; which, joined to a mind distinguished for its strength and fortitude, rendered him as invaluable auxiliary in defense of the liberty of his country." About 1768 he had married Esther MAUND at the home of Aquilla Sugg near Tarboro. She was born in Norfolk County, Virginia, and died in Edgecombe County on January 19, 1841, aged eighty-nine years. She had been left a widow in 1779 with five small children. Her executor was Jonas J. Carr who sold her personal property on February 6, 1841. (T. P. January 30, 1841)

Alfred JOINER, son of Howell JOINER, died at the home of Moses Beckwith of Edgecombe County on January 29, 1841. (T. P. February 13, 1841)

Allen JONES died in Edgecombe County on October 11, 1856, aged about sixty-seven years, leaving a wife, three sons, and three daughters. (S. October 18, 1856)

Benjamin JONES died at Scotland Neck on August 10, 1828. (F. P. August 22, 1828)

Frederick JONES died in Edgecombe County on December 15, 1839, aged forty-two years and leaving a widow, two sons, and three daughters. His funeral sermon was preached by the Rev. William Hyman. (T. P. December 21, 1839)

Dr. Jesse F. JONES died at Spring Green in Martin County on August 15, 1832, in his sixty-eighth year. (N. C. F. P. September 4, 1832)

Mrs. Martha JONES, wife of James JONES, Jr., died in Halifax County on May 30, 1829. (F. P. June 12, 1829)

Mrs. Pherebee JONES died in Edgecombe County on January 24, 1838, aged seventy-six years, and for many years a member of the Baptist Church. (T. P. February 2, 1838)

Robert Allen JONES, Esq., died in Halifax County on September 20, 1831. (N. C. F. P. September 27, 1831)

Mrs. Lucy A. JORDAN, wife of William B. JORDAN and daughter of Colonel F. L. DANCY of Florida, died at Rocky Mount on September 4, 1858, aged about twenty-three years. (S. September 11, 1858)

Valentine S. JORDAN died near Pactolus on October 11, 1852. He had been born on August 4, 1782. (S. October 30, 1852)

Mrs. Temperance JOYNER, wife of Colonel Andrew JOYNER, died in Halifax County on March 8, 1834. (T. F. P. March 14, 1834)

Joseph B. JUDKINS of Pitt County died at Greenville "a short time since." (T. P. November 12, 1836)

Willie KEEL died of consumption in Martin County on September 13, 1863, aged about sixty-one years. (S. September 19, 1863)

W. G. KILKELLY of Goldsboro, agent for the Adams Express Company, was killed on March 10, 1856, when the Seaboard and Roanoke train was wrecked. (S. March 15, 1856)

_____ KING was presumed drowned at Smithfield on February 15, 1853, after the explosion of a steam-boiler. (S. February 19, 1853)

Warren T. KING died on October 18, 1853. (S. November 12, 1853)

William Coffield KING, son of Coffield KING, died at his father's residence near Tarboro on June 26, 1862. He had been born on July 21, 1841, and at the time of his death was serving as Commissary Sergeant of the 44th North Carolina Regiment. (S. July 5, 1862) His obituary appeared on August 9, page 2, columns 3/4.

Mrs. Eliza KIRTLAND died on November 5, 1829. She was the wife of H. L. KIRTLAND and the daughter of E. D. MACNAIR. (F. P. November 6,1829)

Allen J. KNIGHT, gig-maker, died at Tarboro on September 10, 1828. Concord Masonic Lodge, No. 58, held funeral rites for him at the Old Church in Tarborough on November 2, 1828. (F. P. September 12, 1828, and October 24, 1828)

Andrew C. KNIGHT, son of Jesse C. KNIGHT, died on January 26, 1840, aged about nineteen years. (T. P. February 1, 1840)

Andrew J. KNIGHT died in Edgecombe County on August 3, 1858, aged about twenty-seven years. (S. August 7, 1858)

Arthur KNIGHT died "at an advanced age" on June 24, 1834. (T. F. P. June 27, 1834)

Mrs. Asa KNIGHT, wife of John KNIGHT and daughter of the late Eli HOWELL, died in Edgecombe County on November 14, 1843. (T. P. November 18, 1843)

Benjamin KNIGHT died in Edgecombe County on April 1, 1854, aged about twenty-five years, leaving a wife and two children. (S. April 8, 1854)

Benjamin Franklin KNIGHT died at the residence of his father Jesse C. KNIGHT, Esq., on May 1, 1854, in his twenty-ninth year. (S. May 6, 1854)

Charles W. KNIGHT died in Edgecombe County on February 9, 1848, aged nearly seventy-three years. (T. P. February 19, 1848)

Colbert C. KNIGHT died in Edgecombe County on August 14, 1839, leaving a wife and two children. (T. P. August 17, 1839)

Daniel KNIGHT died at Tarboro on March 15, 1843, aged about forty-five years. (T. P. March 18, 1843)

David B. KNIGHT died of consumption at Williamston on June 6, 1859. He was born on December 23, 1832. (S. June 25, 1859)

Elizabeth KNIGHT, eldest daughter of Charles W. KNIGHT, Esq., died on February 20, 1832, in her twentieth year. (N. C. F. P. February 21, 1832; February 28, 1832)

Gariot KNIGHT died in Edgecombe County on June 27, 1834, aged about sixty-two years. (T. F. P. July 18, 1834)

James KNIGHT died in Edgecombe County on June 25, 1847. (T. P. July 10, 1847)

Jesse C. KNIGHT, "a prominent and useful citizen," died in Edgecombe County on October 28, 1859, aged about sixty years. (S. November 5, 1859)

John KNIGHT, Sr., died in Edgecombe County on April 21, 1859, aged about fifty-five years, leaving a wife and three children. (S. April 23, 1859)

Mrs. Martha Ann KNIGHT, wife of John KNIGHT, Jr., and daughter of the late Elisha CROMWELL, died on May 30, 1859, aged about thirty-eight years. (S. June 18, 1859)

Mrs. Peter E. KNIGHT died in Edgecombe County on February 6, 1844. (T. P. February 10, 1844)

Mrs. Sally KNIGHT, widow of Arthur KNIGHT, died in Edgecombe County at the home of A. K. Barlow, Esq., on July 16, 1847, in her seventy-fifth year. (T. P. July 17, 1847)

Sarah KNIGHT, daughter of John KNIGHT, died in Edgecombe County on January 22, 1849, aged about twelve years. (T. P. January 27, 1849)

Mrs. Spicey KNIGHT, widow of James KNIGHT, died in Edgecombe County on October 15, 1848. (T. P. October 21, 1848)

Walker KNIGHT died on March 24, 1833, in his seventy-third year. (N. C. F. P. March 30, 1833)

William KNIGHT, son of James KNIGHT, died on March 2, 1837, aged about twenty years. (T. P. March 11, 1837)

William F. KNIGHT died in Edgecombe County on August 29, 1846, aged about thirty-five years. (T. P. September 2, 1846) On August 25, 1846, he had secured a marriage bond to marry Nancy Lawrence.

Willis KNIGHT died in Edgecombe County on March 4, 1846, aged about seventy years. (T. P. March 11, 1846)

Churchill KNOX of Pitt County died at Holmes's Hotel in Wilmington on August 31, 1856. (S. September 6, 1856)

Joseph LACKEY of Tarboro died on January 14, 1829. (F. P. January 16, 1829)

Henry LANCASTER, "an Officer of the Revolution," died in Edgecombe County "recently, at the advanced age of eighty-four." (T. P. February 20, 1836)

Daniel LAND, a member of the Baptist Church for forty years, died on September 12, 1857, aged sixty-four years. (S. September 19, 1857, and October 3, 1857)

David LANE died in Edgecombe County on October 2, 1837, aged about forty-five years, leaving a wife and several children. (T. S. October 6, 1837. T. P. October 7, 1837)

Martha LANE died near Enfield on September 15, 1826, being a daughter of Joseph LANE. (T. P. September 19, 1826)

Colonel Robert LANE died at Waynesville in Haywood County on July 17, 1845, in his eighty-fifth year. (T. P. August 6, 1845)

William LANGSTON died in Goldsboro on July 9, 1860, leaving a widow. (S. August 4, 1860)

John LANIER, son of William A. LANIER, died on April 17, 1845, aged sixteen months. (T. P. April 19, 1845)

Clement H. LASSITER was murdered in Hyde County on December 6, 1852, by Elder George Washington Carawan. (S. December 11, 1852)

Mrs. Penelope LASSITER of Greene County was murdered at night in her bed in the week preceding, "with a hole the size of a pistol ball through her skull, just above one of her ears." (T. P. February 9, 1842)

Noah LATHAM, "a revolutionary soldier," died in Pitt County on April 8, 1835, aged seventy-seven years. (T. P. April 18, 1835)

Thomas LATHAM, Jr., was murdered about five miles from Williamston on the night of August 29, 1850, aged twenty-one years, recently married, and a nephew of Colonel Thomas Latham. (T. P. August 31, 1850)

Annie L. LAWRENCE, daughter of Thomas D. and Mary F. LAWRENCE, died in

Edgecombe County on September 29, 1863, aged three years and eight months. (S. October 10, 1863)

Edmund Mullen LAWRENCE, son of Peter P. LAWRENCE, died at Tarboro on August 5, 1829, aged eleven months. (F. P. August 7, 1829)

Mrs. Emily G. LAWRENCE, wife of David LAWRENCE, died in Greenville on January 2, 1850, leaving six children. (T. P. January 19, 1850)

John LAWRENCE of Edgecombe County died "at an advanced age" on June 19, 1844. (T. P. June 22, 1844)

John G. LAWRENCE, aged about thirty, was murdered by Napoleon Cromwell on February 3, 1836, leaving a family. (T. P. February 6, 1836)

John Paul LAWRENCE, son of James J. and Adeline LAWRENCE, was born on December 31, 1849, and died on September 10, 1854. (S. September 16, 1854)

Joseph J. LAWRENCE died in Edgecombe County on July 31, 1860, aged about thirty years, leaving a family. (S. August 4, 1860)

Lemuel LAWRENCE died in Edgecombe County on June 12, 1838, leaving a wife and three small children. His funeral sermon, sponsored by Concord Masonic Lodge, No. 58, would be preached by Elder William Hyman on December 30, 1838, at "the residence of his father, Elder Joshua LAWRENCE." (T. P. June 16, 1838; and December 8, 1838)

Louisa Jennsie LAWRENCE, daughter of William and Emily LAWRENCE of South Quay, Virginia, died at the home of Coffield King on February 13, 1860, having been born on January 20, 1860. (S. February 18, 1860)

Mrs. Martha LAWRENCE, wife of Peter P. LAWRENCE, died on October 31, 1831. (N. C. F. P. November 8, 1831)

Mrs. Mary LAWRENCE, wife of Peter P. LAWRENCE, died at Tarboro on February 6, 1838. (T. P. February 10, 1838)

Mrs. Mary LAWRENCE, widow of the Rev. Joshua LAWRENCE, died in Edgecombe County on May 11, 1851. (T. P. May 17, 1851)

Peter P. LAWRENCE, for many years Cashier of the Tarboro' Branch of the State Bank, died at Tarboro on February 3, 1855, in his seventy-sixth year. (S. February 17, 1855)

Quincy LAWRENCE died in Edgecombe County on March 28, 1856, aged about thirty-five years. (S. April 12, 1856)

Thomas D. LAWRENCE died in Edgecombe County on November 8, 1859, aged thirty-two years, and leaving a wife and two children. (S. November 19, 1859)

Mrs. _____ LEE died in Edgecombe County on June 19, 1844, aged about ninety-two years. (T. P. June 22, 1844)

Willie LEE, son of Levi LEE of Edgecombe County, died on November 13, 1843. (T. P. November 18, 1843)

Mrs. Elizabeth LEGGETT, wife of Levin LEGGETT, died in Edgecombe County on August 12 (or 13), 1837, leaving a husband and "a large family of children." (T. S. August 18, 1837. T. P. August 19, 1837)

Levin LEGGETT died in Edgecombe County "at an advanced age" on January 6, 1855. (S. January 13, 1855)

William R. LEGGETT of Martin County died at J. Wood's Tavern at Louisburg on March 30, 1835. (T. P. April 4, 1835)

Mrs. Amy LEIGH, wife of William C. LEIGH, Esq., died in Edgecombe County on December 25, 1838. (T. P. January 5, 1839)

Miss Rhoda LEIGH was born on June 17, 1788, and died in Edgecombe County on July 27, 1852. (S. July 31, 1852)

William C. LEIGH, Esq., died in Edgecombe County on February 2, 1855, aged about fifty-five years. (S. February 10, 1855)

William W. LEWELLING died at Greenville on October 13, 1831. His Masonic Funeral was announced for November 27. (N. C. F. P. October 18, 1831, and November 8, 1831)

Mrs. _____ LEWIS, widow of Exum LEWIS, died at Mount Prospect in Edgecombe County at "an advanced age" on December 16, 1843. (T. P. December 23, 1843)

Exum LEWIS died on January 18, 1839, aged about seventy years. He had "held a conspicuous station in society for many years, was chairman of the County Court, &c." (T. P. January 26, 1839)

Frederick Wiggins LEWIS, son of Dr. H. E. LEWIS, died of diptheria on October 16, 1862, in his thirteenth year, in Edgecombe County. (S. October 18, 1862)

Dr. John Wesley LEWIS, formerly of Edgecombe County, died at Raleigh on November 22, 1842, after two or three years of residence there. (T. P. November 26, 1842)

J. LEWIS was killed by lightning near Faucett's in Halifax County on June 17, 1853. (S. July 16, 1853)

Mary Foreman LEWIS, wife of Richard Henry LEWIS, Esq., died at Greensborough, Alabama, on September 24, 1840, aged thirty years. She was a native of Edgecombe County and left four small children. (T. P. October 10, 1840)

Richard Henry LEWIS, Esq., died in Pitt County on January 18, 1857, aged about fifty years. (S. January 24, 1857) A later issue stated that he died of consumption on January 19, 1857, in his fifty-first year. (S. February 7, 1857)

Robert H. LEWIS, Esq., died at Milton of consumption on September 3, 1860, aged thirty-three years, and leaving a widow and two small children. He was a member of the Presbyterian Church. (S. September 22, 1860)

Robert H. LEWIS, only child of the late Robert H. LEWIS, of Milton, died at Tarboro on November 7, 1860, aged six months. (S. November 10, 1860)

Thomas L. LIDDON, bricklayer and formerly of Tarboro, died at Washington on April 24, 1855, aged about thirty-five years, leaving a wife and five children. (S. April 28, 1855)

Mrs. Sarah P. LIPSCOMBE, wife of George B. LIPSCOMBE, died in Tarboro on November 14, 1862, aged about thirty-seven years, leaving one child. (S. November 18, 1862)

Dempsey LITTLE of Pitt County died on August 3, 1834. (T. F. P. August 22, 1834)

Mrs. Elizabeth LITTLE died at the William Lodge home on September 5, 1859, aged about sixty years. (S. September 10, 1859)

Mrs. Frances LITTLE, wife of the late Jesse LITTLE, died in Edgecombe County on September 19, 1843, in her seventy-second year, leaving five children and many grandchildren and great-grandchildren. For forty years she had been an "exemplary member of the Predestinarian Baptist Church." (T. P. September 23, 1843)

Frederick D. LITTLE of Edgecombe County died suddenly on January 17, 1855, leaving a wife and ten children. (S. January 20, 1855) A later issue indicated that he had been born on May 28, 1800, and died at Conetoe on January 18, 1855. (S. February 3, 1855)

Major Gray LITTLE died near Tarboro on August 13, 1824. He was for many years Sheriff of Edgecombe County. (F. P. September 3, 1824)

Major Gray LITTLE had been in the North Carolina Legislature in 1829 and 1830 and was a native of Edgecombe County. He died at Bladen Springs, Alabama, on April 18, 1857, in his fifty-fifth year, leaving a wife and several children. He was a Mason and also a member of the Methodist Church in Sumter County. (S. May 23, 1857)

Josephine LITTLE, daughter of Colonel L. G. LITTLE of Pitt County, died in Tarboro of the measles on July 10, 1862, aged about eighteen years. (S. July 12, 1862)

Margaret LITTLE, wife of William LITTLE, died "a few days since" aged about fifty years. (T. P. November 30, 1844) (William LITTLE had married Margaret Drake on November 20, 1829)

William LITTLE, Jr., of Edgecombe County died on August 10, 1857, aged about twenty-seven years. (S. August 15, 1857)

Joseph B. LITTLEJOHN, originally from Granville County, lost his wife in Tennessee on October 16, 1840. (T. P. October 24, 1840)

Robert Vernon LITTLEJOHN, son of Gen. Joseph B. LITTLEJOHN of Franklin County, died in Tarboro on May 25, 1850, aged about nineteen months. (T. P. June 1, 1850)

Mrs. Chloe LLOYD, wife of David LLOYD, died at Tarboro on May 17, 1829. (F. P. May 22, 1829)

George M. LLOYD died in Tarboro on October 27, 1856, aged about twenty-three years. (S. November 1, 1856)

Joseph R. LLOYD, Esq., President of the Branch of the State Bank at Tarboro, died near there on February 5, 1841, leaving a wife and five children. (T. P. February 6, 1841)

Polly LLOYD, daughter of David LLOYD of Tarboro, died on September 8, 1827. (F. P. September 15, 1827)

Elder Nathaniel LOCKHEART, a Free-Will Baptist Minister for twenty-one years, died in Pitt County on December 21, 1835, aged sixty-four years. (T. P. February 6, 1836)

Lewis LODGE, a Revolutionary War soldier, died in Edgecombe County on September 27, 1829, aged about sixty-seven years. (F. P. October 2, 1829)

Mrs. Elizabeth LONG died at Halifax on December 4, 1830, having been long a member of the Baptist Church. (N. C. F. P. December 14, 1830)

Emily Ann LONG, daughter of James S. LONG, died in Edgecombe County on June 25, 1845. She had been born on September 21, 1843. (T. P. July 2, 1845)

John LONG died in Martin County on July 6, 1840. His administratrix Mary A. C. LONG sold ten or twelve slaves and other personal property at his residence in the Town of Hamilton. (T. P. July 6, 1840; and November 28, 1840)

John B. LONG, son of James S. LONG of Edgecombe County, died on June 16, 1854. He was born on March 13, 1842. (S. June 17, 1854)

Joseph LONG died in Martin County on June 3, 1834, aged about fifty-five years, leaving a wife and six children. (T. F. P. June 13, 1834)

Mrs. Louisa LONG, daughter of the Rev. Joshua LAWRENCE and wife of James LONG, died in Edgecombe County on January 23, 1837. (T. P. January 28, 1837)

Mary Eliza LONG, daughter of James S. and Welthy LONG of Edgecombe County, died on January 21, 1861, aged fourteen years and seven months. (S. February 2, 1861)

Nancy LONG, daughter of William R. LONG, died in Edgecombe County on December 4, 1839, aged about thirty years. (T. P. December 7, 1839)

Dr. Reading S. LONG, formerly of Tarboro, died near Mars Bluff, South Carolina, on October 12, 1831. (N. C. F. P. November 1, 1831)

William R. LONG died in Edgecombe County, "an aged, worthy, and highly respected citizen," on June 24, 1849. (T. P. June 30, 1849)

Exum L. LOWE, formerly of Tarboro, died at Hamilton on December 24, 1834, aged forty-four years. (T. P. January 2, 1835)

Figures LOWE, Esq., a native of North Carolina, settled in 1840 near Livingston, Mississippi, and died wealthy on April 16, 1852, leaving a wife and one daughter. He was a member of the Methodist Church. (S. May 15, 1852)

Thomas LYON, "an aged and much esteemed planter," died in Edgecombe County "a short time since." (T. P. January 30, 1836)

Thomas LYON'S widow died "at an advanced age" in Edgecombe County on July 25, 1838. (T. P. July 28, 1838)

Captain Baker W. MABREY of the 44th North Carolina Regiment, died of

typhoid fever at the home of his uncle Baker Staton near Tarboro on
September 18, 1862, aged thirty-three years. "He had been twice
married, and was a childless widower at the time of his death."
(S. September 20, 1862)

Colonel Charles MABRY'S wife died in Edgecombe County on June 9, 1838.
(T. P. June 9, 1838)

Colonel Charles MABRY died in Edgecombe County on December 12, 1857, aged
about fifty-six years. (S. December 19, 1857)

Mrs. Lucy B. MABREY, wife of Dr. B. W. MABREY and daughter of John
LAWRENCE, died at Tarboro on March 15, 1857, in her twenty-second
year. (S. March 21, 1857)

Mrs. Mary E. MABREY, wife of Dr. Baker W. MABREY of Tarboro and daughter
of the late Jos. FREEMAN, died on August 5, 1860, aged about eighteen years. (S. August 11, 1860)

Wilkinson MABRY died in Edgecombe County on May 18, 1839, "at an advanced age." (T. P. May 25, 1839)

William Almarine MABREY, formerly of Edgecombe County, died of typhoid
fever in Martin County on October 23, 1855, aged about twenty-eight
years. (S. October 27, 1855)

Edmund D. MACNAIR, Esq., died at "Hope Lodge" near Tarboro on December
6, 1842, in his sixty-sixth year. (T. P. December 10, 1842)

John MACNAIR, son of Edmund D. MACNAIR, shot himself accidentally while
hunting on Thursday and died the next day near Tarboro on November
11, 1836, aged about fourteen years. (T. P. November 12, 1836)

Pauline MACNAIR, daughter of Hugh MACNAIR, died near Tarboro on March
27, 1862, aged about two years. (S. March 29, 1862)

Mrs. Penelope MACNAIR, wife of Dr. A. H. MACNAIR, died near Tarboro on
July 26, 1851, in her twentieth year. (T. P. August 9, 1851)

William Augustus MACNAIR, son of Dr. A. H. and Anna MACNAIR, died at
Tarboro on May 17, 1855. He was born on January 4, 1854. (S. May
19, 1855)

John P. MANNING died in Edgecombe County on March 15, 1839. (T. P.
March 23, 1839)

Harriet MARINER, daughter of William MARINER, died on September 18, 1843,
aged about three years. (T. P. September 23, 1843)

Mrs. Louisa MARINER, wife of William MARINER, died at Tarboro on August
24, 1848, from a spider bite, leaving two children. (T. P. August
26, 1848)

Mrs. Amanda L. MARKS, wife of Jos. J. N. MARKS, died in Edgecombe County
on August 8, 1860, aged about thirty-eight years, leaving eight
children. (S. September 1, 1860)

Rosena Ann MARKS, daughter of James C. MARKS, died in Edgecombe County
on February 27, 1860, aged about sixteen years. (S. March 17, 1860)

Thomas B. MARKS died at Tarboro on September 8, 1827, aged eighteen
years. (F. P. September 29, 1827)

Henry MASON of Scotland Neck was stabbed to death by his overseer Blount
Marshall on December 4, 1834. Both had been drinking before the
fight. (T. F. P. December 19, 1834)

Burrell MATTHEWS was frozen to death "a few days since" in Pitt County.
(T. P. January 21, 1846)

Nathan MATTHEWSON, Clerk of the Superior Court of Edgecombe County and
"one of our oldest and most respected citizens," died on July 5,
1832. (N. C. F. P. July 10, 1832)

Paschal P. MATTHEWSON died "a few days since" of the smallpox in Providence, Rhode Island, being a son of the late Nathan MATTHEWSON of
the Edgecombe County Court. (T. F. P. August 1, 1834)

Benjamin MAY, Esq., a native of Edgecombe County, died near Macon, Georgia, on January 9, 1852, in his seventy-sixth year. (S. January
31, 1852)

Benjamin MAY of Pitt County was accidentally killed by a gunpowder explosion on March 9, 1860. (S. March 10, 1860)

Elizabeth MAY, daughter of Alvin and Susan MAY of Pitt County, died at the home of John F. Hughes, Esq., in Edgecombe County on September 8, 1843, aged about twenty-three years. (T. P. September 23, 1843)

Drewry MAYO died in Edgecombe County on August 12, 1834. (T. F. P. August 22, 1834)

Mrs. Elizabeth MAYO, widow of Colonel Nathan MAYO, died in Edgecombe County on September 24, 1815, in her eightieth year. (P. S. October 5, 1815, and October 9, 1815)

Elizabeth MAYO, daughter of Mrs. Susan MAYO, died on August 31, 1843, aged about twenty years. (T. P. September 16, 1843)

Elizabeth MAYO, wife of John MAYO, died in Edgecombe County on December 10, 1855. (S. December 15, 1855)

Frederic MAYO, son of Reuben MAYO, died in Edgecombe County on July 1, 1854, aged about twenty years. (S. July 8, 1854)

F. W. MAYO was born on March 15, 1804, and died in Fayette County, Tennessee, on November 21, 1853, leaving a wife and children. (S. January 7, 1854)

James MAYO from Martin County died in Fayette County, Tennessee, on August 30, 1848, in his fifty-third year, leaving a wife and eleven children. He had been a Baptist for thirty-one years. (T. P. October 28, 1848)

John MAYO died in Edgecombe County on December 12, 1855, aged about sixty-five years. (S. December 15, 1855)

John MAYO died in Edgecombe County "a few days since." His funeral sermon would be held by the Concord Masonic Lodge, No. 58, at the Luke Ward home on December 28, 1828. (F. P. December 5, 1828)

Lawrence MAYO died at the home of F. P. Redmond in Hardiman County, Tennessee, on September 6, 1840, aged forty-seven years. He was buried on his brother James MAYO'S farm near Lagrange in Fayette County. (T. P. October 3, 1840)

Louisa MAYO, daughter of John MAYO, died in Edgecombe County on July 14, 1846, aged about twenty years. (T. P. July 15, 1846)

Mrs. Sally E. MAYO, wife of the late James MAYO, died in Fayette County, Tennessee, on March 30, 1850. (T. P. April 27, 1850)

Thomas MAYO died in Edgecombe County on August 5, 1856, aged about forty-five years, leaving a wife and eight children. (S. August 30, 1856)

William Henry MAYO, son of Frederick W. MAYO, formerly of Martin County, died in Fayette County, Tennessee, on July 18, 1845, having been born on August 9, 1835. (T. P. August 13, 1845)

John MCDOWELL died in Edgecombe County on March 15, 1855, aged about twenty-three years. (S. March 31, 1855)

Patrick MCDOWELL died in Edgecombe County on February 23, 1857, aged about fifty-five years. (S. February 28, 1857)

Mrs. Susan E. MCKEE, wife of Dr. William H. MCKEE and daughter of the late Joel and Mary P. BATTLE of Edgecombe County, died at Raleigh on December 12, 1851, leaving four small children. (T. P. December 20, 1851)

Richard MCKINNE died at the home of his uncles J. and H. McKinne in Alabama of typhoid fever on January 17, 1852, aged nineteen years. (S. February 21, 1852)

Levi H. MCLEAN died at the home of Absalom B. Whitaker in Halifax County on September 17, 1826, aged twenty-eight years. (T. P. September 26, 1826)

James MCMAHON died suddenly in the woods on March 5, 1835. (T. P. March 14, 1835)

George MCWILLIAMS died at Tarboro on December 19, 1834, leaving a wife and three children. (T. P. January 2, 1835)

Mrs. Mary MCWILLIAMS died at Tarboro on May 17, 1848, aged about fifty-two years. (T. P. May 20, 1848)

Inez MEHEGAN, infant daughter of James MEHEGAN, died in Tarboro on September 4, 1846. (T. P. September 9, 1846)

James Thomas MEHEGAN, son of James MEHEGAN, died in Edgecombe County on August 26, 1843, aged about three years. (T. P. September 2, 1843)

Mrs. Mary MEHEGAN, wife of James MEHEGAN, died on December 8, 1848, leaving a husband and four children. (T. P. December 9, 1848)

John MERCER, Esq., died in Edgecombe County on March 28, 1864, aged eighty-three years. (S. April 2, 1864)

John D. MERCER died near Autrey's Creek Meeting House on August 23, 1845, in his thirty-second year, leaving a wife and six small children. (T. P. September 3, 1845)

Mrs. Margaret MERCER, daughter of the late Isaac NORFLEET, died in Edgecombe County on October 30, 1852. (S. November 13, 1852)

Mrs. Nancy MERCER, wife of John MERCER, Esq., died in Edgecombe County on February 17, 1850, aged about sixty years. (T. P. February 23, 1850)

William MERCER of Edgecombe County died in Portsmouth, Virginia, on June 21, 1848, aged about sixty years. (T. P. July 1, 1848)

Mrs. William MERCER died in Edgecombe County on June 29, 1846. (T. P. July 8, 1846)

Mary Ann MILLER, daughter of Pleasant MILLER, Esq., of West Tennessee, died at Tarboro on May 6, 1830. (F. P. May 7, 1830)

Jesse MINSHUR died at Stantonsburg on January 27, 1828, aged about fifty years. His widow became sick the day after his death and died on February 4, 1828. (F. P. February 15, 1828)

Augustus MOORE, Esq., of Williamston died "a few days since" in Jacksonville, Florida, of consumption and aged about twenty-three years. He had represented Martin County in the last General Assembly. (S. April 21, 1860)

Mrs. Elizabeth MOORE died in Pitt County on January 1, 1833, in her one hundred and first year. (N. C. F. P. January 29, 1833)

Lavinia Olife MOORE, daughter of John O. MOORE recently from Norfolk, died at Tarboro on August 30, 1853. She had been born on June 28, 1843. (S. September 3, 1853)

Mrs. Louisa MOORE, wife of Bartholomew F. MOORE and daughter of George BODDIE, Esq., of Nash County, died on November 5, 1829. (F. P. November 13, 1829)

Nathan MOORE, son of S. E. MOORE, died of brain fever at Tarboro on July 20, 1862, aged about four years. (S. July 26, 1862)

Mrs. Ruth MOORE, wife of John R. MOORE, and formerly Mrs. Carney, died near Tarboro on September 17, 1850. (T. P. September 21, 1850)

Telitha MOORE, daughter of the late Roderick MOORE of Pitt County, died at Tarboro on April 15, 1845, aged about fourteen years. (T. P. April 19, 1845)

William G. MOORE, grandson of William and Telitha GRIMES, died of typhoid fever in Edgecombe County on September 13, 1855, aged twenty-two years. (S. September 15, 1855)

John H. MOORING died in Martin County on October 31, 1845, aged about twenty-two years, having been shot accidentally on his return with friends from a deer-hunting party on the Roanoke River. (T. P. November 19, 1845)

Mrs. Elizabeth C. MORGAN, wife of Laertes MORGAN of Halifax County, died of cancer of the mouth on October 25, 1827. (F. P. November 24, 1827)

William MORGAN, "a colored man, much respected by his neighbors, a revolutionary soldier and pensioner," died in Edgecombe County on October 2, 1837, aged about eighty-seven years. (T. S. October 6, 1837, and T. P. October 7, 1837)

Robert MORRISS of Wayne County died on November 7, 1826, in his thirty-first year, leaving a wife and four small children. (F. P. November 14, 1826)

William MORRIS, shoemaker, died at Halifax on September 1, 1827. He was a native of New Jersey. (F. P. September 8, 1827)

Louisa Virginia MOYE, daughter of General Wyatt MOYE, died at her father's residence in Aberdeen, Mississippi, on March 25, 1852, "on the day she was to have been married. Her bridal robes were her burial clothes." (S. April 3, 1852, and April 17, 1852)

Mrs. Louisa MOYE, wife of General Wyatt MOYE of Aberdeen, Mississippi, was born in Pitt County on May 9, 1812. She married about 1828 General Jesse SPEIGHT (he died on May 1, 1847), and moved South in 1836. She died on October 5, 1856, at Aberdeen. (S. October 25, 1856)

Mrs. Martha MOYE, wife of General Wyatt MOYE, was born on February 10, 1804, and died on May 25, 1845, in Edgecombe County at the age of forty-one years, leaving a husband and two daughters. (T. P. June 4, 1845)

Lt. William H. MOYE of Company A, North Carolina Volunteers, and from Edgecombe County, died at New Orleans on August 9, 1847. (T. P. August 28, 1847, and September 11, 1847)

Maria Louisa MURPHY, daughter of the late William S. MURPHY of Pitt County, died at New Bern on July 27, 1827, in her twenty-first year. (F. P. August 4, 1827)

Joseph P. NEAL, son of C. E. and Pernetta NEAL, died at Tarboro on July 9, 1857, having been born on March 20, 1857. (S. July 11, 1857)

Mary NEAL, daughter of David NEAL, died in Tarboro on May 29, 1862, aged about fourteen months. (S. June 14, 1862)

Mrs. Pernette NEAL, wife of Charles E. NEAL of Tarboro, died in Edgecombe County at the home of her father S. P. JENKINS on January 25, 1861, aged about thirty-five years, leaving two small children. (S. January 26, 1861)

Allen NETTLE died in Edgecombe County on April 14, 1860, aged about eighty years. (S. April 21, 1860)

Jacob NETTLE died in Edgecombe County on May 19, 1838, aged about sixty-two years. (T. P. May 26, 1838)

John NETTLES died "a few days since, at an advanced age." (F. P. February 12, 1830)

James Thomas NEVIL died in Edgecombe County on October 6, 1854. He was born on November 6, 1851. (S. October 14, 1854)

Francis NEWBY of Perquimans County, "a soldier of the revolution," was kicked in the head by his horse on March 23, 1830, and died on March 26, aged seventy-three years, leaving a widow. (F. P. April 23, 1830)

James NEWBY of Perquimans County died "in the prime of life" on September 6, 1828, two hours after "his horse ran away and threw him." (F. P. October 3, 1828)

Thomas NEWBY of the firm of Newby & Horne, died at Rocky Mount on November 14, 1852. (S. November 20, 1852)

Miss Celia NEWTON died in Pitt County on November 25, 1845, and was memorialized by an acrostic poem. (March 11, 1846)

Mrs. Catharine NICHOLSON was born and reared in Edgecombe County. She married Anderson NICHOLSON and had resided for thirty years in Raleigh, where she died on April 16, 1848. (T. P. April 22, 1848)

Peter NIXON died in Tarboro "at an advanced age" on September 6, 1845. (T. P. September 10, 1845)

Mrs. Olivia NOBLES, wife of Dr. John NOBLES, died in Wilson County on March 15, 1857, aged about twenty-five years, and leaving two children. She died of a congestive chill. (S. March 21, 1857)

John NORCOTT, Esq., of Pitt County died at White Sulphur Springs, Virginia, "where he had gone for the benefit of his health," on July 6, 1845, in his fifty-second year. (T. P. July 23, 1845)

Mrs. Christiana NORFLEET, widow of Isaac NORFLEET, died on April 15, 1853, aged sixty-three years. (S. April 23, 1853)

George Townsend NORFLEET, son of Robert NORFLEET, died at Tarboro on September 20, 1851, aged seven days. (T. P. September 27, 1851)

Isaac NORFLEET of Edgecombe County died near Philadelphia on October 11, 1844, aged sixty-four years. (T. P. October 26, 1844)

James NORFLEET, eldest son of Isaac NORFLEET, died in Edgecombe County on June 3, 1832, aged about twenty-one years. (N. C. F. P. June 12, 1832)

Joseph NORFLEET of Edgecombe County died in Philadelphia on September 7, 1859, aged twenty-nine years. (S. September 24, 1859)

Sarah Elizabeth NORFLEET died at her mother's home near Tarboro on March 17, 1852, in her twentieth year. (S. March 20, 1852)

Charles OAST of Wilson was killed in an explosion near Sparta on October 24, 1859. (S. October 29, 1859)

Caroline OBERRY, daughter of Green OBERRY, died at Tarboro on August 24, 1856. She was born on June 12, 1855. (S. August 30, 1856)

Mrs. Elizabeth OBERRY, wife of Green OBERRY, died at Tarboro on February 24, 1850, aged about seventeen years. (T. P. March 2, 1850)

Elizabeth OBERRY, daughter of Green OBERRY, died at Tarboro on April 25, 1855, aged about three years. (S. April 28, 1855)

Mrs. Nancy O'BRIEN, long a member of the Methodist Church, was burned to death in front of her fireplace on March 4, 1858, aged seventy-seven years. (S. March 6, 1858)

John O'NEAL died in Edgecombe County on February 24, 1863, aged about thirty-eight years. (S. March 7, 1863)

Dr. F. W. H. OSBORNE of North Carolina died in Mobile, Alabama, "of the prevailing fever" on September 30, 1829, aged about twenty-eight years. (F. P. November 6, 1829)

Elder James OSBOURN of Baltimore died at Williamston on August 24, 1850, aged about seventy-three years and a Primitive Baptist minister. (T. P. August 31, 1850)

David OUTLAW, Esq., died at the home of his kinsman and heir Dr. Joseph OUTLAW of Nash County on March 2, 1849, aged about sixty years. (T. P. April 7, 1849)

Nathan PAINE of Virginia was killed by an explosion near Sparta on October 24, 1859. (S. October 29, 1859)

Daniel PARISH died in Halifax County on November 23, 1847, "for many years past a teacher in this and the adjoining counties." (T. P. November 27, 1847)

Andrew Mills PARKER, son of Richard R. and Mary PARKER of Edgecombe County, died at Enfield on June 17, 1852. He had been born on September 21, 1828, and was a Mason. A Masonic Funeral was conducted at his father's residence on July 18, 1852, by the Rev. Thomas Lowe. (S. June 26, 1852, and July 3, 1852)

Mrs. Ann PARKER, widow of Cader PARKER, died in Edgecombe County at the home of Hardy PARKER on March 20, 1846, in her ninety-seventh year leaving a large number of children and "upwards of 110 descendants." (T. P. March 25, 1846, and April 1, 1846)

Arthur PARKER, son of Arthur PARKER, died in Edgecombe County on February 4, 1837. (T. P. February 11, 1837)

Arthur PARKER died "at an advanced age" on March 2, 1849, in Edgecombe County. (T. P. March 3, 1849)

Briscoe PARKER died on September 14, 1829, and George PARKER died on

September 7, 1829, both being infant children of Weeks PARKER, Jr.
(F. P. September 18, 1829)

Eli PARKER died in Edgecombe County on January 15, 1845, leaving a wife
and two children. (T. P. January 18, 1845)

George B. PARKER was accidentally shot to death by his brother Mark
PARKER in Edgecombe County on the night of July 21, 1856. (S.
August 9, 1856)

Hardy PARKER died in Edgecombe County on June 17, 1854, in his eighty-
second year, leaving a wife, four children, grandchildren and great-
grandchildren. He had been a Primitive Baptist for forty-five
years. (S. July 1, 1854)

Irwin PARKER, son of Theophilus PARKER, died at Tarboro on July 27, 1828,
aged about three years. (F. P. August 1, 1828)

Rev. J. Haywood PARKER, oldest son of the late Theophilus PARKER of Tarboro, was born there on January 21, 1813, graduated in 1832 from
U. N. C., became a minister at the age of thirty-three years, and
was Rector of St. Luke's Church in Salisbury at the time of his
death on September 16, 1858. (S. October 2, 1858)

Jethro PARKER died in Halifax County on September 19, 1855, aged eighty-
three years. (S. September 29, 1855)

John PARKER died at Tarboro on June 7, 1848, aged about sixty years.
(T. P. June 10, 1848)

John PARKER died in Halifax County on June 24, 1849, aged about seventy
years. (T. P. July 7, 1849)

John PARKER died in Edgecombe County at the home of his father-in-law
Britton Howell on August 31, 1853, aged about twenty-five years and
leaving a wife and one child. (S. September 3, 1853)

Dr. John H. PARKER, a native of Edgecombe County, had settled in or near
Pensacola, Florida, where in November of 1837 he was axed to death
by slaves Lewis and Henry who threw his body into the Escambia
River, in which it floated for about twenty-five miles before being
found. (T. P. September 1, 1838)

Joseph J. PARKER, son of John PARKER of Tarboro, died on October 23,
1846. He was born on October 5, 1833. (T. P. November 4, 1846)

Mrs. Lucy PARKER, wife of John PARKER, died at Tarboro on September 6,
1826. (T. P. September 12, 1826) (Sheriff John PARKER had married
Lucy Bell on April 12, 1825)

Mrs. Margaret B. PARKER, wife of M. K. PARKER, Esq., died in Sumter
County, Alabama, on April 22, 1844, in her forty-fifty year. She
was from Edgecombe County and left a husband and four children.
(T. P. May 18, 1844)

Mrs. Mary PARKER, widow of Theophilus PARKER, died in Tarboro on December
29, 1859, in her seventy-second year, leaving several children in-
cluding a daughter married to the Rev. R. B. Drane, D. D., at
Wilmington, and one to the Rev. J. B. Cheshire of Tarboro. (S.
January 8, 1859)

Paul A. PARKER, formerly of Edgecombe County, died in Tipton County,
Tennessee, on September 20, 1844, in his thirty-fourth year, leaving
a wife and five children. (T. P. November 2, 1844)

Richard H. PARKER, son of John PARKER, died at Tarboro on June 4, 1848,
in his twentieth year. (T. P. June 10, 1848)

Richard PARKER died in Edgecombe County on September 10, 1858, aged
about seventy years, "a worthy and highly respected citizen." (S.
September 18, 1858)

Sabra PARKER, daughter of S. Baker PARKER, died in Edgecombe County on
August 31, 1845, aged about five years. (T. P. September 3, 1845)

Sally PARKER, daughter of John PARKER, died at Tarborough on September
24, 1826, having been born on August 11, 1825. (T. P. September
26, 1826)

Simmons B. PARKER died in Edgecombe County on May 5, 1846, aged thirty-four years, leaving a widow, one child, and an aged mother. He had been partially incapacitated for many years as the result of an accidental wound received while hunting. (T. P. May 13, 1846)

Theophilus PARKER died in Tarboro on February 9, 1849, in his seventy-fourth year. (T. P. February 17, 1849)

Weeks PARKER died in Edgecombe County on January 16, 1844, aged seventy-five years. (T. P. January 27, 1844)

William PARKER died in Edgecombe County on August 27, 1827, aged thirty-seven years, leaving a wife and two children. (F. P. September 1, 1827)

James PARKES of Wayne County died on July 9, 1860, leaving a widow and three children. (S. August 4, 1860)

George C. PATTERSON, formerly of Tarboro, died "a few weeks since" in Mississippi. (T. P. April 1, 1837)

James PEACOCK was killed at Pikeville in Wayne County on February 19, 1857, "while engaged in an affray with two brothers, James and Needham Tarleton. James has given security to answer in the sum of $1,000." (S. February 21, 1857)

Zadoc PEACOCK died near Stantonsburg on July 23, 1852, leaving a wife and children. (S. July 31, 1852)

Mrs. Elizabeth PEARCE, widow of Jesse PEARCE, died in Johnston County on February 8, 1833, aged about one hundred and eleven years. (N. C. F. P. February 19, 1833)

Emily Jane PEARCE, daughter of the Rev. William PEARCE, died at Tarboro on January 1, 1843, aged five months. (T. P. January 7, 1843)

William PEARCE, son of the Rev. William PEARCE, died of scarlet fever at Tarboro on December 18, 1841, aged about four years. (T. P. December 25, 1841)

Anderson H. PEEBLES, a native of Warren County, died of brain fever at Tarboro on March 8, 1856, aged about twenty-seven years. On February 27, 1856, he had married Elizabeth Ann Cherry, daughter of the late Cader Cherry. (S. March 15, 1856)

Joseph J. PEEBLES of Pitt County died at Franklinton Institute on July 31, 1856, in his eighteenth year. (S. August 9, 1856)

John PEELE, a native of Edgecombe County, died on February 16, 1857, in his sixty-eighth year, at Douglassville in Cass County, Texas, where he had resided for three years. (S. May 9, 1857)

David PENDER died on February 28, 1834, aged about thirty-seven years. (T. F. P. March 7, 1834)

Miss Elizabeth PENDER died "at an advanced age" at the Spencer L. Hart Esq., residence on October 9, 1836. (T. P. October 15, 1836) (Spencer L. Hart is known to have married Delphia Pender, daughter of Joseph Pender.)

Florence PENDER, daughter of Robert H. PENDER of Tarboro, died on December 11, 1848. She had been born on January 10, 1845. (T. P. December 16, 1848)

Florida PENDER, daughter of Robert H. PENDER, died at Tarboro of the measles on July 2, 1862, aged about six months. (S. July 12, 1862)

India Louise PENDER, daughter of Josiah S. and Marie L. PENDER, died at Tarboro on June 4, 1852, aged eight months and twenty-three days. (S. June 19, 1852)

Dr. Joshua PENDER died on November 29, 1845, aged about twenty-one years and son of William PENDER of Edgecombe County. He "had just completed his medical studies and entered on the duties of his profession." (T. P. December 3, 1845)

Colonel Joshua PENDER died in Edgecombe County on August 5, 1847, in his fifty-seventh year, leaving a wife and seven children. (T. P. August 7, 1847)

Josiah PENDER, son of Jo. S. PENDER, died at Tarboro on July 1, 1854, aged about eight months. (S. July 8, 1854)

Mrs. Lucy PENDER, wife of Cullen PENDER, died in Edgecombe County on July 4, 1850, leaving two children. (T. P. July 20, 1850)

Margaret PENDER died on December 30, 1839, aged about twenty years. (T. P. January 11, 1840)

Mrs. Margaret PENDER died at the home of her son Captain T. C. HYMAN of Edgecombe County on April 24, 1864, aged seventy years. (S. April 30, 1864)

Mrs. Mary PENDER, wife of Colonel Joshua PENDER, died in Edgecombe County on August 13, 1837, leaving a husband and seven small children. (T. S. August 18, 1837, and T. P. August 19, 1837)

Miranda PENDER, daughter of the late Colonel Joshua PENDER, died at Tarboro on May 22, 1849, in her fourteenth year. (T. P. May 26, 1849)

Robert W. PENDER died of consumption at Tarboro on September 3, 1853, in his twenty-sixth year. (S. September 10, 1853)

Routh PENDER, nine-days-old son of Robert H. PENDER, died at Tarboro on November 29, 1848. (T. P. December 9, 1848)

Mrs. Sarah PENDER, widow of Josiah PENDER, died "at an advanced age" on December 17, 1835. (T. P. December 19, 1835)

Sarah E. PENDER, daughter of the late Joshua PENDER, died in Edgecombe County at Tarboro on December 29, 1852, aged sixteen years. (S. January 1, 1853)

Sarah Ellen PENDER, daughter of Robert H. PENDER, died at Tarboro on July 13, 1862. She was born on January 26, 1847. (S. July 19,1862)

Captain Solomon PENDER, Assistant Quarter Master, U. S. A., died at Saltillo, Mexico, on September 21, 1847. (T. P. November 6, 1847)

Solomon PENDER died at Tarboro on the morning of September 8, 1852, aged sixty-nine years. (S. September 11, 1852)

William PENDER, Sr., died in Edgecombe County on June 16, 1852, in his eighty-fourth year. (S. July 24, 1852)

Mrs. Elizabeth PERKINS died at Greenville on July 16, 1862, in her seventieth year. (S. August 23, 1862)

William D. PETWAY, former Sheriff of Edgecombe County, died on October 18, 1858, aged about sixty years. (S. October 23, 1858)

David PHILIPS died suddenly in Edgecombe County on September 8, 1828. (F. P. September 19, 1828)

Figures PHILIPS, Esq., died on April 26, 1833, aged about forty-five years. (N. C. F. P. May 11, 1833)

Frederick PHILIPS died in Edgecombe County on October 1, 1837, aged about sixty-six years. (T. S. October 6, 1837. T. P. October 7, 1837) T. C. Hearn, Secretary of Concord Masonic Lodge, announced later that on Sunday, October 29, "the Rev'd Joshua Lawrence will preach the Funeral of Bro. Frederick PHILIPS, at the residence of his son Dr. James J. PHILIPS. The Brethren of Concord Lodge and the adjacent Lodges are respectfully invited to attend." (T. S. October 27, 1837)

Dr. James J. PHILIP'S residence was stated as the place for a Funeral Sermon to be preached by the Rev. S. Y. McMasters on Sunday, February 23, 1845. (T. P. February 1, 1845)

Mary Jane PHILIPS, daughter of Dr. James J. and Harriet PHILIPS of "Mount Moriah" in Edgecombe County died on the evening of March 15, 1844, aged four years. (T. P. March 23, 1844)

Susan S. PHILIPS, youngest child of Dr. James J. PHILIPS, died in Edgecombe County on October 12, 1837. (T. P. October 14, 1837)

Thomas PHILIPS, Sheriff of Martin County, died at Williamston on October 7, 1839. (T. P. November 2, 1839)

William Burt PHILIPS, son of Dr. James J. PHILIPS, died in Edgecombe County on January 29, 1856, aged about eleven years and six months. (S. February 2, 1856)

Flavius Alexander PIPPEN, sixth son of the late J. J. and Talitha PIPPEN, died of typhoid fever in Edgecombe County on June 13, 1864. He was born on August 9, 1837. (S. June 18, 1864)

Henry William PIPPEN, son of Joseph John PIPPEN, died on May 28, 1829, aged eight years. (F. P. June 12, 1829)

Jessie PIPPEN, daughter of William M. PIPPEN of Tarboro, died on August 10, 1857, aged about one year and four months. (S. August 15,1857)

Joseph PIPPEN, "an officer of the Revolution," died on April 10, 1833, in his eighty-second year. (N. C. F. P. April 13, 1833)

Joseph PIPPEN, youngest son of Joseph H. and Sarah E. PIPPEN, died in Edgecombe County on June 28, 1862. He was born on May 17, 1859. (S. July 5, 1862)

Joseph John PIPPEN, Esq., merchant of Tarboro, died on October 24, 1853, in his fifty-seventh year, leaving twelve children. He was for many years a Justice of the Peace, former member of the North Carolina General Assembly, and Deacon in the Cross Roads Baptist Church. (S. October 29, 1853)

Mary PIPPEN, daughter of William M. PIPPEN, died of the measles in Tarboro on July 9, 1862, aged about ten months. (S. July 12, 1862)

David Garrett PITT, son of John P. and Mary PITT, died on November 5, 1839. He was born on September 27, 1833. (T. P. November 23, 1839)

Elizabeth PITT, wife of Colonel Joab P. PITT, died in Edgecombe County on October 7, 1841, aged about thirty-six years, and leaving a husband and eight children. (T. P. October 9, 1841)

James PITT, Jr., died in Edgecombe County on October 5, 1831, in his twentieth year. (N. C. F. P. October 11, 1831)

Colonel Joab P. PITT died near Sparta on August 23, 1854, aged about fifty-six years. (S. August 26, 1854)

Mrs. Rebecca PITT, widow of James PITT, died on December 7, 1855, aged forty-nine years. (S. December 15, 1855)

Sally Ann PITT, wife of Dr. Franklin PITT and daughter of Jordan KNIGHT, died on September 17, 1851, aged about eighteen years, leaving an infant of about five weeks. (T. P. September 20, 1851)

Warren PITT of Edgecombe County was "found dead in the road" on December 30, 1855, and had presumably frozen to death while intoxicated. (S. January 5, 1856)

Lt. William PITT, son of Bennet P. PITT of Edgecombe County, died in the Winder Confederate Hospital at Richmond on August 3, 1862, aged about twenty years. He was a member of Company F, 30th North Carolina Regiment, C. S. A. (S. August 9, 1862)

William S. PITT, Clerk of the Edgecombe County Court, died suddenly on March 24, 1856, in his twenty-fifth year and unmarried. (S. March 29, 1856)

Benjamin Coffield PITMAN, third son of Reddin PITMAN, Esq., died on September 27, 1842, aged about six years. (T. P. October 8, 1842)

Gresham PITMAN, "one of our most wealthy and respected planters," died in Edgecombe County on February 1, 1853, in his seventieth year. (S. February 5, 1853)

Thomas PITMAN died at Tarboro on September 1, 1847. (T. P. September 4, 1847)

Harrison PITTMAN died in Edgecombe County on May 20, 1859, in his eighty-fifth year. (S. May 28, 1859)

Harrod PITTMAN was fatally wounded in an argument with Joseph George near Teat's Bridge on November 30, 1836. (T. P. December 3, 1836)

Martha PITTMAN, daughter of the late Reddin PITTMAN, died at her mother's home in Edgecombe County on May 28, 1857, aged about twelve years. (S. May 30, 1857)

Mrs. Mary PITTMAN, wife of Grisham C. PITTMAN, died on April 15, 1843, in her sixty-sixth year, leaving a husband and one son. (T. P. April 29, 1843)

Mrs. Mary PITTMAN, wife of Dr. N. J. PITTMAN, died at Tarboro on January 10, 1861, in her twenty-third year. (S. January 19, 1861)

Oliver PITTMAN, son of G. C. PITTMAN, died "recently" in Edgecombe County. (F. P. October 2, 1829)

Reddin PITTMAN, Esq., died in Edgecombe County on April 18, 1854, aged fifty-two years, and leaving a widow and six children. He was enterprising and wealthy and served in the North Carolina House of Commons in 1831. (S. April 22, 1854)

Mrs. Susan PITTMAN, wife of William PITTMAN, Jr., died in Edgecombe County on May 8, 1827, aged about thirty years. (F. P. May 19,1827)

Wiley POLLARD was killed in Pitt County by Elisha Briley on February 20, 1858, at a log-rolling. His skull had been fractured in several places by a hand-spike. (S. March 6, 1858)

John POPE died in Greene County on August 21, 1827, in his fiftieth year, and two hours after the death of one of his little sons. (F. P. September 22, 1827)

Jacob POPE of Halifax County was shot on August 25 and died on August 26, 1834, aged about fifty-seven years, leaving a wife and ten children. (T. F. P. September 5, 1834)

P. Wesley POPE died in Edgecombe County on September 15, 1845, in his twenty-second year. (T. P. September 24, 1845)

William Allen POPE died at Rocky Mount in Edgecombe County on July 11, 1848. (T. P. July 15, 1848)

Elisha PORTER, formerly of Pitt County, died in Onslow County on December 17, 1856, aged seventy-one years and nine months. (S. January 3, 1857)

Ely PORTER, merchant and Baptist, died at Tarboro on February 6, 1843, aged about sixty-five years, and leaving a wife and three children. His funeral was preached by the Rev. William Pearce. (T. P. February 11, 1843)

Mrs. Martha PORTER,widow of Ely PORTER, died on September 15, 1845, aged fifty-eight years. (T. P. September 17, 1845)

Mrs. Susan PORTER, wife of Joseph J. PORTER, died at Tarboro on February 25, 1846, leaving a husband, two small children, and a sister. (T. P. March 4, 1846) (Joseph J. PORTER had married Susan Wilkins on February 15, 1837, in Edgecombe County.)

William Jeffreys PORTER, son of Joseph J. PORTER, died near Tarboro on May 3, 1855. He was born on March 2, 1854. (S. May 5, 1855)

Willis W. PORTER, son of Joseph John PORTER, died at Tarboro on January 27, 1844. (T. P. February 3, 1844)

Dr. John W. POTTS, lately of Tarboro, died at Little Rock, Arkansas, on July 13, 1835, attended by his brother-in-law T. P. Hawkins. (T. P. August 22, 1835)

Mrs. Eliza POWELL, wife of Jesse H. POWELL, died of consumption on February 15, 1857, aged forty-one years. (S. February 28, 1857)

Frederick POWELL, son of Jesse H. POWELL, died at Tarboro on September 24, 1853, aged about fourteen years and a student at the Tarboro Male Academy. (S. October 8, 1853)

Henry W. POWELL, son of the late Dr. J. J. W. POWELL of Edgecombe County enlisted in Pitt County on March 18, 1864, in Company G, 3rd North Carolina Cavalry Regiment, C. S. A., and was killed at Petersburg on August 21, 1864, aged about eighteen years. (S. August 27,1864)

Mrs. Hester POWELL, wife of Jesse H. POWELL, died on July 31, 1836, leaving four small children. (T. P. August 6, 1836)

Joseph POWELL, son of William H. POWELL, died at the home of Dr. Jos. Lawrence in Tarboro on July 4, 1860, aged about two years. (S. July 7, 1860)

Mrs. Mary POWELL died near Greenwood in Halifax County on July 17, 1837, aged about sixty-two years. (T. P. July 29, 1837)

Richard POWELL died in Greene County on August 25, 1826, in his twenty-first year, and being a son of the late James POWELL of Pitt County. (T. P. September 19, 1826)

Willie POWELL died in Nash County on September 4, 1860, having been born on August 15, 1769. (S. September 15, 1860)

Mrs. Sarah PRESHO died near Beaufort on July 27, 1845, in her one hundred and seventh year. (T. P. August 20, 1845)

Martha PRICE died of consumption in Edgecombe County on December 2, 1841, aged about twenty-one years. (T. P. December 11, 1841)

Moses PRICE died in Edgecombe County on August 16, 1845, aged about sixty-three years, leaving a son and two daughters. He was "for many years an active and energetic Justice of the Peace." (T. P. August 20, 1845)

William PRICE died in Martin County on November 30, 1846, in his eighty-fifth year and "a Revolutionary soldier." (T. P. December 8, 1846)

Miss Mary Jane PROUTY of Newberry, Vermont, and teacher of Music in "The Wilson Schools," died of congestion of the brain at the D. S. Richardson home in Wilson on September 29, 1859. (S. October 8, 1859)

Mrs. Mary Whitmell PUGH, widow of Dr. Whitmell H. PUGH and mother of the Hon. W. W. PUGH, was born in Martin County in 1776, and died on November 22, 1854, at the home of her son-in-law General R. C. Martin in the Parish of Assumption, Louisiana. The PUGHS had settled in 1820 "on the Lafourche." (S. January 6, 1855)

Thomas PUGH died in Martin County on June 8, 1836, aged about twenty-eight years. (T. P. June 18, 1836)

William PURKINSON was killed at Smithfield when a steamboiler exploded on February 15, 1853. (S. February 19, 1853)

Mrs. Eliza PURVIS, wife of John PURVIS, died in Martin County on March 7, 1858, aged about thirty-three years. (S. March 13, 1858)

William PURYEAR, carpenter, died suddenly in Goldsboro on February 24, 1858, aged fifty or more years. (S. March 6, 1858)

Elizabeth RAGSDALE of Tarborough died at Raleigh on August 30, 1834, in her eighteenth year. (T. F. P. September 5, 1834)

Mrs. Elizabeth RAGSDALE, widow of Benjamin RAGSDALE, former Chief Clerk of the State Bank, died at the home of Joiner Watkins while on her way from Tarboro to Raleigh on July 7, 1835, in her sixtieth year. (T. P. July 18, 1835)

Samuel RALSTON, a native of Ireland and merchant of Yankee Hall in Pitt County, died on February 11, 1829. (F. P. February 20, 1829)

Mrs. _____ RANDOLPH, an aged widow, died in Tarboro on October 4, 1828. (F. P. October 10, 1828)

Captain David RANDOLPH died at Major John G. Blount's home on August 11, 1828, aged about forty-five years. (F. P. August 15, 1828)

John S. RANDOLPH was killed in a fight by Bythal R. Bell at Marianna, Florida, on Saturday morning, March 27, 1841. Both men were from Edgecombe County. (T. P. April 10, 1841, and April 24, 1841)

Mrs. Lydia Olivia RANDOLPH, wife of John RANDOLPH, Esq., and daughter of James F. EBORN, Esq., died in Pitt County on October 20, 1849, in her twenty-fourth year. (T. P. November 3, 1849)

Willis RANDOLPH died in Pitt County on October 25, 1834, aged about eighty-five years. (T. F. P. October 31, 1834)

Henry Tilman REDDITT, son of Seth REDDITT of Martin County, was drowned in the Roanoke River on April 18, 1840, aged about eighteen years.

Mrs. Catharine REDMOND, wife of James M. REDMOND, died at Tarboro on November 7, 1856, leaving a husband and four children. (S. November 8, 1856)

George REYNOLDS died of consumption in Tarboro on October 9, 1859, aged about twenty-eight years. (S. October 15, 1859)

Charlie G. RHODES died of the croup in Wilson on November 4, 1859, aged four years and two months, and being the eldest son of Archibald G. and Louisa M. RHODES. (S. November 12, 1859)

Jesse R. RHYMES died at Colonel Andrew Joyner's home in Halifax County on August 24, 1829, in his twenty-first year. (F. P. September 4, 1829)

John RICE, Sr., died near Vicksville in Nash County on October 27, 1845, aged sixty years. (T. P. November 19, 1845)

Mrs. Mary R. RICHARDS, wife of Danford RICHARDS, died on September 29, 1833, in her nineteenth year, together with her infant of one hour. (T. F. P. October 4, 1833)

Captain David RICKS died in Nash County on June 24, 1829, aged about forty years. (F. P. July 3, 1829)

Edmund RICKS, "a soldier of the Revolution," died "recently" in Pitt County. (T. P. November 12, 1836)

Isaac W. RICKS died at Battleboro on April 5, 1858. (S. April 10, 1858)

Mrs. Olive RICKS, formerly of Halifax County, died at the home of Isaac Fort in Lawrence County, Alabama, on October 19, 1826. (F. P. October 24, 1826)

Major J. C. RIDLEY of Granville County and son-in-law of the late Geraldus Toole of Edgecombe County, died in Washington, D. C., on June 27, 1837. (T. P. July 1, 1837)

Clara RIVES, wife of Richard E. RIVES of Pitt County and daughter of Captain Benjamin BROWN of Pitt County, died on October 4, 1857. She had been born on January 23, 1778, and had married on March 25, 1817. (S. October 10, 1857)

Peter RIVES died in Pitt County on April 21, 1827, in his fiftieth year, leaving a wife and six children. (F. P. May 12, 1827)

Sallie Dancy RIVES, daughter of Dr. John G. and wife Lucie RIVES, died of diptheria at Mrs. Sarah E. Foxhall's home on October 31, 1863. She was born on November 16, 1859. (S. November 14, 1863)

William F. RIVES, son of John G. and Lucie RIVES, died on August 15, 1853. He was born on May 11, 1853. (S. August 20, 1853)

William F. RIVES, son of John G. and Lucie D. RIVES, died in Edgecombe County on June 27, 1863. He was born on December 13, 1861. (S. August 28, 1863)

Henry Irvin ROBARDS, son of William H. ROBARDS, died on June 10, 1835, aged nine months. (T. P. June 13, 1835)

William ROBBINS, Sr., "an old revolutionary soldier," died on January 7, 1831, in his eighty-sixth year. (N. C. F. P. January 11, 1831)

Private Jesse B. ROBERSON, a private of "The Edgecombe Guards," Company A, 1st North Carolina Regiment, C. S. A., died of typhoid fever at Yorktown on June 22, 1861, aged nineteen years. (S. June 29, 1861)

William ROBERSON died in Edgecombe County on May 31, 1837, aged about twenty-three years. (T. S. June 2, 1837)

John L. ROBINSON died in Vicksburg, Mississippi, on September 16, 1837, in his twenty-second year. (T. S. November 3, 1827)

Hester Ann ROGERS, daughter of Isaac B. BRADY, formerly of Tarboro, died in Martin County on September 3, 1837. She was born on September 23, 1836. (T. S. September 15, 1837)

John ROGERS, son of John P. ROGERS of near Tarboro died on August 9, 1857, aged about one year and five months. (S. August 15, 1857)

Turner ROGERS died in Edgecombe County on September 23, 1843, aged about thirty-five years. (T. P. September 30, 1843)

William ROGERS died in Pitt County on March 18, 1846, leaving a wife and two small children. (T. P. March 25, 1846)

Captain William ROSS died at the B. J. Spruill residence in Halifax County at an advanced age on December 14, 1831. (N. C. F. P. December 20, 1831)

Elizabeth ROUNDTREE of Edgecombe County died at Louisburg Female Academy on August 19, 1853, aged about sixteen years. (S. September 3, 1853)

Jesse ROUNTREE, Sr., died in Pitt County on April 12, 1831, in his sixty-sixth year. "He was a soldier of the Revolution, and served faith-fully until the end of the war." (N. C. F. P. May 24, 1831)

Jesse ROUNTREE died of cholera morbus in Pitt County on September 10, 1858. "He was a strict member of the Disciples Church." (S. September 25, 1858)

Nathan H. ROUNTREE died at Tarboro on September 6, 1837, in his thirty-eighth year, leaving a family consisting of a wife and two children. He served for about ten years as Post Master before entering the mercantile business. (T. S. September 8, 1837. T. P. September 9, 1837)

John ROWE'S Masonic Funeral was preached "At his late residence in this county" on November 23, 1845, as announced by Secretary John G. Williams of the Joseph Warren Lodge. (T. P. November 5 and November 12, 1845)

Lamon RUFFIN, "an old and highly respectable inhabitant" of Edgecombe County, died on May 24, 1828. (F. P. June 6, 1828)

William J. RUFFIN, son of the late Samuel RUFFIN, Esq., died in Edge-combe County on September 20, 1826. (T. P. September 26, 1826)

Miss Catharine RUTH, sister of Mrs. Nancy Mercer, died on February 18, 1850, aged about fifty years. (T. P. February 23, 1850)

Reuben SANDERS, Esq., Senator from Johnston County, died at Raleigh on December 28, 1829. (F. P. January 8, 1830)

Mrs. Emily Pittman SARSAMON, formerly of Tarboro, died in Livingston County, Kentucky, on January 10, 1843. (T. P. February 18, 1843)

Mrs. Martha Grimes SASNETT, wife of Reddin SASNETT, died in Edgecombe County on August 18, 1850. (T. P. August 24, 1850)

Zachariah SASNETT died on October 2, 1837, aged about fifty-five years. (T. P. October 7, 1837)

Arthur SASSER, "an aged man" of Wayne County, was killed by a falling limb on March 3, 1856. (S. March 22, 1856)

Joshua SASSNETT was drowned accidentally in the millpond of his brother Zachariah SASSNETT on March 27, 1834. (T. P. April 4, 1834)

Zachariah SASSNETT died in Edgecombe County on October 2, 1837, aged about fifty-five years. (T. S. October 6, 1837)

Margaret Louisa SAUNDERS, daughter of Dr. L. K. and Mary A. SAUNDERS, died in Tarboro of scarlet fever on May 18, 1863. She was born on March 17, 1858. (S. May 23, 1863)

Alavena SAVAGE, daughter of Alston SAVAGE, died on December 2, 1837, aged six years, in Edgecombe County. (T. S. December 8, 1837. T. P. December 9, 1837)

Alston SAVAGE of Edgecombe County was found on the evening of February 21, 1859, "at the road near the gate near his house, in a helpless condition, and on being carried into the house died in about fifteen minutes. He had been to Palmyra in a buggy and it is conjectured that on his return an hour or two before sundown, his horse ran away with him, and on turning into the gate, he was thrown out, the horse continuing up to the house with the buggy still fastened to him. Mr SAVAGE was about sixty years of age and has left a wife and several children." (S. February 26, 1859)

Mrs. James Murphy SAVAGE, wife of Richard A. SAVAGE, died in Tarboro on February 28, 1849, leaving a daughter a few hours old. (T. P. March 3, 1849)

Corporal James M. SAVAGE of Company I, 17th North Carolina Regiment, C. S. A., died of typhoid fever at the Hospital in Wilmington on December 7, 1863, aged twenty-nine years. (S. March 5, 1864)

Mr. and Mrs. Larkey SAVAGE of Edgecombe County died a few days before

April 26, 1845. (T. P. May 3, 1845)

Mrs. Pheribee SAVAGE, wife of James SAVAGE, Esq., and youngest daughter of the late Rev. Joshua LAWRENCE of Edgecombe County, died at Pittsboro at the residence of H. H. Burke, Esq., on October 27, 1851. (T. P. November 8, 1851)

James SAVIDGE died in Edgecombe County on October 9, 1834, aged sixty-five to seventy years. (T. F. P. October 17, 1834)

Major James SCARBOROUGH died at 1:15 a. m. on March 1, 1836, in his eighty-eighth year. (T. P. March 5, 1836) (He was a Revolutionary War soldier and pensioner and resided near Saratoga in the present Wilson County.)

Mary Ann SCOTT, wife of Lunsford W. SCOTT and daughter of the late James SIMMONS, Sr., Esq., of Halifax County, died in Hardiman County, Tennessee, on April 1, 1841, in her thirty-second year, leaving five children, one only a few hours old. (T. P. May 1, 1841)

Benjamin A. SELBY, Esq., formerly Sheriff of Pitt County, died at Greenville "at an advanced age" on June 17, 1856. (S. June 21, 1856)

Hannah B. SELBY, daughter of Benjamin M. SELBY, died at Rocky Mount on September 1, 1862, aged fifteen years and nine months. She was formerly a resident of Washington. A poem was written and published in her memory by "Sallie." (S. September 6, 1862; September 20, 1862)

Celia SESSOMS, daughter of Nathan SESSOMS, died on December 27, 1826, aged nine years. (F. P. January 9, 1827)

Mrs. Elizabeth SUSSUMS died at Tarboro on May 21, 1835, "at an advanced age." (T. P. May 23, 1835)

Dr. Isaac T. SESSUMS'S wife died at Nashville on July 22, 1837. (T. P. July 29, 1837)

Nathan SESSUMS died in Edgecombe County on March 22, 1836, aged about sixty years. (T. P. March 26, 1836)

Wilson SESSUMS died of pneumonia in Edgecombe County on January 24, 1849. (T. P. January 27, 1849)

John SHARP died in Edgecombe County on June 26, 1842, aged about forty-eight years, leaving a wife and children. (T. P. July 2, 1842)

Abraham SHARPE died on July 15, 1831, aged about forty-eight years, leaving a wife and eight children. (N. C. F. P. July 26, 1831)

Mrs. Ann SHARPE, wife of Colonel Benjamin SHARPE, died on April 17, 1837. (T. P. April 22, 1837)

Colonel Benjamin SHARPE died on April 24, 1843, aged fifty-nine years, leaving a wife and four children. He had represented Edgecombe County in both Houses of the North Carolina General Assembly. (T. P. April 29, 1843)

Eason SHARPE died near Joyner's Depot in Wilson County on April 28, 1860, leaving four children. (S. May 5, 1860)

John P. SHARPE died in Edgecombe County on December 22, 1845, aged about twenty-five years and leaving a wife. He had graduated from U. of N. C. in 1840. (T. P. December 24, 1845)

Mrs. Martha R. Pender SHARPE died on August 12, 1831. (N. C. F. P. August 23, 1831) (On August 19, 1828, Benjamin SHARPE, Jr., had taken out a bond to marry her.)

John SHAW, overseer of the Roanoke Navigation Company, died at Weldon on August 15, 1829. (F. P. August 21, 1829)

Lavina SHELTON, daughter of Burrell SHELTON, died in Edgecombe County of typhoid fever on August 31, 1862, aged about twenty-five years. (S. September 6, 1862)

Major James SHEPPARD died near Greenville in Pitt County on November 25, 1830, in his fiftieth year. (N. C. F. P. December 7, 1830)

Ann Amanda B. SHERROD, wife of William SHERROD and daughter of Goold and Martha HOYT, died at Greenville on August 20, 1844, aged eighteen years, leaving two children. (T. P. August 31, 1844)

Colonel Benjamin SHERROD died at "Cotton Garden" near Courtland, Alabama, on March 21, 1847, in his seventy-first year. He was from Halifax County, went to Georgia in his youth, and in 1820 continued onward to Alabama. (T. P. April 10, 1847)

Calvin SHERROD, son of John SHERROD of Martin County, died of burns on March 1, 1835, aged about five years. (T. P. March 7, 1835)

Harriet A. SHERROD, daughter of William R. W. and Mary SHERROD of Martin County, died of pneumonia at the Britton Howell residence in Edgecombe County on May 20, 1859. (S. May 28, 1859)

John SHERROD drowned in Martin County near Hamilton on April 12, 1841. (T. P. April 17, 1841)

Henry SHIRLEY, an extensive and successful farmer, died near Tarboro on October 13, 1854, aged about seventy-three years. (S. October 21, 1854)

Jacob SHULTZ died in Stokes County on July 15, 1848, aged fifty-seven years. (T. P. August 12, 1848)

Geraldus SHURLEY died on May 6, 1843, aged about thirty-seven years, leaving a wife and four children. (T. P. May 6, 1843)

Mrs. Temperance SHURLEY, wife of Geraldus SHURLEY, died in Edgecombe County on June 7, 1839. (T. P. June 15, 1839)

David SILLS died in Nash County on June 13, 1833, in his sixtieth year, leaving a wife and six children. (N. C. F. P. June 29, 1833)

Mrs. Elizabeth SIMMONS, wife of William SIMMONS, died in Hyde County on February 27, 1848, aged thirty-seven years. (T. P. April 29, 1848)

James SIMMONS, "a soldier of the Revolution," died in Halifax County "at an advanced age" on April 9, 1836. (T. P. April 16, 1836)

Colonel Jesse H. SIMMONS, Clerk of the County Court, died at Halifax on January 25, 1840, aged forty-two years. (T. P. February 8, 1840)

Mrs. Maria SIMMONS, wife of Willoughby SIMMONS from Halifax County and daughter of the late Joab BRADDY, died in Hardiman County, Tennessee, on September 5, 1842, aged about thirty-five years. (T. P. November 19, 1842)

Mrs. Mary SIMMONS died in Halifax County on November 21, 1833, in her sixty-fifth year, leaving numerous children and grandchildren. (T. F. P. December 6, 1833)

Mrs. Nancy SIMMONS, wife of Enoch SIMMONS from Halifax County, died in Hyde County on October 13, 1843. (T. P. November 18, 1843)

Robert SIMMS died in Wayne County on June 6, 1848. (T. P. July 1, 1848)

Mrs. M. D. A. E. SINGLETARY, wife of the Reverend John SINGLETARY and daughter of the late Dr. Robert WILLIAMS of Pitt County, died at Washington, North Carolina, on September 19, 1842. (T. P. October 1, 1842)

Rev. John SINGLETARY, formerly of Washington, North Carolina, died in Henderson County on June 21, 1845, aged fifty-three years. (T. P. July 9, 1845, and July 16, 1845)

Dempsey SKINNER, Sr., "a Patriot of the Revolution" and for thirty years a member of the Old Town Creek Baptist Church, died on May 14, 1827, aged eighty-four years, survived by a wife of sixty-one years, and fifty-five children and grandchildren (from fifteen children and sixty-three grandchildren.) (F. P. May 26, 1827)

Henry SLADE, Esq., "a very respectable and useful citizen" died in Martin County on October 10, 1835, aged sixty-five years. (T. P. October 24, 1835)

William SLADE died near Williamston on October 25, 1852, aged forty-five years, leaving a widow and children. He was a member of the M. E. Church. (S. November 13, 1852)

Mrs. Margaret A. SMAW, wife of John G. SMAW, died near Tarboro on March 19, 1863. She had been born on January 24, 1841. (S. April 4, 1863)

Ann Knight SMITH, daughter of Thomas SMITH, died on April 23, 1838, "aged a few weeks." (T. P. April 28, 1838)

Mrs. Elizabeth SMITH, daughter of the late Samuel SKINNER, of Chowan County, and wife of Thomas SMITH, died of pneumonia at Sparta on February 17, 1856. She was for twenty-four years a member of the Presbyterian Church at Washington, North Carolina. (S. March 1, 1856)

Elizabeth N. SMITH, daughter of the late William R. SMITH, Esq., died at her mother's home in Scotland Neck on December 15, 1851. (T. P. December 20, 1851)

Henry T. SMITH, son of L. H. and Ann SMITH, died in Edgecombe County on March 7, 1851, aged two years and six months. (T. P. March 8, 1851)

Martha Maria SMITH, daughter of Thomas SMITH, died on September 24, 1842, aged about three years. (T. P. October 1, 1842)

Philip SMITH of Pitt County on the early night of June 12, 1828, lost in the burning of his home four children under the age of ten years, and the daughter of ten years was seriously burned. (F. P. June 27, 1828)

Mrs. Priscilla SMITH, wife of Moses SMITH, Esq., died in Halifax County on November 16, 1859. She had been born on October 13, 1779, and was a member of the Old Side (Primitive) Baptist Church. (S. December 10, 1859)

Mrs. Thomas SMITH died near Sparta in Edgecombe County on February 16, 1856, aged about forty-five years. (S. February 23, 1856)

William SMITH, son of Thomas SMITH, died at Tarboro on September 22, 1836, in his tenth year. (T. P. October 1, 1836)

William SMITH of Edgecombe County was fatally crushed by a heavy piece of timber on October 7 and died on October 9, 1841, leaving a wife and three or four small children. (T. P. October 16, 1841)

William SMITH of Chowan County died at the residence of his son near Sparta on January 21, 1851. (T. P. January 25, 1851)

Colonel Ebenezer SMITHWICK died at Williamston on July 15, 1829. (F. P. July 31, 1829)

Mrs. Anna SOREY, formerly Anna Wiggins, died in Nash County on June 2, 1854, aged about sixty-five years and leaving her husband Robert SOREY. She was for about twenty-five years a member of the Falls of Tar River Baptist Church. (S. August 5, 1854)

Joshua SPAIN from Pitt County was kicked in the stomach by a horse at Mrs. Gregory's Hotel in Tarboro on December 5, 1839, and died about a half-hour later at the age of nineteen or twenty years. He was the driver of the stage between Tarboro and Enfield. (T. P. December 7, 1839)

Mrs. Martha SPARKS, wife of A. J. SPARKS of Edgecombe County, died suddenly on March 13, 1860, aged about twenty-six years, and leaving three small children. (S. March 17, 1860)

Benjamin SPEIGHT died at Washington City on May 25, 1846, being a son of Senator Jesse E. SPEIGHT of Mississippi, and in his twenty-sixth year. (T. P. June 3, 1846)

Mrs. Charity SPEIGHT, widow of Lemon SPEIGHT, died in Greene County on November 19, 1830. (N. C. F. P. November 30, 1830)

Charles G. SPAIGHT, Esq., died at New Bern on August 24, 1831. (N. C. F. P. August 30, 1831)

Mrs. Edwin G. SPEIGHT died in Greene County on October 22, 1846, at her mother's home. (T. P. October 28, 1846)

Joseph SPEIGHT was murdered by Andrew Harrell of Nansemond County, Virginia, on December 20, 1837. SPEIGHT was from Gates County. (T. P. January 19, 1838)

Lemon SPEIGHT died in Greene County on June 1, 1830, aged about forty years. (F. P. June 25, 1830)

Mrs. Margaret SPEIGHT, wife of William V. SPEIGHT, Esq., of Greene County, died on September 15, 1826. (T. P. September 26, 1826)

Mrs. Mary SPEIGHT, wife of General Jesse SPEIGHT, died in Greene County on September 5, 1826, leaving a husband and five children. (T. P. September 19, 1826)

William Vines SPEIGHT died in Greene County on October 31, 1836, in his fifty-eighth year. He was for fifteen years in the North Carolina Senate. (T. P. November 5, 1836)

William Vines SPEIGHT, son of Edwin G. SPEIGHT, Esq., died in Greene County on September 25, 1844. He was born on March 16, 1841. (T. P. October 5, 1844)

John SPELL died in Pitt County on June 1, 1835, aged ninety-three years. "He never took a dose of medicine in his life." (T. P. June 20, 1835)

Moses SPICER died in Edgecombe County "a few days since, at an advanced age." (T. P. February 17, 1838)

Margaret SPRUILL, wife of Benjamin SPRUILL, died at Tarboro on September 7, 1838, leaving three small children. She was a member of the Episcopal Church. (T. P. September 8, 1838, and September 29,1838)

Reverend John STADLER of Caswell County died on March 7, 1860, being a "distinguished minister of the Primitive Baptist Church." (S. March 24, 1860)

Mrs. Elizabeth STALLINGS died in Edgecombe County on August 31, 1858, aged forty-nine years. (S. September 4, 1858)

Mrs. Julia STANLY, wife of Congressman Edward STANLY, died in San Francisco, California, on December 20, 1854. (S. February 3, 1855)

Captain Williams STANSELL died in Pitt County on September 30, 1843, aged about thirty-two years, leaving a wife and several small children. (T. P. October 7, 1843)

John Henry STANTON, son of Washington M. STANTON, died on September 7, 1841, aged about three years. (T. P. September 18, 1841)

Mary STANTON, daughter of Washington M. STANTON, died on September 5, 1841, aged about seven years. (T. P. September 18, 1841)

Washington M. STANTON died at Stantonsburg on March 28, 1854, in his forty-sixth year, leaving a wife and eight children. (S. August 26, 1854)

Bythal STATON, Jr., died in Edgecombe County on August 16, 1830, aged twenty-seven or -eight years. (N. C. F. P. August 24, 1830)

Bythal STATON died on April 26, 1834, in his fifty-fifth year. His Masonic Funeral was held on August 31, 1834. (T. F. P. May 2, 1834, and August 1, 1834)

Mrs. Drucilla STATON, wife of Colonel Simmons B. STATON, died in Edgecombe County on July 22, 1841, leaving four small children, the youngest about one month old. (T. P. July 24, 1841)

Ezekiel STATON died in Edgecombe County on August 22, 1843. (T. P. August 26, 1843)

Mrs. Gatsey STATON, wife of John STATON and daughter of the Rev. John H. DANIEL, died of consumption near Tarboro on October 5, 1857, aged about twenty-five years, and leaving three small children. (S. October 10, 1857)

Mrs. Isabella STATON, widow of Reddin STATON, died in Edgecombe County on October 20, 1831, leaving five small orphans. (N. C. F. P. October 25, 1831)

Mrs. Julia STATON, wife of W. D. STATON, Esq., died in Halifax County on June 11, 1850, aged about fifty-eight years. (T. P. June 22, 1850)

Martha Elizabeth STATON, daughter of William John STATON, died in Edgecombe County on July 7, 1853, aged about eleven months. (S. July 9, 1853)

Redding STATON died in Edgecombe County on November 2, 1829. (F. P. November 6, 1829)

Richard STATON died in Edgecombe County on August 20, 1852, aged twenty-two years. (S. August 21, 1852)

Roderick STATON died in Edgecombe County on May 3, 1851, aged about fifty-five years. (T. P. May 17, 1851)

Colonel Simmons B. STATON died in Edgecombe County on October 5, 1850, aged about forty years, and leaving three children. (T. P. October 12, 1850)

Thomas C. STATON died in Edgecombe County on August 21, 1854, aged about twenty-five years. (S. August 26, 1854)

William STATON, planter, died in Edgecombe County on February 10, 1828, aged about fifty years. (F. P. February 15, 1828)

Winfield D. STATON of Halifax County and formerly of Edgecombe County, died "a few days since." (S. May 12, 1855)

Edmond H. STEPHENS died in Wilson on June 9, 1853, in his forty-third year, leaving a wife and four children. He was a member of the Missionary Baptist Church, Mt. Lebanon Masonic Lodge, No. 117, Winchester Lodge, No. 16, and the I. O. O. F. of Rocky Mount. (S. June 25, 1853)

Mrs. Jannett STEWART of Tarboro died at the home of her mother Mrs. Bryant near Bethel Meeting House in Pitt County on January 23, 1852. (S. January 31, 1852)

Miss Adelaide STILLMAN died of consumption at Tarboro on January 25, 1857, aged about thirty years. (S. January 31, 1857)

Samuel STILLMAN died in Connecticut on August 20, 1827, leaving a wife and two children. (F. P. September 8, 1827)

Seth W. STODDARD, teacher at the Greenville Academy and a native of Broome County, New York, died on September 30, 1838. (T. P. October 6, 1838)

Mrs. Frances STONE, widow of Thomas G. STONE, Esq., died at Nashville on July 19, 1831, leaving a husband and two children. (N. C. P. August 16, 1831)

James STRICKLAND was killed by Thomas GRAY in Halifax County on February 18, 1833. (N. C. F. P. March 5, 1833)

Marmaduke STRICKLAND, "an honest man," died "in the lower end of Halifax County" on December 26, 1831, aged sixty-four years. (N. C. F. P. January 3, 1832)

Mrs. Mary L. STUBBS, wife of Jesse R. STUBBS, Esq., died at Williamston on June 3, 1861, of the consumption. (S. June 29, 1861)

George A. SUGG died in Pitt County on April 8, 1835, "a wealthy and respectable citizen." (T. P. April 18, 1835)

Joel S. SUGG died in Edgecombe County on April 11, 1843. (T. P. April 15, 1843)

Joseph SUGG of Greene County was to be hanged on November 24, 1842, for the murder of "a free man named Dick Jones." (T. P. November 5, 1842)

Mrs. Margaret SUGG, widow of the late Reddin SUGG, died in Edgecombe County on August 18, 1850, aged about sixty-three years. (T. P. August 24, 1850)

Mrs. Mary SUGG died near Tarboro on March 5, 1824, in her seventy-sixth year. (F. P. March 26, 1824)

Phesanton SUGG, son of Dr. Phesanton SUGG, died on June 1, 1838, aged a few weeks. (T. P. June 9, 1838)

Dr. Phesanton SUGG died on October 14, 1855, in his fifty-first year, leaving a widow and eleven children. He had been a Justice of the Peace, a Delegate to the North Carolina Convention of 1835, and had not practiced medicine for about three years. (S. October 20, 1855)

Reading SUGG, son of Reading SUGG, died in Edgecombe County on October 29, 1831, aged about four years. (N. C. F. P. November 1, 1831)

Reddin SUGG died on June 20, 1841, in his sixty-third year, being "one of our most wealthy and enterprising farmers." (T. P. June 26, 1841)

Captain John E. SULZMAN, a native of Germany and formerly of Nashville, died of cholera at Georgetown, Mississippi, on March 22, 1850, aged forty years. (T. P. April 20, 1850)

Starling SUMMERELL lost the oldest two of his five children when his home burned on October 27, 1834. (T. F. P. November 7, 1834)

Bryant SUTHERLAND was killed at William Outlaw's mill in Wayne County on February 14, 1853, leaving a wife and seven children. (S. March 5, 1853)

William SUTTON, Esq., died in Edgecombe County on November 27, 1833. (T. F. P. November 29, 1833)

William TANNAHILL, merchant of Washington, died in Havana on January 8, 1845, in his forty-fifth year, leaving a wife and six children. (T. P. January 25, 1845)

Elnathan TARTT, formerly of Edgecombe (now Wilson) County, died "a few weeks ago" at the age of thirty-six in Sumter County, Alabama. (T. P. March 21, 1835)

Thomas E. TARTT, Esq., of the House of Tartt, Stuart & Co., died of apoplexy at Mobile on May 6, 1842, aged forty-six years. "Mr. TARTT was formerly of this County, and a very enterprising and worthy citizen, and much respected by all who knew him." (T. P. May 28, 1842)

Charles TAYLOR of Edgecombe County died on October 3, 1831, aged about forty years. (N. C. F. P. October 11, 1831)

Dempsey TAYLOR died in Nash County on April 2, 1845, aged seventy-one years, leaving five children. (T. P. April 12, 1845)

Irvin TAYLOR died in Edgecombe County on August 3, 1857, aged about fifty-seven years, leaving a large family. (S. August 8, 1857)

Mrs. John TAYLOR died in Edgecombe County on September 30, 1840. (T. P. October 3, 1840)

Mrs. Mary TAYLOR, wife of Kinchen TAYLOR, Esq., died in Nash County on May 27, 1829, leaving a husband and eight children. (F. P. June 19, 1829)

Mrs. Rosamond TAYLOR died in Nash County on July 13, 1829, aged about eighty years. (F. P. July 24, 1829)

William A. "Ned" TAYLOR was stabbed to death by James Dancy at Battleboro on July 28, 1853. (S. August 6, 1853)

Aurelius Wilmot TERRELL, son of Nathaniel M. TERRELL, died at Tarboro on October 9, 1844, aged three years and seven months. (T. P. October 12, 1844)

William Lewis TERRELL, son of N. M. TERRELL, died at Tarboro on April 26, 1838, aged about four months. (T. P. April 28, 1838)

Lucy Murray TERRELL, daughter of Robert G. and M. B. TERRELL, died at Stanhope on July 7, 1846. She was born on June 30, 1845. (T. P. July 22, 1846)

Cornelia THIGPEN, daughter of Kenneth THIGPEN, Esq., died in Edgecombe County on December 22, 1857, aged two years and one month. (S. January 9, 1858)

James THIGPEN died in Sumter County, Alabama, recently. (T. P. November 7, 1840)

Rufus C. THIGPEN died in Edgecombe County on July 15, 1854, aged about twenty-seven years, and leaving a wife and one child. (S. July 22, 1854) A later issue said that Rufus C. THIGPEN, Esq., was twenty-eight and died on July 16, 1854. (S. August 26, 1854)

Rufus Harriet Louisa THIGPEN, only child of the late Rufus C. THIGPEN, died at the residence of the Rev. John Henry Daniel in Edgecombe County on September 2, 1855, aged about two years. (S. September 8, 1855)

Amanda R. THOMAS, wife of Jacob THOMAS, died on August 24, 1832, in her seventeenth year. (N. C. F. P. August 28, 1832)

Jacob THOMAS died "a few days since" in Edgecombe County. (T. P. May 9, 1840)

James C. THOMAS, infant son of Dr. William George THOMAS, died at Tarboro on September 5, 1846. (T. P. September 9, 1846)

Maria C. THOMAS, daughter of Dr. William G. THOMAS, died of cholera infantum at Tarboro on June 13, 1845, aged about eleven months. (T. P. June 18, 1845)

Edward G. THOMPSON of Tarboro and formerly of Northampton County, died on January 22, 1845. (T. P. January 25, 1845)

Mrs. Eliza THOMPSON, daughter of Spencer D. COTTEN and wife of Noah Thompson, died in Tarboro on June 26, 1835. (T. P. July 4, 1835)

Mrs. Martha THORNE, wife of Dr. Samuel THORNE of Halifax County, died on April 8, 1827, in her fifty-sixth year. (F. P. May 5, 1827)

Mrs. Sarah THORNE, wife of William D. THORNE of Edgecombe County, died on February 28, 1848, leaving one child. (T. P. March 4, 1848)

Herbert B. THORPE of Southington, Connecticut, was injured by the accidental discharge of a cannon on June 11 and died on June 18, 1858. (S. June 19, 1858)

Mrs. Betty T. THURSTON, widow of the Rev. John THRUSTON, and daughter of the late Francis GAINES of King and Queen County, Virginia, died at Halifax on March 20, 1849, in her sixty-eighth year, leaving one daughter. (T. P. March 31, 1849)

Catharine THURSTON died at Tarboro on July 31, 1838, in her eighteenth year. (T. P. August 4, 1838)

Olivia TISON, daughter of the late William TISON, died in Edgecombe County on August 21, 1859, aged about thirty years. (S. August 27, 1859)

Sherrod TISON, merchant, died in Pitt County on March 28, 1842, aged about fifty years. (T. P. April 9, 1842)

Lewis TODD, "the last Revolutionary soldier of this county," died about December of 1851. (S. February 14, 1852)

Mrs. Sarah TOMLINSON of Johnston County died on October 14, 1824, aged eighty-eight years. (F. P. October 29, 1824)

Mrs. Rosa TOMPKINS died in Nash County "at an advanced age" at the residence of her recently deceased brother Bennett BUNN, on May 23, 1849. (T. P. May 26, 1849)

Geraldus TOOLE, Esq., died in Sampson County on August 21, 1832. (N. C. F. P. August 28, 1832)

Geraldus TOOLE, "one of our wealthiest and most respected citizens," died "at an advanced age" on October 9, 1834. (T. F. P. October 17, 1834)

Frances M. TOOLE died at Oxford on August 13, 1832. (N. C. F. P. August 28, 1832)

Henry Irwin TOOLE, Esq., died at Wilmington on December 28, 1850, in his forty-first year. (T. P. January 11, 1851)

Hugh Geraldus TOOLE, son of Henry TOOLE, Esq., died at Washington, North Carolina, on September 7, 1836, aged about six years. (T. P. September 17, 1836)

James TOOLE died at Averasborough on August 18, 1832. (N. C. F. P. August 28, 1832)

Mrs. Margaret Eliza TOOLE, wife of Henry I. TOOLE, Esq., died of cancer of the breast at their residence "The Cottage" in Pitt County on July 16, 1848, aged thirty-six years. She was a member of the Episcopal Church. (T. P. July 22, 1848)

Wiley TOOLE died at Averasborough on August 14, 1832. (N. C. F. P. August 28, 1832)

Captain Alexander D. TUMBRO, a printer by trade, died in Edgecombe County at the residence of his father-in-law F. H. Knight on October 17, 1862. He was a member of Company D, 4th North Carolina Regiment, C. S. A. (S. October 18, 1862)

Mrs. Bettie S. TUMBRO, wife of A. D. TUMBRO, Esq., Editor of the Newbern Enquirer, died at the home of her father F. H. KNIGHT in Edgecombe County on July 5, 1860, aged twenty-two years and leaving an infant of ten days. (S. July 7, 1860)

Mrs. Louisa TUNNELL, wife of B. B. TUNNELL, Esq., died at Rocky Mount on July 8, 1846, leaving three children. (T. P. July 15, 1846)

William TURNER died in Nash County on December 31, 1843, aged ninety-two years. "The deceased was a Revolutionary soldier, and a more patriotic spirit never inspired the breast of man than he possessed, having lived and died in full faith of Democracy." (T. P. January 13, 1844)

William TURNER of Rocky Mount died on January 23, 1856, after having been run over by a train on January 18 preceding. (S. January 26, 1856)

Mrs. Louisa TYLER, wife of Johnson TYLER, died on March 3, 1860, aged twenty-five years. (S. March 17, 1860)

Benjamin TYSON, Esq., died in Pitt County on January 11, 1846, in his sixty-first year, leaving a wife and one infant child. (T. P. January 21, 1846)

Ichabod TYSON died in Pitt County on December 4, 1826, aged sixty-nine years. "The dec'd was a soldier in the American Revolution." (F. P. December 19, 1826)

William TYSON of Edgecombe County died on December 13, 1827, aged about thirty years, leaving a wife and one child. (F. P. December 28, 1827)

Mrs. Camilla H. VAUGHAN, wife of the Rev. Maurice H. VAUGHAN, died at Tarboro of scarlet fever on May 21, 1863, aged twenty-one years. (S. May 23, 1863)

Belfield W. VICK, son of the late Sheriff Samuel W. VICK, of Nash County, died "Near Wilson in this county" on June 22, 1852. He was born on March 2, 1839. (S. July 17, 1852)

Josiah VICK died in Nash County on August 11, 1845. (T. P. August 27, 1845)

Providence VICK died in Edgecombe County on August 31, 1843, aged about seventy years. (T. P. November 11, 1843)

Samuel W. W. VICK died in Nash County on June 9, 1845, being "one of our most worthy citizens," and leaving a wife and ten children. (T. P. June 18, 1845)

Louisa VINES, daughter of John A. VINES, died on January 7, 1844, aged about five years. (T. P. January 13, 1844)

Samuel VINES of Greene County died on November 17, 1844, aged about sixty years. (T. P. November 30, 1844)

James Stewart VIPON, merchant of New Bern, died at Greenville on January 21, 1827, in his twenty-fourth year. (F. P. February 3, 1827)

James WADDELL, only child of Matthew and Maria T. WADDELL of Tarboro, died at the home of Mrs. L. P. Cotten near Raleigh on September 4, 1857, aged two years and two months. (S. September 12, 1857)

Mrs. Martha Ann WALKER, wife of Dr. J. R. WALKER of Mecklenburg County, Virginia, and daughter of the late Spencer L. HART of Edgecombe County, died at her mother's home on July 11, 1857, leaving two infant children. She had been born on September 18, 1831. (S. July 18, 1857)

Sterling WALLER, "an aged and respectable citizen," died on September 21, 1826. (T. P. September 26, 1826)

Warren WALLER, died in Edgecombe County on March 29, 1860, aged seventy-two years. (S. April 7, 1860)

Mary Ann WALSTON, daughter of Willie and Mary WALSTON, died in Edgecombe

County on September 11, 1863. (S. September 19, 1863)

Mrs. Margaret S. WALTER, wife of Richard WALTER, Esq., and a native of Accomac County, Virginia, died at Portsmouth on April 19, 1846, in her thirty-first year, and leaving one infant. Her Obituary was signed by "J. C. B." (T. P. September 9, 1846)

Colonel Harman WARD of Edgecombe County died on October 28, 1850, in his fortieth year. He was Colonel of the Militia, Chairman of the Board of Superintendents of Common Schools, and his funeral was preached by the Reverend William Hyman. (T. P. November 2, 1850)

Henry WARD, infant of John F. and Lucy WARD, died at Tarboro on September 12, 1863. (S. September 19, 1863)

Dr. John F. WARD, formerly of Tarboro, died in Madison County, Tennessee, on February 25, 1834. (T. F. P. March 21, 1834)

Joseph WARD, only child of Mrs. Charlotte WARD, died of typhus fever on August 7, 1831, aged about nineteen years. (N. C. F. P. August 9, 1831)

Joseph John E. WARD, only survivor from the three marriages of his widowed mother, died on August 7, 1831, aged almost twenty-one years. (N. C. F. P. September 6, 1831)

Laura WARD, daughter of Dr. John F. WARD, formerly of Tarboro, died in Salem on January 29, 1844, in her thirteenth year. A poetic Elegy of forty-eight lines was dedicated to her memory. (T. P. February 10, 1844)

Elder Luke WARD died "at an advanced age" in Edgecombe County on March 4, 1839. (T. P. March 9, 1839)

Maria WARD, wife of Dr. WARD and only child of Samuel VINES of Greene County, died at Stantonsburg on November 6, 1844. (T. P. November 23, 1844)

Mrs. Nancy WARD, widow of Elder Luke WARD, died in Edgecombe County on March 21, 1854, aged about seventy years. (S. April 8, 1854)

Mrs. Zilpha WARREN, widow of Samuel WARREN, died in Edgecombe County on February 9, 1861, aged about fifty-five years. (S. February 16, 1861)

John A. WARRINGTON, Tavern Keeper of Plymouth, died in Tarboro on December 8, 1831, "he having been drinking and carousing for two or three days previous." (N. C. F. P. December 13, 1831)

Mrs. Alice B. WATSON, wife of Joshua WATSON, died in Nash County near Rocky Mount on June 10, 1859, in her fifty-seventh year. (S. June 25, 1859)

Thomas WATSON died in Halifax County on August 21, 1827, in his sixtieth year; and Temperance WATSON died on September 5, 1827, aged fifteen years. (F. P. September 22, 1827)

William WATSON was hanged at Williamston on September 30, 1842. (T. P. October 8, 1842)

Major William WATTS died "a few days since" at Williamston. He had been "for many years a hotel keeper in that town" and was about seventy-five years of age. (S. October 15, 1859)

William McG. WEATHERSBEE'S Masonic Funeral sponsored by the Skewarkey Lodge, No. 90, was to be held at his late residence in Martin County about one and one-half miles from Log Chapel Meeting House, on Sunday, May 16, 1849. (T. P. April 21, 1849)

Benjamin WEAVER died on August 28, 1834, aged fifty years, and leaving a wife and three children. (T. F. P. September 5, 1834)

Richard H. WEAVER, Esq., Clerk of Northampton County, died near Jackson on June 13, 1835. (T. P. June 27, 1835)

Frances C. E. WEBB, wife of C. N. WEBB, died at Halifax on March 21, 1856. (S. April 12, 1856)

John WEBB, Sr., "a soldier of the Revolution," died in Edgecombe County on October 7, 1842, aged about eighty years. (T. P. October 15, 1842)

Mrs. Sally WEBB, wife of William WEBB, died on March 9, 1855, aged about fifty-four years and a member of the Baptist Church. (S. March 17, 1855)

William E. WEBB, Esq., died at Hyde Park in Halifax County on May 30, 1829. (F. P. June 12, 1829)

Arabella WEDDELL, daughter of Matthew WEDDELL, died at Tarboro on April 25, 1855, aged about one year and eight months. (S. April 28,1855)

Henrietta WEDDELL, daughter of James WEDDELL, died at Tarboro on May 6, 1849, aged about three years. (T. P. May 12, 1849)

James WEDDELL, son of James WEDDELL, died at Tarboro on June 29, 1850, aged nine weeks. (T. P. July 6, 1850)

Laura Ward WEDDELL, daughter of James WEDDELL, died in Tarboro on March 21, 1849, aged about seven weeks. (T. P. March 24, 1849)

Mrs. Maria T. WEDDELL, wife of Matthew WEDDELL, died of consumption at Tarboro on June 16, 1859, in her forty-sixth year. Her father was the late James W. CLARK. (S. June 18, 1859)

Mary WEDDELL, daughter of James WEDDELL, died at Tarboro on July 19, 1846, aged twenty-two months. (T. P. July 22, 1846)

Captain Virginius L. WEDDELL, son of James WEDDELL who was for many years a resident of Tarboro, died of typhoid fever at his father's residence on Sycamore Street in Petersburg on July 22, 1862, aged about twenty-one years. He was serving in the Confederate Cadets. (S. July 26, 1862)

Mrs. Olive WEEKS died in Edgecombe County on December 12, 1848, aged sixty-nine years. (T. P. December 16, 1848)

Mrs. Margaret WELLS died in Halifax County on February 1, 1835, aged eighty-nine years and a member of the Baptist Church for over fifty years. (T. P. February 14, 1835)

Thomas WELLS, former Magistrate of Edgecombe County, died on December 19, 1838, aged seventy-two years. (T. P. December 22, 1838)

Mary WEST, daughter of William W. WEST, Esq., died at New Hope in Halifax County on June 29, 1827. (F. P. July 14, 1827)

Cary WHITAKER of Edgecombe County died on March 7, 1860, aged about fifty-two years. (S. March 17, 1860)

Mary WHITAKER, daughter of Colonel Spier WHITAKER, died at Davenport, Iowa, on August 22, 1855. (S. October 20, 1855)

Mrs. Charlotte WHITE, wife of Ezekiel WHITE and daughter of the late David BRADLEY, died in Edgecombe County on November 17, 1853, aged about thirty-three years, and leaving seven children. (S. November 26, 1853)

James WHITE of Edgecombe County was shot near Scotland Neck by his brother Shan WHITE on October 22, 1859, leaving a wife in feeble health and seven children. The brother was later sentenced to six months of imprisonment. (S. October 29, 1859, and November 12, 1859)

S. B. WHITE died in Edgecombe County on June 26, 1860, aged about twenty-four years. (S. July 7, 1860)

Augustin "Austin" WHITEHEAD died in Edgecombe County on August 30, 1846, aged seventy-five or eighty years. (T. P. September 9, 1846)

Major J. S. WHITEHEAD, son of Howell WHITEHEAD, Esq., of Pitt County, died in Wilson on August 7, 1862. James S. WHITEHEAD was Major of the 55th Regiment, North Carolina Troops, C. S. A. (S. August 23, 1862)

L. B. WHITEHEAD was fatally shot near Penny Hill in Pitt County by John Edmondson, "under the excitement of a contention about a ten dollar debt," on July 1, 1852, aged about thirty-two years. (S. July 3, 1852)

Mrs. Margaret WHITEHEAD, wife of Henry WHITEHEAD, died in Halifax County on September 26, 1829. (F. P. October 16, 1829)

Mrs. Polly WHITEHEAD, wife of Robert WHITEHEAD, and daughter of Josiah FREEMAN, died in Edgecombe County on May 19, 1829. (F. P. May 22, 1829)

Reuben WHITEHEAD, overseer on the plantation of Dr. K. H. Dicken of Edgecombe County, was killed on March 17, 1859, "by his horse running away with him in a buggy." (S. March 19, 1859)

William WHITEHEAD of Halifax County died on April 20, 1845, in his eighty-first year. (T. P. April 26, 1845)

Charles WHITEHURST, son of Robert WHITEHURST from Washington, died near Tarboro on July 6, 1862, aged about eighteen months. (S. July 12, 1862)

Mrs. Nancy WHITEHURST, wife of James WHITEHURST and daughter of Winfield STATON, Esq., died in Edgecombe County on June 30, 1854. (They had been married on February 17, 1842.) (S. July 1, 1854)

Mrs. Sallie A. WHITEHURST, daughter of Wilson HOWARD, died in Martin County on March 20, 1862, in her twenty-eighth year, leaving a husband and four children. (S. April 5, 1862) (Newton WHITEHURST had married Sarah A. HOWARD on October 20, 1852, in Edgecombe County.)

George Wimberley WHITFIELD, son of George W. and Mary L. WHITFIELD, died in Edgecombe County on August 24, 1856, aged five years. (S. August 30, 1856)

Robert WHITFIELD, son of George W. WHITFIELD, Esq., died in Edgecombe County on July 5, 1860, aged about nineteen months. (S. July 7, 1860)

Miss Ruth WHITFIELD, formerly of Nashville, died recently in Sumter County, Alabama. (T. P. November 7, 1840)

Thomas WHITFIELD died in Pitt County on October 25, 1857, aged about thirty years, leaving a wife and two children. (S. October 31, 1857)

William WHITFIELD of Wayne County hanged himself in his front yard on August 27, 1851. (T. P. September 20, 1851)

_____ WHITLEY, daughter of Willie WHITLEY, died recently in Edgecombe County, aged about twenty-one years. (T. P. November 11, 1843)

Mrs. Nancy Ann WHITLEY, wife of John B. WHITLEY of Pitt County and daughter of the Rev. John H. DANIEL of Edgecombe County, died on September 28, 1853, aged about twenty years, leaving a child of eleven months. (S. October 1, 1853)

Blake H. WIGGINS died on September 4, 1827. (F. P. September 8, 1827)

James WIGGINS of Halifax County was killed by a free mulatto named Morgan on August 23, 1834. (T. F. P. September 5, 1834)

Jesse B. WIGGINS died at Crowell's Crossroads in Halifax County on October 3, 1829. (F. P. October 16, 1829)

Lawrence WIGGINS died in Edgecombe County on June 27, 1847. (T. P. July 10, 1847)

Samuel Lawrence WIGGINS, son of Mason L. WIGGINS, died at Farmwell in Halifax County on May 16, 1850, aged fifteen years. (T. P. June 8, 1850)

Mrs. Littleberry WILCOX died in Halifax County on September 13, 1827. (F. P. September 29, 1827)

James B. WILKINS died in Edgecombe County on May 20, 1849, aged forty-three years. (T. P. May 26, 1849)

Thomas M. WILKINS, "an industrious, attentive and obliging citizen," was mangled and killed by the grist mill at Battle & Sons Cotton Factory, where he had worked for about twenty years, on June 1, 1854, aged about forty-five years and unmarried. (S. June 3, 1854)

Willis WILKINS, Esq., "a wealthy, extensive, and enterprising farmer," died about fifty-five years, and a Justice of the Peace. (T. P. October 1, 1845)

Mrs. Willis WILKINS died in Edgecombe County on February 15, 1832. (N. C. F. P. February 21, 1832)

Colonel Benjamin WILKINSON died in Edgecombe County on February 27, 1837. (T. P. March 4, 1837)

Benjamin WILKINSON seems to have died shortly before November 28, 1837, and Secretary T. C. Hearn of the Concord Masonic Lodge at Tarboro announced funeral rites to be conducted "at his late residence" by Elder William Hyman on December 17, 1837. (T. S. December 1, 1837. T. P. December 2, 1837)

Benoni M. WILKINSON died at Hamilton on February 5, 1854. (S. February 18, 1854)

Charles WILKINSON, Esq., died in Edgecombe County on September 14, 1834. (T. F. P. September 19, 1834) Charles WILKINSON'S funeral was preached by the Reverend Joshua Lawrence on December 15, 1834, while Administrator Silas Wilkinson gave notice that his personal property would be sold on December 18, 1834. (T. F. P. November 28, 1834)

Henrietta WILKINSON, daughter of the late Charles WILKINSON, died on September 23, 1834, in her twelfth year. (T. F. P. October 10,1834)

Howard WILKINSON, son of James and Julia WILKINSON, died at Petersburg on March 14, 1851, aged about three years. (T. P. March 22, 1851)

James WILKINSON died of consumption at Tarboro on March 31, 1855, in his forty-second year, leaving a wife and two children by an earlier marriage. He was a native of Rahway, New Jersey, and had been a confectioner at Petersburg before coming to Tarboro. His remains were sent to Petersburg on April 2, and he was buried at Blandford after a funeral conducted by the Reverend Mr. Gibson. (S. April 7, 1855)

Lafayette WILKINSON, son of the late Charles WILKINSON, died on March 15, 1838, aged about twelve years. (T. P. March 24, 1838)

Levi WILKINSON died in Edgecombe County on November 8, 1833, aged about twenty-five years. (T. F. P. November 15, 1833)

Benashly WILLIAMS, son of the late David WILLIAMS of Martin County, died of yellow fever at Richmond, Louisiana, on October 12, 1855, aged twenty-six years. (S. November 17, 1855)

Benjamin WILLIAMS, son of Benjamin WILLIAMS of Tarboro, died on September 24, 1829, aged about four years. (F. P. September 25, 1829)

Mrs. Caroline WILLIAMS, daughter of Major John H. DRAKE and wife of Dr. Robert WILLIAMS of Pitt County, died near Falkland on September 22, 1844, leaving a husband and five children. (T. P. September 28, 1844)

Charles WILLIAMS, son of the late Benjamin WILLIAMS of Tarboro, died of typhoid fever at Petersburg on August 1, 1862, aged about twenty-two years. He was a member of Lloyd's Battery, 40th North Carolina Regiment, C. S. A. (S. August 9, 1862)

David WILLIAMS died in Martin County on September 28, 1835. (T. P. October 3, 1835)

David WILLIAMS, youngest son of John G. WILLIAMS, Esq., died of typhoid fever in Edgecombe County on October 6, 1854. He was born on October 20, 1839. (S. October 14, 1854)

Egbert H. WILLIAMS died in Henderson County, Tennessee, on September 20, 1838. He was a native and former resident of Edgecombe County. (T. P. October 27, 1838)

Hezekiah T. WILLIAMS died at his father's home near Hamilton on July 23, 1844, aged twenty-two years. (T. P. August 31, 1844)

Howard WILLIAMS, son of Captain Orren WILLIAMS, died in Tarboro on September 2, 1862, aged nine months. (S. September 6, 1862)

James WILLIAMS died at the hands of Mark Jones near River Bridge in Pasquotank County on October 14, 1833. (T. F. P. October 18, 1833, and October 25, 1833)

James J. WILLIAMS of Tarboro died of yellow fever at Galveston, Texas, on October 14, 1859, aged thirty-two years. He had resided for many years earlier at Montgomery, Alabama. His Obituary seems to suggest that he participated in the defense of Texas during the Mexican War. (T. M. November 9, 1859. S. November 12, 1859)

John WILLIAMS, son of Thomas WILLIAMS, died on January 8, 1839, aged about forty years. (T. P. January 12, 1839)

John WILLIAMS, former merchant of Tarboro, died in Edgecombe County on November 4, 1848, aged about sixty years, leaving a wife and four children. (T. P. November 11, 1848)

John Lee WILLIAMS died at Philadelphia on October 26, 1857, in his twenty-fifth year. The Edgecombe Lodge, No. 50, I. O. O. F., published a warm note of regret. (S. November 7, 1857)

Joseph H. WILLIAMS died at Tarboro on March 4, 1857, in his thirty-fourth year. (S. March 6, 1857)

Lewis WILLIAMS, son of Lewis A. WILLIAMS of Martin County, died on September 12, 1831, in his thirteenth year. (N. C. F. P. September 27, 1831)

Lewis WILLIAMS, son of Benjamin WILLIAMS, died at Tarboro on May 21, 1845 aged thirteen months. (T. P. May 24, 1845)

Mrs. Louisa WILLIAMS, wife of Senator William P. WILLIAMS and daughter of Geraldus TOOLE of Edgecombe County, died in Franklin County on February 23, 1832, in her thirty-fourth year. She was a Methodist. (N. C. F. P. March 6, 1832)

Mark WILLIAMS, son of Benjamin WILLIAMS, died on March 16, 1843, aged about four months. (T. P. March 18, 1843)

Mrs. Nancy WILLIAMS, wife of Dr. William W. WILLIAMS of Martin County, died at the residence of General Hawkins in Warren County on September 24, 1835, leaving a husband and children. She was a member of the Methodist Church. (T. P. October 3, 1835)

Mrs. Nancy WILLIAMS, wife of Roderick WILLIAMS of Edgecombe County, was burned to death on March 11, 1844, leaving a husband and three children. (T. P. March 16, 1844)

Nicholas WILLIAMS, son of the late Dr. Robert J. WILLIAMS, died "with a fit" at Greenville on February 3, 1858, aged about twenty-two years. (S. February 6, 1858)

Mrs. Priscilla WILLIAMS, wife of Dr. Robert WILLIAMS, Jr., died in Pitt County on October 23, 1829. (F. P. November 6, 1829)

Dr. R. F. J. H. WILLIAMS died in Pitt County on March 18, 1853, aged about fifty-four years. (S. April 2, 1853)

Richard WILLIAMS was killed by lightning at Greenville on June 14, 1856. (S. June 21, 1856)

Robert WILLIAMS, son of Benjamin WILLIAMS, died at Tarboro on September 17, 1832, aged about seventeen months. (N. C. F. P. September 25, 1832)

Dr. Robert WILLIAMS died in Pitt County on October 12, 1840, in his eighty-third year. He long represented his County in the State Legislature and was a zealous patriot during the Revolutionary struggle. (T. P. October 24, 1840)

Samuel WILLIAMS died in Martin County on April 1, 1850. (T. P. April 13, 1850)

General William WILLIAMS died in Warren County on March 5, 1832. (N. C. F. P. March 13, 1832)

William WILLIAMS died in Pitt County on July 22, 1850, aged about sixty-five years. (T. P. August 3, 1850)

Meedy WILLIFORD, Esq., died in Edgecombe County on September 6, 1846, aged sixty-three years, leaving a wife and eleven children. (T. P. September 9, 1846)

Thomas WILLIFORD of Edgecombe County died on September 11, 1844. (T. P. September 14, 1844)

James W. WILSON died in Edgecombe County on May 1, 1831. (N. C. F. P. May 3, 1831)

Miss Polly WILSON died at Tarboro on June 2, 1855, aged about sixty years. (S. June 9, 1855)

Mrs. Catherine L. WIMBERLEY, a native of Edgecombe County, died at the residence of George W. Whitfield at Gainesville in Sumter County, Alabama, on February 12, 1840, aged about sixty years. She went to Alabama in 1836 and was a member of the Baptist Church for about forty years. (T. P. March 14, 1840)

George WIMBERLEY died in Johnston County on March 28, 1834. He was born on December 20, 1769, and had been a member of the Baptist Church for over twenty-two years. (T. F. P. April 18, 1834)

Mrs. Mary Ann Louisa WIMBERLEY, wife of George WIMBERLEY, died on February 3, 1828, in Robertson County, Tennessee. She was formerly of Halifax County. (F. P. March 14, 1828)

Mary Ann WIMBERLEY, daughter of Robert D. WIMBERLEY, died on June 5, 1855, aged about sixteen years. (S. June 9, 1855)

Mrs. _____ WINBURN died at Tarboro on May 16, 1855, "at an advanced age." (S. May 19, 1855)

Mrs. Mary Ann WINBURN, wife of Henry G. WINBURN and daughter of Darling CHERRY of Martin County, died at the home of Moses Price, Esq., of Edgecombe County on November 10, 1837, aged eighteen years, and leaving one small child. She became ill just as they were leaving for West Tennessee. (T. P. November 18, 1837)

Caswell WINDHAM, son of Cannon WINDHAM, died on August 7, 1832, aged one year and seventeen days. (N. C. F. P. August 14, 1832)

M. A. E. WINSTEAD, eldest daughter of W. W. WINSTEAD, died in Wilson on July 3, 1859, aged seventeen years and nine months. (S. July 9, 1859)

Aquilla WOMBLE of Halifax County died in Petersburg on March 28, 1835, in his forty-eighth year. (T. P. April 4, 1835)

Mrs. Dianner WOMBLE, wife of A. WOMBLE of Halifax, died on January 19, 1835. (T. P. January 24, 1835)

Mrs. Warren WOMBLE died "a few days since." (N. C. F. P. April 17, 1832)

George W. WOODMAN, merchant, died at Tarboro "at an advanced age" on November 19, 1833. (T. F. P. November 22, 1833)

Amos H. WOOTEN, son of Amos WOOTEN, Jr., died on September 20, 1843. (T. P. September 30, 1843)

Ephraim WOOTEN died of yellow fever at Autry's Creek in Edgecombe County on October 26, 1862, aged nearly thirty-five years, leaving a wife and one child. He had volunteered in Captain Andrew Moore's Company and had been "employed as a nurse in the Hospital" at Wilmington until he became ill and returned home. (S. November 18, 1862)

Levi WORRELL died on August 19, 1838, after having been struck on the head by a piece of fencerail in the hands of his wife Sally WORRELL. He was aged about fifty years. (T. P. August 25, 1838)

Mrs. Emeliza WORSLEY, wife of John WORSLEY and daughter of Moses SPICER, Esq., died near the Falls of Tar River in Edgecombe County on May 17, 1837, leaving a husband and one small child. (T. S. May 19, 1837. T. P. May 27, 1837)

Mrs. Nancy WORSLEY, wife of Mayo WORSLEY, died in Edgecombe County on July 26, 1841, leaving four small children. (T. P. July 31, 1841)

John S. YOUNG, a native of Scotland, died in Tarboro on August 12, 1862, aged about thirty-five years. He was a harness-maker at Washington until it was captured by the Federal Army. "His wife died a few months ago, when she became intemperate, and soon drank himself to death." (S. August 16, 1862)

INDEX TO THE MARRIAGES

IN

TARBORO NEWSPAPERS

1824-1865

by

Hugh Buckner Johnston

Wilson, North Carolina

1983

Robert AARON married Sarah WHITAKER, daughter of Robert WHITAKER, on February 14, 1828, in Halifax County, by Benjamin W. Davis, Esq. (F. P. February 22, 1828)

Hardiman ABINGTON of Halifax County married Elizabeth BIGGS, daughter of James BIGGS, Esq., in Edgecombe County on February 8, 1830, by James Downing, Esq. (F. P. February 12, 1830)

Corporal Elisha ABRAMS of the Edgecombe Volunteers married Mary F. DUPREE daughter of William R. DUPREE, on August 24, 1848, by Kenneth Thig-pen, Esq. (T. P. August 26, 1842)

John ADAMS of Alexandria, Virginia, married Mary L. EBORN of Beaufort County in Greenville on September 16, 1856, by Rev. T. B. James. (S. October 11, 1856)

William ADAMS, Sr., married Mary ROBBINS, daughter of Jacob ROBBINS "a few days since" in Edgecombe County. (T. P. January 12, 1839)

John ADKINS married Margaret MADDERA in Halifax County on December 19, 1837, by L. B. K. Dicken, Esq. (T. P. December 23, 1837)

Lacy ALFORD married Sally MAYO in Edgecombe County on February 4, 1838, by W. C. Leigh, Esq. (T. P. February 17, 1838)

James V. ALLEN married Eliza M. JOHNSTON in Halifax County on May 6, 1829, by T. S. Brownlow, Esq. (F. P. May 29, 1829)

John ALLEN, aged about sixty years, married Miss _____ BROWNING, aged about twenty, in Franklin County "a short time past." (F. P. September 26, 1828)

Alexander P. ALSOBROOK of Tarboro married Mary E. GRAY in Halifax County on September 11, 1838, by Thomas Ousby, Esq. (T. P. September 22, 1838)

Newsom ALSOBROOK of Martin County married Mrs. James A. PARKER, daughter of Britton HOWELL, in Edgecombe County on June 20, 1855, by Elisha Cromwell, Esq. (S. June 23, 1855)

George W. ANDERSON married Elizabeth FOUNTAIN on May 29, 1845, by William D. Bryan, Esq. (T. P. June 11, 1845)

Joshua L. ANDERSON married Catharine BRADLEY of Edgecombe County on December 25, 1828, by Dempsey Bryan, Esq. (F. P. January 2, 1829)

Micajah ANDERSON, Jr., married Absilla A. DENTON, daughter of Campbell DENTON, in Edgecombe County, January 31, 1861, by John W. Johnson, Esq. (S. February 9, 1861)

Alford ANDREWS married Winnefred HYMAN at the John Hyman home in Martin County on March 12, 1829, by J. L. G. Baker, Esq. (F. P. March 20, 1829)

William J. ANDREWS of Edgecombe County married Virginia HAWKINS, daughter of John D. HAWKINS, in Franklin County on May 8, 1833, by Rev. Joseph H. Saunders. (N. C. F. P. May 25, 1833)

Dr. Joseph J. ANTHONY of Hamilton married Caroline E. GATLIN, daughter of the late Thomas GATLIN, at Tarboro, on May 30, 1854, by Rev. T. R. Owen. (S. June 3, 1854)

Major Whitmel H. ANTHONY married Charity BARNES in Halifax County on August 2, 1831. (N. C. P. August 9, 1831)

W. W. ANTHONY married Charity D. WILLIAMS in Martin County on December 15, 1857. (S. December 19, 1857)

William J. ARMSTRONG married Mrs. Catharine BAKER on January 29, 1846, in Edgecombe County. (T. P. February 11, 1846)

Archibald H. ARRINGTON of Nash County married Catherine Elizabeth WIMBERLEY, daughter of Robert D. WIMBERLEY of Edgecombe County on March 14, 1855, by Rev. T. R. Owen. (S. March 17, 1855)

Arthur ARRINGTON of Nash County married Elizabeth IRWIN, daughter of the late J. A. IRWIN, near Tarboro on December 7, 1830, by Benjamin Boykin, Esq. (N. C. F. P. December 14, 1830)

Peter ARRINGTON, Jr., married Sally Ann BURT, daughter of William BURT of Nash County on June 23, 1831. (N. C. F. P. June 28, 1831)

Richard ARRINGTON married Mrs. Temperance WHITEHEAD in Nash County on
    May 29, 1827. (F. P. June 9, 1827)

Samuel ARRINGTON married Eliza NICHOLSON of Nash County on December 19,
    1826, by Lawrence Battle, Esq. (F. P. December 26, 1826)

John ATKINSON married Mrs. Esther TYSON "a few days since." (N. C. F. P.
    December 20, 1831)

Peyton A. ATKINSON married Susan Virginia STREETER, daughter of Benjamin
    STREETER, in Greene County, on July 27, 1843, by Rev. Spivey. (T.
    P. July 29, 1843)

Willie ATKINSON married Sally WILKINSON on January 6, 1829, by Dempsey
    Bryan, Esq. (F. P. January 9, 1829)

Robert H. AUSTIN married in Franklin County on January 29, 1840, Janett
    JEFFRIES, daughter of William JEFFRIES, Esq., by Elder P. W. Dowd.
    He was of Tarboro. (T. P. February 8, 1840)

Zebidee BAILEY married Matilda GRANBERRY of Halifax County on January 22,
    1829. (F. P. February 6, 1829)

David G. BAKER married Catharine H. WILLIAMS, daughter of Egbert H.
    WILLIAMS, on January 26, 1834, by Joab P. Pitt, Esq. (T. F. P.
    January 31, 1834)

Dr. Joseph H. BAKER married Susan A. FOXHALL, daughter of the late
    William FOXHALL, in the Tarboro Episcopal Church on May 15, 1855, by
    Rev. J. B. Cheshire. (S. May 19, 1855)

William S. BAKER married Julia SHURLEY, daughter of Henry SHURLEY near
    Tarboro on January 11, 1831, by James Biggs, Esq. (N. C. F. P.
    January 18, 1831)

Dr. William S. BAKER married Sarah R. POWELL, daughter of Jesse H. POWELL
    of Edgecombe County at the residence of R. D. Winberley, Esq., on
    July 9, 1848. (T. P. July 22, 1848)

Alvin BALLANCE of Johnston County married Sarah BOYETT at the George
    Boyett residence in Wilson County on September 25, 1859, by Stanly
    Kirby, Esq. (S. October 1, 1859)

Thomas BANKS, "a revolutionary soldier" aged eighty, married in Edge-
    combe County on January 22, 1828, Patsey CONE, aged twenty-five, by
    H. Austin, Esq. (F. P. February 1, 1828)

Ethington BARFIELD married Margaret BELL in Edgecombe County on Septem-
    ber 20, 1831, by William C. Lee, Esq. (N. C. F. P. September 27,
    1831)

Horace BARFIELD married Mary HOWARD, daughter of Wilson HOWARD in Edge-
    combe County on February 5, 1857, by William S. Long, Esq. (S.
    February 14, 1857)

David BARLOW, Esq., married Margaret H. BELL, daughter of the late Jos-
    eph BELL, at Wilson on June 7, 1863, by Rev. J. Blount Cheshire.
    (S. August 28, 1863)

David BARLOW married Peninah SHIRLEY, daughter of Henry SHIRLEY, on
    January 30, 1834, by Benjamin Boykin, Esq. (T. F. P. January 31,
    1834)

Col. A. K. BARLOW, formerly of Edgecombe County, married Elvira P. REID,
    aged twenty, daughter of John REID, Esq., from Halifax County, on
    May 14, 1851, in Hinds County, Mississippi, by Rev. O. L. Nash.
    BARLOW'S letter to Editor George Howard said that she "has an
    accomplished and finished education. So much for Temperance and
    steady habit." (T. P. June 7, 1851)

Arthur K. BARLOW of Edgecombe County married Winifred ATKINSON, daughter
    of Joel ATKINSON of Scotland Neck, on February 25, 1830, by S. M.
    Nickels, Esq. (F. P. March 5, 1830)

Arthur BARNES, Esq., of Wilson, married Joana MANER, daughter of Thomas
    L. MANER, Esq., in Edgecombe County on February 26, 1860, by Rev.
    N. A. H. Goddin. (S. March 3, 1860)

B. B. BARNES, Esq., of Wilson married Lyde PROUDFIT at Brownsville,
    Tennessee, on September 9, 1858, by Rev. William Shelton. (S.

October 2, 1858)

Caswell Hines BARNES married Nancy BOTTOMS "recently" in Nash County. (T. P. April 13, 1844)

Charles BARNES, aged seventy-one, married Piety GAY, aged thirty, at Tarboro on February 20, 1838. (T. P. March 17, 1838)

Elias BARNES married Mahala F. SHARPE, daughter of Col. Benjamin SHARPE, on March 16, 1830, by Willis Wilkins, Esq. (F. P. March 19, 1830)

George BARNES married Zylphia SHARPE in Edgecombe County on May 10, 1851, by B. B. Barron, Esq. (T. P. May 17, 1851)

James BARNES married Mary BARNES in Edgecombe County on May 10, 1851, by B. B. Barron, Esq. (T. P. May 17, 1851)

John R. BARNES married Margaret RUFFIN, daughter of the late Samuel RUFFIN, Esq., on February 13, 1831, in Edgecombe County. (N. C. F. P. February 22, 1831)

Joseph BARNES of Nash County married Elizabeth EXUM, daughter of the late John EXUM, in Edgecombe County on December 4, 1850) (T. P. December 7, 1850)

Josiah BARNES married Elizabeth HINNANT at her father's residence in Wilson County on November 3, 1859, by Simon Barnes, Esq. (S. November 12, 1859)

Simon BARNES married Mary C. ATKINSON in Wilson County on April 21, 1859, by Stanly Kirby, Esq. (S. April 30, 1859)

William BARNES married Jane WILKINS, daughter of Willis WILKINS, Esq., on December 3, 1833, by Benjamin Sharpe, Esq. (T. F. P. December 6, 1833)

Wright BARNES married Mrs. Mary A. S. SHARPE in Edgecombe County on February 13, 1844, by J. C. Knight, Esq. (T. P. February 17, 1844)

Col. Bolin B. BARRON married Mary E. A. THOMAS, daughter of the late Jacob THOMAS, on July 8, 1851, at the residence of Rev. Mark Bennett. (T. P. July 12, 1851)

Turner BASS of Halifax County married Mrs. Susan DICKEN of Edgecombe County on January 11, 1827, by Eli Howell, J. P. (F. P. January 16, 1827)

R. B. BASSETT married Mary Jane WILSON, daughter of the late Mr. John WILSON, on September 17, 1862, at Tarboro, by Rev. J. P. Simpson. (S. September 20, 1862)

Daniel BATCHELOR, aged seventy-five married Miss Elizabeth CRICKMAN in Nashville on August 27, 1839, by Henry Blount, Esq. (T. P. September 14, 1839)

Amos J. BATTLE married Margaret H. PARKER, daughter of Weeks PARKER, on January 7, 1830, by Rev. P. W. Dowd. (F. P. January 15, 1830)

James L. BATTLE of Edgecombe County married Louisa PEEBLES of Sussex County, Virginia, at Scotland Neck on November 26, 1856, by Rev. E. G. Barclay. (S. November 29, 1856)

Dr. James P. BATTLE married Katie Ruth HORNE, daughter of Joshua L. HORNE, on January 12, 1858, by Rev. Joel B. Tucker, Methodist. (S. February 6, 1858)

James R. BATTLE of Nash County married Elizabeth ARRINGTON in Halifax County on November 14, 1826. (F. P. December 5, 1826)

James W. BATTLE from Edgecombe County married Diana FORT, daughter of Dr. J. W. FORT, at Myrtle Springs, Texas, on January 22, 1852, by Rev. Thomas F. Selby. (S. March 20, 1852)

John J. BATTLE married Susan S. PHILIPS, daughter of Dr. James J. PHILIPS, on February 19, 1861, in Edgecombe County, by Rev. Jos. Blount Cheshire. (S. February 23, 1861)

Demp BATTLE, Esq., of Raleigh, married Martha E. BATTLE, daughter of the late James S. BATTLE, on November 28, 1855, by Rev. J. B. Cheshire. (S. December 1, 1855)

T. W. BATTLE, Esq., of Edgecombe County, married Lavinia B. DANIEL, second daughter of the late Judge DANIEL, at Halifax, on May 1, 1850, by Rev. J. B. Cheshire. (T. P. May 4, 1850)

William S. BATTLE married Elizabeth M. DANCY, youngest daughter of Francis L. DANCY, Esq., on June 25, 1845, by Rev. Thomas R. Owen. (T. P. July 2, 1845)

William F. BATTLY of Nash County married Mary Eliza JENKINS of Edgecombe County on July 17, 1839, by Rev. William H. Wills. (T. P. August 3, 1839)

Benjamin B. BATTS married Matilda GARDNER on June 1, 1848, by John S. Dancy, Esq., in Edgecombe County. (T. P. June 3, 1848) She died on June 26, 1848. (T. P. July 1, 1848)

Benjamin B. BATTS married Mrs. Lucy PITTMAN in Tarboro on November 9, 1848, by L. C. Pender, Esq. (T. P. November 11, 1848)

I. F. BATTS married Fannie O. LITTLE, daughter of Col. Gray LITTLE, in Pitt County on February 2, 1864, by Elder T. R. Owen. (S. March 5, 1864)

Henry BELCHER married Martha E. SHURLEY, daughter of the late Geraldus SHURLEY, on April 18, 1844, by Rev. Thomas Dupree. (T. P. April 20, 1844)

Lewis BELCHER married Rebecca S. PITT, daughter of Colonel Joab P. PITT, at Sparta "a few days since," by Rev. Thomas Dupree. (T. P. September 16, 1843) (The marriage bond was taken out on July 5, 1843.)

Robert BELCHER married Emily COTTEN, daughter of the late Alexander S. COTTEN, on February 5, 1837, by Rev. Thomas Dupree. (T. P. February 11, 1837)

Robert BELCHER married Mary E. H. MAYO, daughter of John MAYO, in Edgecombe County on December 21, 1853. (S. December 24, 1853)

Bennet B. BELL married Susan TURNER, daughter of the late Matthew TURNER, on October 17, 1832, at Stantonsburg, by Frederick F. Robbins, Esq. (N. C. F. P. October 23, 1832)

David B. BELL married Margaret PETWAY, daughter of William D. PETWAY, Esq., on October 12, 1848, by Rev. T. R. Owen. (T. P. October 14, 1848)

David C. BELL married Mary WILLIAMS, daughter of Benjamin WILLIAMS, on February 10, 1839, by L. D. Wilson, Esq. (T. P. February 16, 1839)

Jordan BELL married Delaney BARNES near Wilson on August 23, 1855, by Thomas C. Davis, Esq. (S. September 1, 1855)

Lorenzo D. BELL married Julia BELL at Tarboro on June 4, 1840, by C. G. Hunter, Esq. (T. P. June 6, 1840)

Marmaduke N. BELL married Catharine BODDIE of Nash County on January 23, 1827. He was from Edgecombe County. (F. P. January 27, 1827)

McGilbry BELL married Lavinia BELL, daughter of the late Frederick BELL in Halifax County "a few days since" (about January 1846). (T. P. February 4, 1846)

Richard BELL married Sally JONES on August 18, 1836, by S. B. Staton, Esq. (T. P. August 27, 1836)

Dr. Richard BELL, formerly of Edgecombe County, married Mrs. Pamelia SMITH in Cartaret County on January 25, 1832. (N. C. F. P. February 7, 1832)

William BELL married Caroline WATSON, daughter of the late Thomas WATSON in Halifax County on May 22, 1838, by John Young, Esq. (T. P. June 2, 1838)

William D. BELL married Elizabeth BELL, daughter of Frederick BELL, in Edgecombe County on October 17, 1839, by Patrick McDowell, Esq. (T. P. October 26, 1839)

Alexander S. BELLAMY married Sally BOYKIN at Tarboro on December 15, 1829, by James J. Philips, Esq. (F. P. December 18, 1829)

Dr. Edward C. BELLAMY, M. D., married Ann B. CROOM, eldest daughter of Gen. William CROOM, at Newington in Lenoir County on December 8,

1829. (F. P. December 25, 1829)

Dr. John F. BELLAMY of Nash County married Mrs. Sarah COFFIELD on March 23, 1836, by James George, Esq. (T. P. April 2, 1836)

Dr. John T. BELLAMY married Sarah S. W. COFFIELD of Edgecombe County on November 8, 1858, at Whitaker's Chapel in Halifax County, by L. H. B. Whitaker, Esq. (S. November 13, 1858)

Dr. Samuel C. BELLAMY of Nash County married Elizabeth Jane CROOM in Lenoir County on June 26, 1834, by Isaac Croom, Esq. (T. F. P. July 11, 1834)

Dr. William E. BELLAMY married Mary L. HOWELL, daughter of Bythal HOWELL, at the home of Mrs. Lucy Dancy of Edgecombe County on March 12, 1857, by Orren Williams, Esq. (S. March 14, 1857)

John A. BENFORD married Mrs. Priscilla WEST in Halifax County on November 30, 1830. (N. C. F. P. December 14, 1830)

Dr. S. Cooper BENJAMIN married Mrs. GODLEY "recently" in Pitt County. (T. P. March 8, 1845)

Dr. S. G. BENJAMIN of Hamilton married Hattie D. MAY, daughter of Robert W. MAY, Esq., formerly of Pitt County, on December 10, 1857, at Jackson, Tennessee, by Rev. Aaron Jones. (S. January 16, 1858)

Charles E. BENNETT married Emily PALAMOUNTAIN at Tarboro on April 26, 1860, by Rev. T. R. Owen. (S. May 5, 1860)

Lemuel B. BENNETT of Nash County married Elizabeth SLEDGE, daughter of James SLEDGE of Warren County, on January 21, 1827) (F. P. January 27, 1827)

Rev. Mark BENNETT of Edgecombe County married Ann L. POPE at Cononary Church in Halifax County on June 30, 1855, by Rev. Joseph Barkley. (S. July 7, 1855)

Rev. Philemon BENNETT married Lucretia POPE on April 15, 1837, by William S. Baker, Esq. (T. P. May 6, 1837)

Stephen BENNETT married Mrs. Elizabeth BELL, widow of Whitmell BELL, on November 19, 1829, by Lunsford R. Cherry, Esq. (F. P. November 27, 1829)

William B. BENNETT of Williamston married Deborah M. HARDISON on July 20, 1830, at Plymouth, by Ezekiel Hardison, Esq. (F. P. August 6, 1830)

Thomas BENSON married Martha KING in Edgecombe County on May 24, 1832, by L. R. Cherry, Esq. (N. C. F. P. May 29, 1832)

Dr. William BERNARD married Eliza EASTON in Pitt County on June 28, 1853. (S. July 9, 1853)

Dr. William A. BERNARD married Mary A. H. SMITH at St. Paul's Church in Greenville on August 17, 1859, by Rev. Edwin Geer. (S. August 27, 1859)

R. BEST of Conwayboro, South Carolina, formerly from Greene County, married Miss A. C. BYNUM in Wilson County on September 11, 1855, at the Reuben Bynum residence, by Rev. Nathan Anderson. (S. September 22, 1855)

Robert S. BEST married Harriet STATON, daughter of Winfield D. STATON, Esq., on May 20, 1841, by Rev. William Hyman. (T. P. May 22, 1841)

William BEST of Greene County married Louisa BYNUM, daughter of Reuben BYNUM, Esq., of Wilson County, at the Bynum residence on October 20, 1859, by Rev. Dr. Deems. (S. November 5, 1859)

Asa BIGGS of Williamston married Martha E. ANDREWS of Bertie County on June 26, 1832, by Thomas J. Pugh, Esq. (N. C. F. P. July 10, 1832)

Eli C. BIGGS married Martha C. STEPTOE in Scotland Neck on November 26, 1856, by Rev. J. B. Cheshire. (S. November 29, 1856)

James BILBRY, a teacher, marred Anne WALLER of Edgecombe County on December 5, 1830, "after a courtship of 20 years, or thereabouts." (N. C. F. P. December 7, 1830)

William BILLUPS married Elizabeth ELLINOR on June 29, 1833 by Henry Austin

Esq., (N. C. F. P. June 29, 1833)

Heshborn BISHOP married Mary E. WHITEHEAD at Scotland Neck on January 7, 1858, by Rev. Jos. Blount Cheshire. (S. January 16, 1858)

Imri BLAND married Sarah MEDFORD of Martin County on January 21, 1836, by Joseph R. Ballard, Esq. (T. P. January 30, 1836)

Capt. Charles BLOCKER married Sally Ann CROMWELL, daughter of Col. Elisha CROMWELL near Tarboro on May 13, 1863, by Elder John H. Daniel. (S. May 23, 1863)

John C. BLOCKER of Fayetteville married Julia Ann BRADDY at Tarboro on December 31, 1839, by Rev. W. H. Wills, Jr. (T. P. January 4, 1840)

George L. BLOUNT married Jemima CANNON, daughter of the late Allen CANNON in Pitt County on April 24, 1833. (N. C. F. P. May 11, 1833)

Levi BLOUNT of Plymouth married Susan BROWN, daughter of John BROWN in Edgecombe County on May 6, 1839, by W. C. Leigh, Esq. (T. P. May 18, 1839)

Reading S. BLOUNT of Greenville married Louisa LONG at the home of Mrs. Elizabeth Long near Halifax on October 29, 1828. (F. P. October 31, 1828)

William B. BODDIE of Nash County married Eliza Ann ALSTON in Halifax County on December 20, 1831. (N. C. F. P. January 3, 1832)

Francis L. BOND married Martha E. DANCY, daughter of the late William DANCY on November 20, 1849, by Rev. Thomas R. Owen. (T. P. November 24, 1849)

John M. BOND of Tarboro married Nannie R. KING, daughter of Isham A. KING of Henrico County, Virginia, on December 29, 1857, by Rev. John W. Fussell. (S. January 2, 1858)

Lewis BOND married Polly NORMAN at Tarboro on June 20, 1833. (N. C. F. P. June 22, 1833)

Charles C. BONNER of Beaufort County married Caroline GRAY, daughter of the late Etheldred GRAY, at Rocky Mount on November 20, 1850, by Rev. J. B. Cheshire. (T. P. November 23, 1850)

Lawrence L. BOON married Esther GAY of Edgecombe County "not long since." (T. P. April 13, 1844)

Arnold BORDEN, Esq., of Waynesborough, married Maria BROWNRIGG of Edgecombe County on October 30, 1824. (F. P. November 5, 1824)

Joseph H. BOWDITCH of Tarboro married Elizabeth B. ABBOTT, daughter of George ABBOTT, Esq., on April 2, 1845, at Beverly, Massachusetts. (T. P. April 19, 1845)

William R. BOWERS married Mrs. Mary Ann CLARK, daughter of the late Jordan WATSON, in Martin County on October 9, 1851. (T. P. November 8, 1851)

Payton T. BOYETT married Zilpha HYMAN, daughter of William HYMAN, in Martin County on December 26, 1830. (N. C. F. P. January 4, 1831)

S. D. BOYKIN married Jincie BOYKIN at her father's house in Wilson County by Jesse Fulgham, Esq., on September 22, 1858. (S. October 9, 1858)

Patrick BOYT "late of Tennessee" married Elizabeth BENSON, granddaughter of Elisha WOODARD, Sr., in Edgecombe County on May 27, 1828. (F. P. June 6, 1828)

Richard H. BRADFORD, attorney of Murfreesboro, married Mary FORT, niece of Governor Branch's wife, at Enfield on November 15, 1827. (F. P. December 1, 1827)

Alexander BRADLEY married Elizabeth EDMONDSON, daughter of Thomas EDMONDSON, on January 28, 1834. (T. F. P. February 7, 1834)

Bennett BRADLEY married Sabra GRIFFIN of Edgecombe County on March 22, 1827, by Benjamin Wilkinson, Esq. (F. P. March 24, 1827)

Elias BRADLEY married Mary BRADLEY, daughter of Willis BRADLEY, on June 23, 1836. (T. P. July 2, 1836)

Littleberry BRADLEY married Winnifred EDMONDSON, daughter of Thomas

EDMONDSON, on January 30, 1834. T. F. P. February 7, 1834)

Stephen BRADLEY of Tarboro married Martha WHITAKER in Warren County on May 16, 1839. (T. P. May 25, 1839)

Willie BRADLEY married Mrs. Nancy LYNCH on January 22, 1828, in Edgecombe County. (F. P. February 1, 1828) (She was probably the Nancy Dixon who married Redding Linch on or soon after May 17, 1824).

Isaac B. BRADY of Tarboro married Parthena SHERROD at her mother's home in Martin County on November 21, 1822, by Rev. Luke Ward. (N. C. F. P. November 29, 1833)

Solomon BRADY of Edgecombe County married Eliza TAYLOR, daughter of Kinchen TAYLOR, in Nash County on February 6, 1834, by John H. Drake, Esq. (T. F. P. February 14, 1834)

Nathaniel B. BRAKE, formerly of Raleigh, married Martha A. HINES of Nashville on July 28, 1831. (N. C. P. August 16, 1831)

John BRANCH of Enfield married Mrs. Mary E. BOND at Windsor on November 9, 1853, by Rev. Mr. Hoskins. (S. November 26, 1853)

S. W. BRANCH married Mary WILKINS of Halifax County on December 25, 1827. (F. P. January 18, 1828)

William BRANCH married Elizabeth DUNCAN of Halifax County on May 14, 1829. (F. P. May 29, 1829)

Archelus BRASWELL married Margaret CUTCHIN, daughter of Joseph CUTCHIN of Edgecombe County, on February 24, 1848, by Rev. J. E. Speight. (T. P. February 26, 1848)

Robert S. BRASWELL married Martha BRASWELL in Edgecombe County on March 11, 1858, by William F. Mercer, Esq. (S. April 10, 1858)

William BRASWELL, formerly of Nash County, married Mrs. Emeliza KNIGHT, daughter of Turner BASS of Halifax County, in Edgecombe County on December 10, 1856, by Kenneth Thigpen, Esq. (S. December 20, 1856)

Willie BRASWELL married Polly BULLUCK of Edgecombe County on July 16, 1829, by Moses Baker, Esq. (F. P. July 24, 1829)

Zadock BRASWELL married Evelina GARDNER of Edgecombe County at the Cullen Pender residence by C. C. Bonner, Esq., on March 14, 1854. (S. March 18, 1854)

James M. BREWER married Elizabeth Ann SPARKS at Tarboro on December 9, 1847, by Rev. T. R. Owen. (T. P. December 11, 1847)

Jesse BREWER of Bertie County married Louisa CURRY of Halifax County on December 19, 1837. (T. P. December 23, 1837)

James W. BRIDGERS married Elizabeth GARDNER, daughter of William GARDNER, Esq., in Edgecombe County on January 4, 1853, by William H. Hines, Esq. (S. January 15, 1853)

John L. BRIDGERS, Esq., of Tarboro, married Rebecca Louisa DICKEN, daughter of L. B. K. DICKEN, Esq., of Halifax County on April 27, 1847, by L. H. B. Whitaker, Esq. (T. P. May 1, 1847)

Ralph P. BRIDGERS married Rhoda A. ATKINSON, eldest daughter of the late Willie ATKINSON, in Edgecombe County on August 17, 1852, by Rev. Mark Bennett. (S. August 21, 1852)

Robert R. BRIDGERS married Margaret E. JOHNSTON, daughter of the late Henry JOHNSTON, on December 11, 1849, by Rev. T. R. Owen in Tarboro. (T. P. December 15, 1849)

Bennet BRILEY of Pitt County married Mary BALLARD, daughter of the late Lemuel BALLARD, in Martin County on March 29, 1838, by B. Bennett, Esq. (T. P. April 7, 1838)

Elihu BRILEY of Pitt County married Aneliza Drupeny NELSON, daughter of Jonas NELSON, in Edgecombe County on December 3, 1848, by Harmon Ward, Esq. (T. P. December 9, 1848)

Capt. William BRINKLEY married Elizabeth MOORE of Halifax County on May 1, 1827, by Isham Mathews, Esq. (F. P. May 26, 1827)

Isaac BRINN married Catherine MORGAN, daughter of Henry MORGAN of Edgecombe County, on July 24, 1855. (S. July 28, 1855)

Alfred J. BROWN of Greenville married Fannie STITH, daughter of Dr. B. STITH of Wilson, on October 11, 1859, by Rev. Dr. Nott. (S. October 15, 1859)

Asa BROWN married Louisa HARRELL, daughter of the late Christopher HARRELL, Jr., in Edgecombe County on January 5, 1845. (T. P. January 11, 1845)

Edwin BROWN married Louisa STANSELL, daughter of Godfrey STANSELL, in Pitt County on February 25, 1830. (F. P. March 12, 1830)

Hardy H. BROWN married Mrs. Charity COWEY of Martin County on January 14, 1836, by Arthur S. Cotten, Esq. (T. P. January 30, 1836)

Lunsford BROWN married Bethia PIPPEN, daughter of Joseph J. PIPPEN, on March 6, 1834, by Rev. William Hyman. (T. F. P. March 7, 1834)

Robert C. BROWN married Mary DANIEL, daughter of Rev. John H. DANIEL, in Edgecombe County on December 4, 1860, by David Cobb, Esq. (S. December 15, 1860)

Dr. W. M. B. BROWN married Jane GREENE, daughter of Charles GREENE, at Greenville on November 1, 1854. (S. November 4, 1854)

William R. BROWN of Martin County married Ellen HYMAN, daughter of the late Kenneth HYMAN of Edgecombe County, on December 7, 1835, by Rev. William Hyman. (T. P. December 12, 1835 and January 23, 1836)

Battle BRYAN married Sarah F. JOHNSTON, daughter of Jo. JOHNSTON in Edgecombe County on October 16, 1856, by W. F. Lewis, Esq. (S. October 25, 1856)

Blount BRYAN married Margaret CHERRY, daughter of the late Theophilus CHERRY, on December 16, 1847. (T. P. December 18, 1847)

Capt. D. D. BRYAN married Martha C. JOHNSTON, daughter of Joseph J. JOHNSTON, on September 18, 1856, by L. C. Pender, Esq. (S. October 11, 1856)

Elias BRYAN of Edgecombe County married Anna I. HOWZE at Haywood in Chatham County on February 1, 1836. (T. P. March 5, 1836)

Henry BRYAN married Mary P. BELL, daughter of Jos. BELL at Tarboro on October 11, 1827, by Henry Austin, Esq. (F. P. December 15, 1827)

Henry BRYAN of Edgecombe County married Lucy SAVAGE, daughter of the late William SAVAGE on December 12, 1844, by Rev. John F. Speight. (T. P. December 21, 1844)

Capt. Henry H. BRYAN married Harriet E. DUGGER, daughter of Daniel DUGGER of Nash County, at Nashville on July 12, 1849, by J. H. Drake, Esq. He was from Edgecombe County and "late of the 1st Regiment Mississippi volunteers." (T. P. July 14, 1849)

Henry R. BRYAN, Esq., of Raleigh, married Mary Biddle NORCOTT, daughter of the late John NORCOTT of Pitt County at New Bern on November 12, 1859. (S. December 3, 1859)

Hugh BRYAN of Edgecombe County married Mary P. JENKINS, daughter of Mrs. Sarah JENKINS, at Warrenton on September 5, 1848, by Rev. C. F. McRae. (T. P. September 9, 1848)

Joseph BRYAN of Edgecombe County married Mary Louisa HIGGS, daughter of the late Willie HIGGS, in Scotland Neck on November 14, 1839, by L. B. K. Dicken, Esq. (T. P. November 23, 1839)

Levi BRYAN, formerly of Halifax County, married Mary R. FARMER, only daughter of the late Capt. John FARMER of Martin County, on May 27, 1828, by Joshua Robinson, Esq. (F. P. June 13, 1828)

William D. BRYAN married Peggy BENTON on August 13, 1835, by Rev. William E. Bellamy. (T. P. August 29, 1835)

David BULLUCK married Margaret RUTH on December 15, 1841, by William S. Baker, Esq. (T. P. December 25, 1841)

Capt. Jesse BULLUCK married Lezina WORSLEY, daughter of William WORSLEY, in Edgecombe County on August 13, 1847, by William H. Hines, Esq. (T. P. August 14, 1847)

Joshua K. BULLUCK married Emily VINES, youngest daughter of Samuel VINES, in Pitt County on November 19, 1840, by Benjamin Tyson, Esq. (T. P. December 5, 1840)

W. J. BULLUCK married Jane THORNE, daughter of the late Henry THORNE, on April 19, 1859, by C. B. Killibrew, Esq. (S. April 23, 1859)

Bennett BUNN, Jr., married Sarah Eliza SIMS, daughter of H. SIMS, in Nash County on August 8, 1837, by Rev. Amos J. Battle. (T. P. August 19, 1837)

Redmun BUNN married Mary BRYAN of Edgecombe County on March 20, 1832, by Rev. Mark Bennett. He was a merchant of Nash County. (N. C. F. P. March 27, 1832)

G. BUNTING married Blaney TAYLOR in Edgecombe County on December 29, 1852, by Jesse Harrell, Esq. (S. January 8, 1853)

William BUNTING of Nash County married Mrs. Martha HIGH of Johnston County at the home of B. Richardson, Esq., on September 3, 1833, by Rev. Granberry Vick. (N. C. F. P. September 20, 1833)

Henry BURGES married Charity A. JOYNER in Halifax County on March 18, 1834, by Willie Higgs, Esq. (T. F. P. March 21, 1834)

John M. BURGIS married Mrs. Frances UNDERHILL at Halifax on January 29, 1829, by Thomas Ousby, Esq. (F. P. February 6, 1829)

Harman H. BURKE of Chatham County married Mrs. Louisiana KNIGHT in Edge-combe County on May 16, 1841, by William S. Baker, Esq. (T. P. May 22, 1841)

Benjamin BURNETT, Esq., of Halifax County married Elizabeth POWELL, daughter of Willie POWELL of Edgecombe County, on October 11, 1849, by Rev. Mr. Hutchins. (T. P. October 20, 1849)

William BURNETT married Virginia HOWERTON in Tarboro on September 21, 1837, by L. D. Wilson, Esq. (T. P. September 23, 1837)

Thomas S. BURT of Stantonsburg married Martha GRAHAM, daughter of Dr. GRAHAM, in Greene County on March 6, 1838. (T. P. March 24, 1838)

Conway W. BURTON of New Haven, Connecticut, married Lucinda R. PENDER, daughter of the late Col. Joshua PENDER, in Tarboro on October 10, 1855, by Rev. T. R. Owen. (S. October 13, 1855)

Maj. Robert A. BURTON married Elizabeth Kearney HILLIARD in Halifax County at the residence of Isaac HILLIARD, Esq., on March 18, 1835. (T. P. April 11, 1835)

Hon. Jesse A. BYNUM of Halifax married Mrs. Emeline BRAY of the Parish of Rapide in Louisiana on May 28, 1839. (T. P. June 29, 1839)

J. J. BYNUM married Sue M. BYNUM, eldest daughter of Reuben BYNUM, near Saratoga on May 7, 1857, by Rev. Peter E. Hines. (S. May 23, 1857)

Richard BYNUM married Mary E. COBB, daughter of Edward COBB, in Edgecombe County on February 17, 1857, by Rev. J. H. Daniel. (S. February 21, 1857)

Col. Robert BYNUM of Edgecombe County married Elizabeth Ann HARRISON, daughter of James HARRISON of Nash County, on February 21, 1843. (T. P. March 4, 1843)

Elisha CAIN married Elizabeth JONES, daughter of Asa JONES, in Martin County on November 1, 1838. (T. P. November 10, 1838)

Richard CAIN married Jinsey HOBGOOD "In the lower end of Halifax County" on January 10, 1839, by L. B. K. Dicken, Esq. (T. P. January 10, 1839)

Andrew A. CALHOUN married Nancy BARNES on December 27, 1836, by Robert Barnes, Esq. (T. P. January 7, 1837)

John CANADY married Mildreth FLEMING in Edgecombe County on February 7, 1854, by J. C. Knight, Esq. (S. February 11, 1854)

Bennet CARLISLE married Mary Frances CHERRY, daughter of the late Cador CHERRY, at Tarboro on December 11, 1851, by H. T. Clark, Esq. (T. P. December 13, 1851)

Elisha CARNEY married Elizabeth WHITEHURST, daughter of James WHITEHURST, in Edgecombe County on March 21, 1850, by Elisha Cromwell, Esq. (T. P. April 6, 1850)

James CARNEY married Mrs. Mary HOPKINS in Edgecombe County on January 15, 1850, by Elisha Cromwell, Esq. (T. P. January 19, 1850)

Elias CARR of Edgecombe County married Miss W. E. KEARNEY of Warren County at the residence of William Kearney, Esq., on May 24, 1859, by Rev. Thomas G. Lowe. (S. May 28, 1859)

James CARR of Edgecombe County married Elizabeth K. HILLIARD at Hilliardston in Nash County on September 19, 1832. (N. C. F. P. October 2, 1832)

William B. CARR of Edgecombe County married Elizabeth H. IRVIN, daughter of the late Thomas B. IRVIN, in Nash County on June 10, 1856, by Rev. Jos. Blount Cheshire. (S. June 14, 1856)

Samuel CARRAWAY married Elizabeth SHAW, daughter of Matthew SHAW, Esq., of Washington, on September 27, 1852, by the Rev. Mr. Owen of Tarboro. He was of Lenoir County. (S. October 2, 1852)

Rev. Robert J. CARSON married Mrs. Mary L. C. WILLIAMS in Martin County on March 25, 1840, by Rev. George N. Gregory. (T. P. April 4, 1840)

Dr. Samuel CARSON married Mrs. Sarah FREEMAN at Dr. P. A. R. C. Cohoon's residence in Tarboro on November 26, 1841, by Henry Austin, Esq. (T. P. November 27, 1841)

Cullen CASPER of Bertie County married Mary BOYCE in Martin County on December 22, 1831, by J. L. G. Baker, Esq. (N. C. F. P. December 27, 1831)

James CHAPMAN of Florida married Helen GRAY, daughter of the late Etheldred GRAY, at her mother's home in Rocky Mount on October 6, 1858, by Rev. J. Blount Cheshire. (S. October 9, 1858)

Cador CHERRY of Tarborough married Mary BELL on November 16, 1828, by James Biggs, Esq. (F. P. November 21, 1828)

Elisha CHERRY married Frances TYER on March 2, 1837, and she died of pleurisy on March 7, 1837. (T. P. March 11, 1837)

Erastus CHERRY of Edgecombe County married Delha SAVAGE, daughter of Lemuel L. SAVAGE, Esq., in Halifax County on February 24, 1859, by Elder William Hyman. (S. March 5, 1859)

Maj. Lunsford R. CHERRY married Mary GEORGE on July 5, 1832, by C. W. Knight, Esq. (N. C. F. P. July 17, 1832)

Thomas CHERRY married Emily BELL, daughter of Frederick BELL, on March 4, 1830, by Louis D. Wilson, Esq. (F. P. March 12, 1830)

Thomas F. CHERRY married Emma L. BATTS at her mother's home on April 2, 1863, by Elder John H. Daniel. (S. April 4, 1863)

T. R. CHERRY married Sally Ann JOHNSON in Greenville on November 1, 1853. (S. November 12, 1853)

William R. CHERRY married Frances SAVAGE, daughter of Alston SAVAGE, in Edgecombe County on April 22, 1857, by Kenneth Thigpen, Esq. (S. May 2, 1857)

Rev. Joseph B. CHESHIRE married Elizabeth PARKER, daughter of Theophilus PARKER, in the Tarboro Episcopal Church on February 8, 1843, by Rev. John Singletary. (T. P. February 11, 1843)

John P. CHESSON of Washington County married Eleanor P. ROSS of Edgecombe County on May 1, 1839, at Mrs. Smith's home in Scotland Neck, by Rev. Mr. Forbes. (T. P. May 11, 1839)

Thomas H. CHRISTIE of Halifax County married Martha BARFIELD, daughter of the late John BARFIELD, in Edgecombe County on January 27, 1859, by Rev. John F. Speight. (S. February 5, 1859)

Charles N. CIVALIER of Tarboro married Myra E. LEE of Virginia at the Edgecombe House in Tarboro on August 23, 1864, by Ex-Governor Henry T. Clark, Esq. (S. August 27, 1864) (On May 1, 1861, he had been elected 2nd Lt. of Company G, 13th N. C. Regiment, but resigned by reason of wounds on November 14, 1863.)

Amos CLARK of Edgecombe County married Penina TAYLOR, daughter of Allen
TAYLOR of Nash County on July 24, 1832. (N. C. F. P. July 31, 1832)

Henry S. CLARK, Esq., of Beaufort County married Alavana STATON on May
20, 1835, by Rev. William Clark. (T. P. May 30, 1835)

Henry T. CLARK of Tarboro married Mrs. Mary Weeks HARGRAVE, daughter of
the late Theophilus PARKER, near Lexington, North Carolina, on
February 11, 1850, by Rev. J. Haywood Parker. (T. P. February 23,
1850)

John CLARK married Nancy FLOWERS at Edgecombe House on November 27, 1856,
by L. R. Cherry, Esq. Both were from Wilson County. (S. December
6, 1856)

William CLARK of Edgecombe County married Winifred HIGGS, daughter of
Samuel HIGGS of Halifax County on May 28, 1835, by Willie Higgs,
Esq. (T. P. June 6, 1835)

W. H. CLARKE, Jr., of the Petersburg & Roanoke Rail Road married Emma E.
CHERRY of Pitt County near Greenville "recently" by Rev. Mr.
Gwaltney. (S. September 27, 1856)

Dr. P. P. CLEMENTS married Mrs. Janet Louisa PUGH, daughter of John
CLOMAN, deceased, in Martin County on October 25, 1842. (T. P.
November 5, 1842)

William CLOMAN of Louisiana married Rebecca MABRY, daughter of Col.
Charles MABRY, in Edgecombe County on November 20, 1851, by Rev.
Blount Cooper. (T. P. November 22, 1851)

Amariah B. COBB married Susan J. WILKINSON, daughter of the late Charles
WILKINSON, in Edgecombe County on May 12, 1857, by Thomas Norfleet,
Esq. (S. May 16, 1857)

David COBB married Elizabeth PIPPEN, daughter of Joseph John PIPPEN, Esq.
in Edgecombe County on March 28, 1850, by Rev. John H. Daniel.
(T. P. March 30, 1850)

Capt. Gray COBB married Martha LITTLE, daughter of James LITTLE, in
Edgecombe County on July 16, 1856, by Elisha Cromwell, Esq. (S.
July 19, 1856)

James COBB, formerly of Bertie County, married Elvy BARTEE of Edgecombe
County on December 7, 1826, by Henry T. Stanton, Esq. (F. P.
December 19, 1826)

Jonas G. COBB married Martha SHELTON, daughter of Burwell SHELTON in
Edgecombe County on December 19, 1849, by Kenneth Thigpen, Esq.
(T. P. December 22, 1849)

Dr. Reuben COBB married Margaret SAVAGE, daughter of Lemuel L. SAVAGE,
Esq., in Halifax County on January 17, 1861, by Rev. T. R. Owen.
He was of Tarboro. (S. January 19, 1861)

John COGGIN married Margaret BEDFORD on September 19, 1830, at Conetoe
on September 19, 1830, by Daniel Hopkins, Esq. (N. C. F. P. September 21, 1830)

William COKER married Charlotte NEALE in Edgecombe County on June 22,
1837, by L. R. Cherry, Esq. (T. S. June 23, 1837. T. P. July 1,
1837)

Joseph D. W. COMANN, Esq., of Halifax County married Susan S. ARRINGTON
of Nash County on March 8, 1849, at the residence of the Hon. A. H.
Arrington, by Rev. Thomas G. Lowe. (T. P. March 24, 1849)

L. M. CONYERS of Franklin County married Margaret HART, daughter of the
late Spencer L. HART, in Edgecombe County on October 22, 1856, by
Rev. Thomas R. Owen. (S. October 25, 1856)

Francis M. COOK married Ann E. TYRRELL, daughter of Nathaniel M. TYRRELL,
in Tarboro on February 16, 1859, by Rev. R. S. Moran. (S. February
19, 1859)

Bynum COOPER married Jannette HOWARD, daughter of Wilson HOWARD, in
Edgecombe County on April 29, 1858, by William S. Long, Esq. (S.
May 8, 1858)

Capt. Jesse COOPER married Esther MARINER at Hamilton in Martin County on March 3, 1831. (N. C. F. P. Marcy 22, 1831)

Andrew J. COTTEN married Elizabeth JENKINS, daughter of James F. JENKINS, in Edgecombe County on August 12, 1856, by Rev. Robert J. Carson. (S. August 30, 1856)

Arthur COTTEN married Louisa MAYO at the home of Mrs. Nancy MAYO of Edgecombe County on May 10, 1827. (F. P. May 19, 1827)

Frederick R. COTTEN, Esq., of Florida, married Elizabeth W. COFFIELD of Edgecombe County on October 7, 1846, by the Rev. George Whitaker. He was a son of the late Spencer D. COTTEN of Tarboro. (T. P. October 14, 1846)

John L. COTTEN married Nancy JOHNSON, daughter of Aaron JOHNSON of Edgecombe County, in Martin County on January 4, 1838. (T. P. January 12, 1838)

John L. COTTEN married Emily SAVAGE, daughter of James SAVAGE, on February 11, 1836. (T. P. March 5, 1836)

John W. COTTEN married Laura P. CLARK, daughter of Maj. James W. CLARK, at Tarboro on December 19, 1832, by Rev. William Norwood. (N. C. F. P. December 25, 1832)

Josiah COUNCIL married Charlotte TAYLOR, daughter of the late Thomas TAYLOR, on November 1, 1838. (T. P. November 10, 1838) (The marriage was bonded by Willie Council on October 31, 1838.)

William R. COX of Nashville, Tennessee, married Penelope B. BATTLE at Cool Spring in Edgecombe County on November 27, 1856, by Rev. Joseph B. Cheshire. (S. December 6, 1856)

Wilson CREDLE of Hyde County married Martha A. WILLIAMS, daughter of John G. WILLIAMS, Esq., in Wilson County on February 12, 1861, by William D. Farmer, Esq. (S. February 16, 1861)

Dr. William M. CRENSHAW, M. D., of Wake Forest, married Catharine E. AUSTIN, daughter of Henry AUSTIN, Esq., at Tarboro on February 12, 1839, by Rev. P. W. Dowd. (T. P. February 16, 1839)

Ezekiel CRISP married Louisa COBB on March 5, 1835, by William C. Leigh, Esq. (T. P. March 14, 1835)

Theophilus CRISP married Elizabeth WRIGHT in Edgecombe County on April 3, 1849, by David Cobb, Esq. (T. P. April 7, 1849)

Norman CROFTON married Sarah L. PHILIPS, daughter of Figures PHILIPS, in Edgecombe County on September 1, 1846, by David Barlow, Esq. (T. P. September 9, 1846)

Elisha CROMWELL married Margaret CROMWELL, daughter of Newsom CROMWELL of Edgecombe County, on February 1, 1848, by Rev. Blount Cooper. (T. P. February 12, 1848)

Elisha CROMWELL married Sally Ann KING, daughter of Coffield KING at Tarboro on December 8, 1842, by Elder James Osbourn. (T. P. December 10, 1842)

Epenetus CROMWELL of Edgecombe County married Jane SHERROD of Martin County on December 12, 1839, by Rev. William Hyman. (T. P. December 14, 1839)

Hansel CROSS married Mrs. Susan BRASWELL in Tarboro on January 10, 1839, by H. Austin, Esq. (T. P. January 12, 1839)

Isaac L. CUSHING of Edgecombe County married Margaret S. WHITEHEAD of Scotland Neck at Vine Hill on February 20, 1850, by William R. Smith, Esq. (T. P. March 2, 1850)

Joseph H. CUTCHEN married Eden HART, daughter of the late Spencer L. HART, in Edgecombe County on November 25, 1858, by Rev. John F. Speight. (S. November 27, 1858)

Elijah CUTCHIN married Canzady PARKER, daughter of Arthur PARKER, in Edgecombe County on December 24, 1848, by Harman Ward, Esq. (T. P. January 6, 1849)

Thomas H. CUTCHINS married Hester Ann LYNCH on August 18, 1836, by L. R. Cherry, Esq. (T. P. August 27, 1836)

William T. CUTCHIN married Mary Ann BARFIELD   daughter of the late John
BARFIELD, on January 11, 1855, by William F. Lewis, Esq., in Edgecombe County. (S. January 20, 1855)

John DAFFIN, formerly of Tarboro, married Harriet SANBORN in Decatur
County, Georgia, on January 15, 1853. (S. February 12, 1853)

Lt. Francis L. DANCY, U. S. A., married Florida FORSYTH, daughter of the
Hon. R. R. REID of St. Augustine, Florida, on October 17, 1833.
(T. F. P. November 8, 1833)

George A. DANCY of Greenville married Penelope E. CHERRY in Pitt County
on November 23, 1847, by Joseph John Norcott, Esq. (T. P. December
4, 1847)

John S. DANCY, Esq., married Cornelia V. BATTLE, daughter of James S.
BATTLE at "Cool Spring" in Edgecombe County on December 12, 1843,
by Rev. Thomas Carter, Methodist Minister. (T. P. December 16,1843)

John S. DANCY married Annie E. HYMAN, daughter of the late Henry HYMAN,
at Tarboro on November 11, 1858, by Rev. Jos. B. Cheshire. (S.
November 13, 1858)

William F. DANCY married Mary Eliza BATTLE, daughter of James S. BATTLE
at "Cool Spring" in Edgecombe County on January 14, 1858, by Rev.
Jos. Blount Cheshire. (S. January 16, 1858)

William F. DANCY of North Carolina married Martha C. MOYE, daughter of
Gen. MOYE, at Columbus, Mississippi, on May 7, 1850, by Rev. S. R.
Frierson in the Presbyterian Church. (T. P. May 25, 1850)

Dr. John J. DANIEL of Edgecombe County married Martha P. DANIEL, daughter of Col. David DANIEL, in Nash County on November 15, 1838, by
Redmun Bunn, Esq. (T. P. November 24, 1838)

Dr. John J. DANIEL married Sally Ann DONALDSON of Edgecombe County at
the Figures Lowe residence in Martin County on January 7, 1832, by
J. J. Williams, Esq. (N. C. F. P. January 10, 1832)

Justice G. DANIEL of Greene County married Julia BYNUM, daughter of the
late Joseph BYNUM of Edgecombe County on June 29, 1848. (T. P.
July 1, 1848)

Nathan P. DANIEL of Stantonsburg married Margaret BYNUM, daughter of the
late Gideon BYNUM, in Pitt County on April 9, 1846, by William Blow,
Esq. (T. P. April 15, 1846)

William DANIEL married Sally Ann ROBASON in Martin County on May 31,
1832, by Elder Joseph Biggs. (N. C. F. P. June 12, 1832)

Moses DAUGHTRIDGE married Rhoda JOINER of Nash County "not long since"
(bonded on January 4, 1844). (T. P. April 13, 1844)

George DAVENPORT of Pitt County married Mary Ann TAYLOR, oldest daughter
of Frederick TAYLOR, in Edgecombe County on March 6, 1845, by
Harman Ward, Esq. (T. P. March 15, 1845)

Edward DAVIS of the steamer NORTH CAROLINA married Mary WILLIAMS, daughter of John C. WILLIAMS, of Martin County, near Williamston on
October 28, 1830, by Peter E. Madera, Esq. (N. C. F. P. November
2, 1830)

James DAVIS married Susan M. GAY, daughter of the late Eli GAY, near
Wilson on July 9, 1855, by Rev. T. H. Lowe. (S. July 28, 1855)

Robert DAVIS of Pitt County married Russia Ann NETTLE, daughter of Allen
NETTLE, in Edgecombe County on January 13, 1841. (T. P. January
23, 1841)

Commodore Stephen Decatur DAVIS of Franklin County married Rachel GAY of
Edgecombe County "not long since." (T. P. April 13, 1844)

Dr. Thomas DAVIS of Franklin County married Mary Ann SLADE, daughter of
the late Dr. Ebenezer SLADE of Martin County, in Warren County on
September 4, 1832. (N. C. F. P. October 2, 1832)

Thomas C. DAVIS married Virginia C. STITH, daughter of Dr. B. STITH, at
Wilson on April 23, 1857, by Rev. William Murphy. (S. May 9, 1857)

Thomas J. DAWSON of Lenoir County married Huldah T. DANIEL, daughter of the late Stephen DANIEL, in Greene County on October 20, 1846, by Elder Swinson. (T. P. October 28, 1846)

John DAY married Margaret MITCHELL on February 14, 1832, by B. Boykin, Esq. (N. C. F. P. February 21, 1832)

William H. DAY, Esq., married Mary JOYNER, daughter of Robert JOYNER of Florida by "formerly of this place," in Halifax County on December 24, 1833, by Rev. Peebles. (T. F. P. January 3, 1834)

Jonathan DEW married Mary STRICKLAND in Nash County on October 8, 1844. (T. P. October 12, 1844)

Benjamin DICKENS from Halifax County married Isabella A. CHAPMAN of Wilmington in Jackson County, Florida, on February 15, 1853, by Rev. Homer Hender. (S. March 19, 1853)

Ephraim DICKEN of Edgecombe County married Charlotte WHITEHEAD of Halifax County "a few days since." (N. C. F. P. November 13, 1832)

Joseph L. DICKEN of Tarboro married Caroline A. BUSH, third daughter of Thomas M. BUSH, Esq., at Marianna, Florida, on July 29, 1858. (S. August 14, 1858)

William H. DICKEN married Lucy THURSTON in Tarboro on March 20, 1834, by Rev. Joshua Lawrence. (T. F. P. March 21, 1834)

John M. DICKIN married Susan Ann LUNDY in Halifax County on September 19, 1839, by S. H. Gee, Esq. (T. P. September 28, 1839)

Thaddeus E. DILLARD of Sussex Court House, Virginia, married William Rebecca Frances ATKINSON of Pitt County at Scotland Neck on October 27, 1845, by William Smith, Esq. (T. P. November 5, 1845)

Dr. Henry DOCKERY from Richmond County married Ann MCKAY from Cheraw County, South Carolina, at Greenville in Pitt County "a few days since." (N. C. F. P. November 23, 1830)

James DORTCH of Nash County married Amanda M. PARKER, daughter of Weeks PARKER, Jr., at Tarboro on December 21, 1837, by Henry Austin, Esq. (T. P. January 5, 1838)

Dr. Lewis J. DORTCH married Nancy J. ADAMS in Edgecombe County on October 10, 1844, by Rev. William Robertson. (T. P. November 2, 1844)

William T. DORTCH, Esq., of Nashville married Mary Elizabeth PITTMAN, daughter of the late Harrison PITTMAN, on March 17, 1846. (T. P. April 1, 1846)

Henry A. DOWD married Laura E. BAKER, daughter of Dr. William S. BAKER, in Tarboro on January 20, 1859. (S. January 22, 1859)

Rev. Patrick W. DOWD of Raleigh married Martha Ann AUSTIN, daughter of Henry AUSTIN, on October 21, 1830, by Rev. John Armstrong at Tarborough. (N. C. F. P. October 26, 1830)

Henry DOWNING of Tyrrell County married Mary COTTEN, daughter of Henry Cotten, deceased, of Edgecombe County, at Hamilton in Martin County on January 24, 1839. (T. P. February 2, 1839)

Edwin DOYLE married Mrs. Creecy WIMBERLEY at Logsborough in Edgecombe County on or after February 18, 1832. (N. C. F. P. February 21, 1832)

Frederick DOZIER of Nash County married Mary A. TREVATHAN, daughter of Dempsey TREVATHAN, in Edgecombe County on May 16, 1848, by B. D. Battle, Esq. (T. P. May 20, 1848)

James H. DOZIER of Tarboro married Catherine JONES, daughter of the late Frederick JONES, in Edgecombe County on January 24, 1855, by Rev. T. R. Owen. (S. January 27, 1855)

William DOZIER married Lucinda J. DRAKE in Nash County on February 3, 1829. (F. P. February 20, 1829)

William L. DOZIER married William Ann KNIGHT, daughter of the late Charles W. KNIGHT, in Tarboro on August 6, 1850, by Rev. Thomas R. Owen. (T. P. August 17, 1850)

Capt. John B. DRAKE married Bettie B. BATTLE, daughter of the late Frederick Battle, in Nash County on October 11, 1853, by Rev. Mr.

Johnson. (S. October 22, 1853)

John H. DRAKE of Nash County married Mary Richard WILLIAMS, on May 27, 1828, at the home of Dr. Robert Williams, Jr., of Pitt County. F. P. July 18, 1828)

Dr. N. J. DRAKE of Nash County married Mrs. Eliza THORNE in Halifax County "a few days ago." (F. P. November 14, 1828)

Rev. Dr. DRANE of Wilmington married Mrs. Caroline HARGRAVE, daughter of the late Theophilus PARKER, in Tarboro on December 3, 1850, by Rev. J. B. Cheshire. (T. P. December 7, 1850)

James H. DRAUGHAN married Arretta BRASWELL on March 11, 1858, by William F. Mercer, Esq. (S. April 10, 1858)

Solomon DREW, aged eighty-eight, married Frances BARNES, aged sixteen, both of Halifax County, on May 1, 1832, in Martin County by Figures Lowe, Esq. (N. C. F. P. May 15, 1832)

James DUGGAN of Halifax County married Mary Ann ALSOBROOK, daughter of Michael ALSOBROOK of Edgecombe County, on January 20, 1835, by Benjamin Batts, Esq. (T. P. January 24, 1835)

Dr. W. A. DUGGAN of Edgecombe County married Lucy LAWRENCE, daughter of Bennett B. LAWRENCE, in Nash County on June 18, 1861, by Rev. N. A. H. Goddin. (S. June 29, 1861)

Daniel A. DUGGER married Lucy B. HINES on August 8, 1832, at the home of Mrs. Elizabeth Anderson in Nash County. (N. C. F. P. August 21, 1832)

Britton DUKE married Mary L. PURRINGTON at Scotland Neck on May 28, 1829, by W. J. Hill, Esq. (F. P. June 19, 1829)

Burrell DUNN married Drucilla DRAUGHN in Edgecombe County on January 22, 1828, by Benjamin Wilkinson, Esq. (F. P. February 1, 1828)

Dr. Lemon S. DUNN married Georgiana GATLIN, daughter of the late Thomas GATLIN, at Tarboro on May 13, 1851, by the Rev. T. R. Owen. (T. P. May 17, 1851)

Stephen DUNN married Elizabeth DEW, daughter of Zachariah DEW (not Dunn) of Edgecombe County on January 18, 1852, by B. B. Barnes, Esq. (S. January 24, 1852)

Allen DUPREE married Mary THIGPEN, daughter of William THIGPEN, in Edgecombe County on August 15, 1843, by William C. Leigh, Esq. (T. P. August 19, 1843)

Lafayette DUPREE married Disha NEWTON, daughter of John NEWTON, Sr. of Pitt County, on March 14, 1839)

Lewis DUPREE married Mary Eliza SHURLEY, daughter of the late Geraldus SHURLEY of Edgecombe County, on June 9, 1846. (T. P. June 10, 1846)

Louis B. DUPREE married Amanda WILLIAMS, daughter of the late Robert WILLIAMS, Jr., of Pitt County, on February 15, 1842, by Rev. Mark Bennett. (T. P. February 26, 1842)

Thomas B. DUPREE married Penina MAY, daughter of the late Alvin MAY of Pitt County, on February 15, 1842, by Rev. Mark Bennett. (T. P. February 26, 1842)

William R. DUPREE married in Edgecombe County on January 29, 1840, Martha TUNNELL, by Louis D. Wilson, Esq. (T. P. February 8, 1840)

Willis DUPREE married Elizabeth MOYE in Pitt County "recently." (T. P. March 29, 1845)

John W. EARLS, merchant, married Martha Carter POPE of Edgecombe County on August 11, 1846, by David Barlow, Esq. (T. P. August 19, 1846)

Harmon EASON married William Irena WYNN, daughter of the late William WYNN, in Williamston on November 15, 1829, by Rev. Wheeler Martin. (F. P. November 27, 1829)

Benjamin F. EBORN, Esq., of Pitt County married Delia Ann LITTLE in Tarboro on July 13, 1858, by Rev. William Closs. (S. July 17, 1858)

Alfred EDMONDSON married Lucinda HAWKINS of Edgecombe County on March

22, 1832, by J. J. Pippen, Esq. (N. C. F. P. March 27, 1832)

Asa EDMONDSON married Nancy PORTER, daughter of the late Moody PORTER, "a few days since." (N. C. F. P. November 20, 1832)

Josiah EDMONDSON married Margaret E. STALLINGS, daughter of Jos. STALL-INGS of Edgecombe County, on August 23, 1860, by H. T. Clark, Esq. (S. September 1, 1860)

Pollard EDMONDSON married Susan HOWARD, daughter of James HOWARD, on October 3, 1839. (T. P. October 12, 1839)

Pollard EDMONDSON married Martha MANNING, daughter of Uriah MANNING, in Edgecombe County on January 8, 1845, by Harman Ward, Esq. (T. P. January 11, 1845)

Willie EDMONDSON married Ann SMITH, daughter of the late William SMITH, in Edgecombe County on December 20, 1853, by Jesse Harrell, Esq. (S. December 24, 1853)

John EDMONSTON married Ann PARKER of Edgecombe County on December 4, 1828, by James Biggs, Esq. (F. P. December 19, 1828)

Charles EDWARDS, Esq., of Greene County, married Charity MCKINNEY in Lenoir County on May 20, 1832, by Elder Robert Bond. (N. C. F. P. June 5, 1832)

Moses EDWARDS married Margaret TURNER of Nash County "not long since." (The marriage bond was dated January 11, 1844.) (T. P. April 13, 1844)

William E. EDWARDS married Mary SUMNER in Nash County on February 17, 1846, by J. H. Drake, Esq. (T. P. February 25, 1846)

William H. EDWARDS married Mary Jane WOODARD, youngest daughter of Mr. James B. WOODARD, in Wilson County on February 25, 1858, by W. W. Batts, Esq. (S. March 6, 1858)

William J. EDWARDS married Jane E. HOWELL, daughter of Bythal HOWELL of Edgecombe County, on January 11, 1857, by David Cobb, Esq. (S. January 17, 1857)

James ELLINOR of Edgecombe County married Mrs. Martha CROMWELL on June 23, 1844, by Rev. Bennett Cooper. (T. P. June 29, 1844)

Joseph ELLINOR of Edgecombe County married Nancy HOPKINS, of Pitt County, on August 28, 1833, by William W. Andrews, Esq. (T. F. P. September 6, 1833)

Josiah ELLINOR married Mary TAYLOR, daughter of Dempsey TAYLOR of Nash County, on October 20, 1841. (T. P. October 23, 1841)

Lawrence J. ELLINOR married Louisa J. CUTCHIN, daughter of the late Eli CUTCHIN, on December 21, 1859, by William F. Lewis, Esq. (S. December 24, 1859)

William T. ELLINOR married Litha HOPKINS of Edgecombe County on January 10, 1834, by William W. Andrews, Esq. (T. F. P. January 10, 1834)

Elijah ELLIOTT of Tarboro married Mrs. Charlotte PATTERSON in Washington on August 15, 1847. (T. P. August 21, 1847)

Elijah ELLIOTT married Mrs. Margaret FORD at Tarboro on October 1, 1837, by Henry Austin, Esq. (T. P. October 7, 1837. T. S. October 6, 1837)

Coffield ELLIS married Eliza FLORA in Wilson County on April 5, 1859, at the residence of James Ellis, by W. W. Batts, Esq. (S. April 16, 1859)

Rev. David ELLIS married Mrs. Eliza WILSON in Pitt County on November 11, 1830, by Rev. George N. Gregory. (N. C. F. P. November 16, 1830)

Hickman ELLIS married Mrs. Queen Esther ELLIS on January 4, 1838, by James Bridgers, Esq. (T. P. January 12, 1838)

Ira Gray ELLIS married Harriet S. ROUNTREE on February 2, 1848, by Jacob S. Barnes, Esq. (T. P. February 12, 1848)

William ELLIS, Esq., member of the House of Commons from Edgecombe County married Sallie Martin PEACOCK, daughter of the late Z. PEACOCK, Esq.

at Stantonsburg on December 29, 1853, by Rev. William Anderson. (S. January 28, 1854)

Francis R. ELY of Plymouth married Fanny A. C. RANDOLPH in Pitt County on April 9, 1835, by Rev. J. Singletary. (T. P. April 18, 1835)

J. A. ENGELHARD of Mississippi married Margaret E. COTTEN, daughter of the late John W. COTTEN, formerly of Tarboro, on September 26, 1855, at Raleigh, by Rev. Dr. Mason. (S. October 6, 1855)

Lewis ETHERIDGE married Eliza PATTERSON in Tarboro on December 24, 1834, by Henry Austin, Esq. (T. P. January 2, 1835)

Ransom ETHERAGE married Elizabeth MOORE in Edgecombe County on December 16, 1846, by W. D. Bryan, Esq. (T. P. December 22, 1846)

Frederick EVANS of Edgecombe County married Arabella ARRINGTON, daughter of Gen. Joseph ARRINGTON of Nash County, on February 13, 1834. (T. F. P. February 21, 1834)

James EVANS married Sally HARRISS in Nash County on or about December 2, 1839, by John J. Tharp, Esq. (T. P. December 7, 1839)

Richard EVANS married Harriet Louisa MOORING in Pitt County on April 2, 1839. (T. P. April 20, 1839)

Seth EVANS married Marina HYMAN of Martin County on January 19, 1836, by Alexander S. Cotten, Esq. (T. P. January 30, 1836)

Alexander H. FALCONER married Mary H. EATON of Warren County on September 11, 1828. (F. P. September 26, 1828)

Joseph B. FARMER of Edgecombe County married Julia Ann BROTHERS of Nansemond County, Virginia, on May 24, 1853, by Rev. W. D. Wellons. (S. June 11, 1853)

Jacob FELDENHEIMER of Tarboro married Rachael ALEXANDER in Richmond on December 8, 1859, by Rev. Seltmer. (S. December 17, 1859)

Joseph FELTON married Charlotte SKINNER at the Henry Barnes residence in Wilson County on April 21, 1859, by Stanly Kirby, Esq. (S. April 30, 1859)

Dixie C. FENNER married Ann P. HARWELL at Halifax on November 1, 1827. (F. P. November 17, 1827)

William FENNER married Anna N. B. SMITH at Scotland Neck on October 28, 1851, by Rev. Jos. B. Cheshire. (T. P. November 8, 1851)

Duncan FERGUSON married Mrs. Martha P. DANIEL in Nash County at the Robert Bryan residence on April 18, 1840. (T. P. April 25, 1840)

Michael FERRALL, merchant, married Mary Eliza EPPES at Halifax on October 31, 1831, by Rev. R. S. Baker, Roman Catholic Priest. (N. C. F. P. November 8, 1831)

William B. FIELDS of Goldsboro married Mary Frances KING, daughter of Coffield KING of Tarboro, on June 5, 1855, by Rev. C. B. Hassell. (S. June 9, 1855)

Edmund P. FINCH of Oxford married Ann D. CULPEPPER of Nash County on December 12, 1826. (F. P. December 26, 1826)

John H. FINCH married N. J. GLOVER, daughter of Benjamin GLOVER, Esq., of Nash County, on February 4, 1849, by E. H. Morgan, Esq. (T. P. March 3, 1849)

W. P. FITZGERALD married Nancy BARBEE at Wilson on September 1, 1859, by Jacob S. Barnes, Esq. (S. September 17, 1859)

Jesse FLEMING of Edgecombe County married Mary PITTMAN, daughter of Frederick PITTMAN of Halifax County, on October 19, 1841. (T. P. October 30, 1841)

Archibald FORBES married Louisa Ann CLARK, daughter of Gen. William CLARK at Greenville on January 21, 1833. (N. C. F. P. January 29, 1833)

Jos. FORBES married Elizabeth EASON, daughter of the late Joseph EASON, on August 29, 1839, by Benjamin Moore, Esq. (T. P. September 7, 1839)

Peter FORBES married Catharine EXUM, daughter of the late John EXUM, on

March 17, 1850. (T. P. April 6, 1850)

Agesilaus S. FOREMAN of Virginia married Delha DANCY, daughter of Francis L. DANCY, in Tarboro on November 10, 1836, by Rev. Samuel Harris. (T. P. November 12, 1836)

John L. FOREMAN, Esq., of Pitt County, married Martha E. HOSKINS, daughter of the late Baker HOSKINS, Esq., of Chowan County, on February 25, 1836, by Rev. William D. Cairnes. (T. P. March 19, 1836)

Maj. Robert R. FOREMAN married Caroline WILLIAMS, daughter of the late Dr. R. F. J. H. WILLIAMS, in Pitt County on June 25, 1853. (S. July 2, 1853)

B. F. FOSTER, Esq., of Franklin County, married Mrs. Mary T. RAWLS in Nash County on February 24, 1850. (T. P. March 23, 1850)

L. F. FOSTER married Elizabeth DAFFIN, daughter of the late Joshua DAFFIN of Edgecombe County, at Tallahassee, Florida, on January 31, 1850, by Rev. Miles Nash. (T. P. February 16, 1850)

John FOX married Rosela POSSUM recently in Martin County. (These are not real names.) (T. S. September 1, 1837)

Joseph H. FOY, Esq., married Kate BATTLE, daughter of Rev. A. J. BATTLE of Wilson, on March 19, 1860. (S. March 24, 1860)

Moses FRANKFORT of Tarboro married B. GOODMAN, daughter of Leopold GOODMAN, at Norfolk on May 29, 1857, by Rev. Mr. Kemp. (S. June 6, 1857)

Henry FREEAR married Mrs. Mary JOHNSTON of Halifax County at the A. Whittaker residence on March 5, 1829. (F. P. March 20, 1829)

Edmund B. FREEMAN, Esq., of Raleigh, married Mrs. Elizabeth FOREMAN, daughter of Dr. Robert WILLIAMS of Pitt County, on November 14, 1837, by Rev. John Singletary. (T. P. November 25, 1837)

Joseph J. FREEMAN married Eliza JONES, daughter of Allen JONES of Edgecombe County, on February 5, 1839, by Henry Austin, Esq. (T. P. February 16, 1839)

John FRIZZLE married Martha Ann NELSON in Greenville on March 6, 1839. (T. P. March 30, 1839)

Capt. J. A. FUQUA, formerly of Tarboro, married Lizzie LEE at Clinton on January 27, 1863, by Rev. Mr. Gibbs. (S. January 31, 1863)

Holman GARDNER married Sally DERRING, daughter of John DERRING, Esq., in Nash County on November 21, 1826. (F. P. December 5, 1826)

William GARDNER married (Cynthia) Eliza BATTS, daughter of Mr. Bailey BATTS of Edgecombe County, on January 22, 1828. (F. P. February 1, 1828)

Col. Isidore V. GARNIE married Mary W. SUTTON, daughter of the late William SUTTON and granddaughter of the late Michael HEARN of Tarboro, "recently" in Jacksonville, Florida. (S. May 7, 1859)

Charles W. GARRETT married Mary SUGG, daughter of Dr. Phesanton SUGG, on June 12, 1851, by Rev. J. B. Cheshire. (T. P. June 21, 1851)

Dr. F. M. GARRETT married Delha WILLIAMS, daughter of Col. David WILLIAMS in Edgecombe County on November 27, 1855, by Rev. R. J. Carson. (S. December 1, 1855)

Henry W. GARRETT married Sarah SASNETT in Tarboro on October 26, 1826, by Jesse C. Knight, Esq. (F. P. November 7, 1826)

James J. GARRETT married Susan KNIGHT, daughter of J. C. KNIGHT, Esq., in Edgecombe County on February 11, 1830, by John Mercer, Esq. (F. P. February 19, 1830)

John GARRETT married Nancy LAWRENCE, daughter of the late John LAWRENCE, in Edgecombe County on January 12, 1854, by Elisha Cromwell, Esq. (S. January 21, 1854)

John GARRETT married Elizabeth NETTLES on April 14, 1836, by Benjamin Sharpe, Esq. (T. P. April 23, 1836)

Dr. Joseph J. GARRETT married Henrietta MERCER, daughter of John MERCER, on September 15, 1851. (T. P. September 27, 1851)

Dr. Joseph GARRETT married Nancy MERCER, daughter of John MERCER, Esq., of Edgecombe County, on May 13, 1846. (T. P. May 27, 1846)

Richard M. GARRETT married Louisa JENKINS, daughter of James F. JENKINS, Esq., in Edgecombe County on October 5, 1852, by Wright Barnes, Esq. (S. November 20, 1852)

Dr. Richard W. GARRETT, formerly of Edgecombe County, married Mary T. LEA, daughter of Woodson LEA, Esq., in Cheatham County on May 21, 1833, by Rev. John W. White. (N. C. F. P. June 1, 1833)

William F. GARVAY married Sallie BURGES in Edgecombe County at the Poland residence in Rocky Mount on October 17, 1858, by G. W. Hammond, Esq. (S. November 6, 1858)

John GARY married Mary IVEY in Halifax County on July 29, 1828, by Willis Johnston, Esq. (F. P. August 8, 1828)

Richard H. GATLIN of Edgecombe County married P. E. PRICE, daughter of S. T. PRICE, near Hamilton on July 19, 1859, by Rev. R. S. Moran. (S. July 23, 1859)

Thomas GATLIN of the merchant tailors King & Gatlin married Julia PENDER on June 18, 1829, by P. S. Sugg, Esq. (F. P. June 26, 1829)

Thomas N. GAUTIER married Rosa A. PITTMAN of Goldsboro on June 24, 1852, by Rev. William J. Ellis. (S. July 10, 1852)

Eli GAY married Mrs. Fanny COBB in Pitt County on December 18, 1828. (F. P. December 26, 1828)

Thomas D. GAY of Edgecombe County married in January 1858 Lou F. FOSTER, youngest daughter of Rev. R. B. FOSTER of Dinwiddie County, Virginia. (S. January 16, 1858)

William M. GAY married Mary O. WILLIAMS in Pitt County on November 9, 1852, by Rev. P. E. Hines. (S. November 13, 1852)

Sterling H. GEE of Alabama married Mary T. WILLIAMS at the home of Henry Williams in Warren County on (or soon after) November 6, 1828. (F. P. November 21, 1828)

Rev. Edwin GEER of Calvary Episcopal Church in Tarboro married Margaret Ann BECKWITH, eldest daughter of Dr. John BECKWITH, M. D., at Raleigh on December 2, 1840. (T. P. December 12, 1840)

Henry A. GILLIAM of Plymouth married Hannah CLEMENTS of Williamston on May 24, 1859, by Rev. B. S. Bronson. (S. June 11, 1859)

George E. GORHAM married Frances E. SELBY, daughter of Benjamin M. SELBY Esq., at Greenville on April 4, 1839, by Rev. Henry S. Spivey. (T. P. April 20, 1839)

Dr. James GORHAM of Pitt County married Frances A. D. DORTCH in Nash County on April 15, 1851, by Rev. Mr. Spivey. (T. P. April 19, 1851)

Thomas A. GORHAM married Susan Z. SELBY, daughter of Benjamin M. SELBY, Sr., of Greenville on January 28, 1844, by Rev. Samuel Pearce. (T. P. February 3, 1844)

William GRAGG, aged ninety, married Nancy COFFEY, aged twenty-two, on July 9, 1837, near Colletsville on the Johns River in Burke County, by Levi Laxton, Esq. "Mr. GRAGG was a Revolutionary soldier; was present at the taking of Burgoyne, and was in the ranks at the sharp shooting at Brandywine, and was on the side of Liberty at Little York, and at the surrender of Cornwallis. He is quite healthy and walked 20 miles on the day before he was married." (The Tarboro' Scaevola, July 28, 1837, I, No. 12, page 3, column 3)

Rev. William F. GRAY of the North Carolina Conference married Lucy JOHNSON, daughter of Joseph J. JOHNSON, in Edgecombe County on October 5, 1858, by Rev. J. F. Speight. (S. October 16, 1858)

William T. GRAY married William Ann PENDER, daughter of the late William PENDER of Edgecombe County on April 8, 1857, by Rev. T. R. Owen. (S. April 11, 1857)

Major Thomas J. GREEN of Warren County and now of Tallahassee, Florida, married Sarah WHARTON on March 8, 1830, at Nashville, Tennessee.

(F. P. April 9, 1830)

Robert GREENE married Eva Sallie SMITH at St. Paul's Church in Greenville on April 18, 1860, by Rev. Edwin Geer of Washington, N. C. (S. April 28, 1860)

Thomas L. B. GREGORY married Mary Frances W. PITTMAN of Halifax County, daughter of Mrs. Ann PITTMAN, on October 7, 1828, by J. H. Simmons, Esq. (F. P. October 24, 1828)

Lovet GRIFFIN married Mrs. Maria BARNES in Martin County on December 9, 1830, by William S. Rayner, Esq. (N. C. F. P. December 21, 1830)

Thomas GRIMES married Mary Eliza COWEY, daughter of Capt. Charles COWEY, in Martin County on October 27, 1831, by William S. Rayner, Esq. (N. C. F. P. November 1, 1831)

Thomas GRIMES married Nancy BEST on August 4, 1835, by Rev. William Hyman. (T. P. August 15, 1835)

Thomas GRIMMER married Nancy WHITEHEAD at Scotland Neck on August 10, 1830, by S. M. Nickels, Esq. (N. C. F. P. August 24, 1830)

James GROVES, aged twenty-three, and Amanda WARD, aged eighteen, daughter of Joseph WARD of Hamilton, were married on August 19, 1855, at the "Edgecombe House" in Tarboro by Henry T. Clark, Esq. (S. August 25, 1855) On September 10, 1855, he wrote at length to Editor George Howard to provide the corrected ages above and to explain the truth about the gossip resulting from her grandmother's malice toward him. (S. September 22, 1855, p. 2, columns 2/3)

William B. GULICK, editor of the Goldsboro' Patriot, married Lucy BLOUNT, only daughter of Benjamin RUNYON, Esq., in Washington on January 15, 1852, by Rev. Mr. Geer. (S. January 31, 1852)

Andrew GUNTER of Edgecombe County married Mary HARRIS in Halifax County on October 26, 1843, by James M. Aaron, Esq. (T. P. November 18, 1843)

Henry GUNTER married Harriet JOSEY on January 8, 1828, by William Doggett, Esq. (F. P. January 18, 1828)

William D. GURGANUS married Lucy A. HYMAN at Jamesville on August 17, 1859, by George Burras, Esq. (S. August 27, 1859)

David GWITHER of Washington County married Maria TAYLOR, daughter of Kinchen TAYLOR, in Martin County on April 10, 1832. (N. C. F. P. April 17, 1832)

Thomas HADLEY of Wayne County married Milley RICHARDSON, daughter of Joseph RICHARDSON, Esq., of Johnston County, on May 16, 1824. (F. P. June 4, 1824) (Their family Bible says May 14, 1824.)

Dr. Alexander HALL of Warrenton married Louisa J. CLARK of Halifax County at Scotland Neck on November 10, 1831, by Rev. Joseph H. Saunders. (N. C. F. P. November 29, 1831)

Dr. Isaac HALL, M. D., married Eliza Imogen EVANS, daughter of Peter EVANS, Esq., of Edgecombe County, on May 15, 1834, by Rev. William Norwood. (T. F. P. May 23, 1834)

Walter S. HANRAHAN, Esq., of Pitt County, married Sarah C. WORTHINGTON, formerly of New Bern, at Greenville on November 2, 1853, by Rev. Stephen Johnson. (S. November 12, 1853)

Parrott HARDY of Lenoir County married Addie TURNAGE at her mother's home in Pitt County "a few days since" by Rev. Peter E. Hines. (S. October 23, 1858)

Franklin HARGRAVE of Lexington married Mary W. PARKER, daughter of Theophilus PARKER, at Tarboro on February 24, 1841, by Rev. John Singletary. (T. P. February 27, 1841)

John L. HARGRAVE of Lexington married Caroline C. S. PARKER, daughter of Theophilus PARKER, Esq., at Tarboro on February 22, 1837, by Rev. John Singletary. (T. P. February 25, 1837)

Gray L. HARGRAVES married Mrs. Martha A. GARDNER, daughter of the late Robert FOXHALL, on March 31, 1853, by Jordan Thigpen, Esq. (S. April 23, 1853)

Gray L. HARGROVE married Felicia LITTLE, daughter of the late Frederick LITTLE, in Edgecombe County on January 27, 1859. (S. January 29, 1859)

Hugh HARPER, Jr., married Gatsey SCARBOROUGH, daughter of David SCARBOROUGH of Greene County, on April 17, 1828, by Charles Edwards, Esq. (F. P. May 2, 1828)

Hugh P. HARPER of Greene County married Marny JOINER, daughter of John JOINER, Esq., in Pitt County on August 19, 1835, by Isaac Joiner, Esq. (T. P. August 29, 1835)

J. J. HARPER married Mrs. Mary A. S. BARNES on August 6, 1857. (S. August 15, 1857)

Kindred HARPER married Mary Eliza STALLINGS, daughter of James STALLINGS of Edgecombe County, on May 6, 1852, by Wright Barnes, Esq. (S. May 22, 1852)

Elisha HARRELL, aged about seventy, married Ann Eliza RAYNER, aged about twenty, in Edgecombe County on August 1, 1854, by R. H. Pender, Esq. (S. August 12, 1854)

Jesse HARRELL married Tabitha SWANNER of Martin County on November 18, 1830. (N. C. F. P. November 23, 1830)

Jesse HARRELL married Sally THIGPEN, daughter of the late Howell THIGPEN, on March 9, 1834, by William C. Leigh, Esq. (T. F. P. March 14, 1834)

John HARRELL, aged sixty-eight, married Rebecca BRAZZIL, aged eighteen, on December 9, 1830, by J. L. G. Baker, Esq. (N. C. F. P. December 21, 1830)

William HARRELL married Temperance LEIGH, daughter of William C. LEIGH of Edgecombe County, on February 16, 1845, by J. J. Pippen, Esq. (T. P. February 22, 1845)

Joshua HARRINGTON married Mary F. ALLEXON in Edgecombe County on December 1, 1859, by E. D. Macnair, Esq. (S. December 17, 1859)

Canfield HARRIS married Mrs. Elizabeth WHITEHEAD in Nash County "a few evenings since" by Asael Vick, Esq. (T. P. December 7, 1839)

Spencer S. HARRIS of Pitt County married Margaret TAYLOR of Edgecombe County on May 20, 1830, by Benjamin Wilkinson, Esq. (F. P. May 28, 1830)

Charles HARRISON married Elizabeth BELL, daughter of Col. Joseph BELL, on July 5, 1832, by Rev. Joshua Lawrence. (N. C. F. P. July 10, 1832)

John A. HARRISON of Nash County married Martha Ann VERELL "recently" at Warrenton. (T. P. October 27, 1849)

Dr. Franklin HART married Sarah BRYAN, daughter of Henry BRYAN, Esq., of Edgecombe County, on November 5, 1845, by Rev. Joseph B. Cheshire. (T. P. November 19, 1845)

Col. Robert H. D. L. HART married Martha A. E. ARRINGTON, daughter of Arthur ARRINGTON, in Nash County on September 10, 1829, by Jos. Arrington, Esq. (F. P. September 18, 1829)

Sheriff Spencer L. HART married Louisiana PENDER on January 18, 1829. (F. P. January 23, 1829)

Spencer L. HART of Edgecombe County married Unity P. ANDREWS of Franklin County at Weldon on November 2, 1857, by Rev. Mr. Graves. (S. November 7, 1857)

James H. HARTMUS married Frances OUTLAW on January 19, 1830, by Henry Austin, Esq. (F. P. January 22, 1830)

John G. HARVEY, Lt. in the United States Army, married Adeline NELMES at Greenville on November 3, 1831, by Gould Hoyt, Esq. (N. C. F. P. November 15, 1831)

Joseph HARVEY married Nancy EASON at Tarboro on March 22, 1842, by Henry Austin, Esq. (T. P. March 26, 1842)

C. B. HASSELL married Mary DAVIS, eldest daughter of the late Durham

DAVIS, in Martin County on May 17, 1832, by Elder Jos. Biggs. (N.
C. F. P. May 22, 1832)

Elder C. B. HASSELL of Williamston married Mrs. Maria M. JEWETT at War-
wick, New York, on March 20, 1849. (T. P. April 21, 1849)

Franklin HATHAWAY married Mrs. Sarah JAMES on May 16, 1848, by J. F.
Hughes, J. P., in Edgecombe County near Sparta. (T. P. June 3,
1848)

Charles HATHCOCK married Sarah BROOKER in Halifax County on June 21,
1829, by William E. Shine, Esq. (F. P. June 26, 1829)

James B. HAWKINS of Warren County married Adella ALSTON, daughter of
Willis ALSTON, on December 16, 1835. (T. P. January 9, 1836)

Hon. Micajah T. HAWKINS married Maria Eaton BAKER, daughter of the late
Blake BAKER, in the Warrenton Episcopal Church on February 20,
1849, by Rev. C. McRae. (T. P. February 24, 1849)

Thomas H. HAWKINS married Martha REED on May 10, 1831, by Rev. William
Bellamy. (N. C. F. P. May 17, 1831)

Jesse HAWLEY of near Fayetteville married Sarah Eliza BRADDY, daughter
of the late Job BRADDY, Esq., of Edgecombe County, on July 30, 1844.
(T. P. August 3, 1844)

William HYLES married Rhoda BRACEWELL, daughter of Jacob BRACEWELL, on
May 16, 1836, by Henry Austin, Esq. (T. P. May 21, 1836)

Henry HAYWOOD married Susan FULCHER, both of Washington, at Williamston
on July 23, 1829, by Rev. Wheeler Martin. (F. P. August 7, 1829)

Lawrence Henry HEARN married Margaret Ann BELL, daughter of the late
Henry BELL, at Tarborough on May 16, 1836, by L. D. Wilson, Esq.
(T. P. May 21, 1836)

Adam HEATH of Johnston County married Maria SIMMS, daughter of the late
James SIMMS, in Edgecombe County on February 14, 1854, by Rev. J.
B. Jackson. (S. March 11, 1854)

Jesse HEDGEPETH married Mary Eliza PARKER, daughter of the late John
PARKER, in Tarboro on January 3, 1849, by L. C. Pender, Esq. (T.
P. January 6, 1849)

Joshua HICKS married Lydia Ann MAYO of Edgecombe County on January 25,
1838. (T. P. February 17, 1838)

Phesanton S. HICKS married Kitturah PROCTOR, daughter of the late William
PROCTOR, in Edgecombe County on December 25, 1856, by Theophilus
Thomas, Esq. (S. January 3, 1857)

Seth S. HICKS of Tarboro married Margaret J. HARRELL, daughter of Jesse
HARRELL, Esq., of Edgecombe County, on December 22, 1857, by David
Cobb, Esq. (S. January 2, 1858)

Jacob HIGGS married Adeline PITTMAN in Halifax County at the James H.
Parker residence on May 5, 1831. (N. C. F. P. May 10, 1831)

Joseph HIGGS married Mary POPE of Halifax County on February 5, 1828, by
John Young, Esq. (F. P. February 15, 1828)

Joseph HIGGS of Halifax County married Phenetta STATON, daughter of the
late Bythal STATON of Edgecombe County, on March 24, 1835, by Joshua
Pender, Esq. (T. P. March 28, 1835)

Southern HIGGS married Rebecca HARRISON in Granville County on January
12, 1830. (F. P. February 5, 1830)

Willie J. HIGGS married Willie Ann SAVAGE of Halifax County at the Edwin
Whitehead residence on February 5, 1861, by John H. Davis, Esq.
(S. February 16, 1861)

Asberry HILL married Emiliza SESSUMS in Edgecombe County on August 2,
1860, by E. D. Macnair, Esq. (S. September 1, 1860)

Daniel HILL married Susan Irwin TOOLE, daughter of the late Geraldus
TOOLE of Edgecombe County, in Franklin County on November 5, 1835,
by Rev. Compton. (T. P. November 14, 1835)

Whitmel J. HILL married Lavinia D. Barnes at Scotland Neck on November
24, 1829, by William R. Smith, Esq. (F. P. December 4, 1829)

James HILLIARD of Nash County married Mary RUFFIN of Edgecombe County on February 10, 1835. (T. P. February 21, 1835)

Louis HILLIARD, Esq., of the Greensboro Bar, married Claudia JORDAN, daughter of the late Henry C. JORDAN of Greenville, at the Baptist Church in Greenville on June 6, 1860, by Elder H. Petty. (S. June 16, 1860)

Peter E. HINES, Esq., married Sarah MACNAIR, daughter of E. D. MACNAIR, at the residence of Mrs. Hunter on February 17, 1834, by Charles G. Hunter, Esq. (T. F. February 21, 1834)

Peter E. HINES of Edgecombe County married Mary MAY, daughter of the late James MAY of Pitt County, on February 18, 1836, by Rev. Thomas Dupree. (T. P. February 27, 1836)

Peter R. HINES, Esq., of Edgecombe County married Emma J. SNOW at Christ Church in Raleigh on March 22, 1842, by Rev. R. S. Mason, D. D. (T. P. April 2, 1842)

Richard HINES, Esq., of Tarboro, married Caroline SNEAD, daughter of John SNEAD, Esq., in New Bern on December 18, 1834, by Rev. John R. Goodman. (T. P. January 2, 1835)

William H. HINES married Malvina MERCER, daughter of John MERCER, Esq., on October 1, 1839, by D. Williams, Esq. (T. P. October 12, 1839)

David HINTON of Wake County married Mary B. CARR, daughter of the late Jonas CARR, at the residence of John B. Williams, by Rev. R. O. Burton. (S. April 10, 1852) The marriage took place on March 31, 1852.

James J. HINTON of Johnston County married Frances A. HART, "formerly of Edgecombe," in Johnston County on June 17, 1830. (F. P. July 9, 1830)

Richard HOCOTT, Jr., of Edgecombe County, aged seventy-two, married Elizabeth DILDA, aged fifty-two, at the home of Willie Dilda, Esq., on Jacob's Branch in Pitt County, about April of 1852, by Allen Exum, Esq. (S. May 8, 1852)

Allen HODGE of Kentucky married Mary BRADY of Edgecombe County on November 7, 1826, by William E. Bellamy, Esq. (F. P. November 14, 1826)

William H. HODGE, attorney of Tarboro, married Frances Ann BOYD of Granville County at the home of Richard Bullock there on December 30, 1828. (F. P. January 9, 1829)

William W. HOLDEN married Louisa V. HARRISON, daughter of the late Robert HARRISON, Esq., at Raleigh on March 7, 1854. (S. March 11, 1854)

Daniel HOPKINS married Mrs. JENKINS in Edgecombe County on December 28, 1827. (F. P. January 18, 1828)

Jarrett HOPKINS, merchant, married Mary STANSELL, daughter of Godfrey STANSELL of Pitt County, on February 2, 1832. (N. C. F. P. February 7, 1832)

Capt. William D. HOPKINS married Julia BEST at the William C. Leigh residence on May 27, 1830, by Louis D. Wilson, Esq. (F. P. June 2, 1830)

Jacob HORN married Martha VINES in Pitt County on December 18, 1828. (F. P. December 26, 1828)

Duke William HORNE of Marianna, Florida, married Mary Amelia Ann LAWRENCE daughter of Peter P. LAWRENCE, at Tarboro on September 29, 1829, by Rev. P. W. Dowd. (F. P. October 2, 1829)

John R. HORNE of Edgecombe County married Eliza Jane BURT, daughter of William BURT of Nash County, at Hilliardston on October 24, 1833. (N. C. F. P. November 15, 1833)

Lawrence HORNE married Elizabeth MERCER, daughter of John MERCER, on November 6, 1832. (N. C. F. P. November 13, 1832)

WHitmel HORNE, formerly of Edgecombe County, married Mary E. TELFAIR in Washington, North Carolina, on December 23, 1834. HORNE was then living in Marianna, Florida. (T. P. January 2, 1835)

Richard T. HOSKINS of Alabama married Elizabeth A. LAWRENCE, daughter of Peter P. LAWRENCE, in Tarboro on October 6, 1846, by Rev. Thomas R. Owen. (T. P. October 7, 1846)

Sennor Don Alonzo Edgar HOWARD, "cosmopolite and itinerant juggler," married Sarah Susan Elizabeth Panza MILLS, daughter of Col. Everitt MILLS, at Tarboro at midnight on February 25, 1853, by John S. Dancy Esq., after one hour of acquaintance and a courtship of fifteen minutes. (S. March 5, 1853)

James P. HOWARD married Martha P. CROMWELL, daughter of the late Thomas CROMWELL of Edgecombe County, in Monroe County, Georgia, about March of 1852. (S. April 10, 1852)

Robert HOWARD married Sarah MOORE in Edgecombe County on November 3, 1857, by William S. Long, Esq. (S. November 21, 1857)

William HOWARD of Edgecombe County married Frances Penelope MARTIN, daughter of Capt. Benjamin MARTIN, near Hamilton on October 4, 1855, by Rev. Mr. Cox. (S. October 20, 1855)

Bythal HOWELL married Henrietta LONG, daughter of William R. LONG, on January 10, 1833, by J. J. Pippen, Esq. (N. C. F. P. January 15, 1833)

James D. HOWELL of Tarboro married Martha E. GRAY, daughter of the late Etheldred GRAY, at Rocky Mount on July 29, 1847, by Rev. Joseph B. Cheshire. (T. P. July 31, 1847)

Levi HOWELL of Martin County married Dolly B. WATSON, daughter of Thomas WATSON, Sr., of Halifax County, on July 24, 1827, by Rev. William Hyman. (F. P. August 11, 1827)

Thomas HOWELL of Martin County married Elizabeth CHERRY, daughter of Roderick CHERRY, Esq., in Pitt County on January 3, 1833, by Rev. William Hyman. (N. C. F. P. January 8, 1833)

William HOWELL of Tarboro married Eliza COOPER, daughter of Jesse COOPER, Esq., in Martin County on April 23, 1835, by J. Ballard, Esq. (T. P. May 2, 1835)

William Ely HOWELL of Edgecombe County married Martha Jane VAUGHAN, daughter of Thomas VAUGHAN of Scotland Neck, on September 23, 1841, by L. B. K. Dicken. (T. P. October 2, 1841)

Baker HOWERTON married Sarah E. BENSON in Edgecombe County at the residence of Mrs. H. King on December 15, 1853, by Rev. John F. Speight. (S. December 17 and December 24, 1853)

Rev. N. Collin HUGHES married Adeline E. WILLIAMS, daughter of the late Dr. Robert WILLIAMS, in Pitt County on October 17, 1848, by Rev. Joseph B. Cheshire. (T. P. October 28, 1848)

Charles G. HUNTER, Esq., of Edgecombe County married Rosalie BARROW, daughter of William R. BARROW, Esq., in East Feliciana Parish, Louisiana, on May 6, 1845. (T. P. May 24, 1845)

Dr. James HUNTER married Sarah BRANCH, daughter of the Hon. John BRANCH, at Enfield on July 16, 1833. (N. C. F. P. August 3, 1833)

Weldon S. HUNTER married Nancy GRIFFITHS at Tarboro on February 14, 1844, by L. D. Wilson, Esq. (T. P. February 17, 1844)

Thomas HURSEY married Mrs. Emeliza ROUNTREE in Tarboro on July 8, 1849, by Rev. T. R. Owen. (T. P. July 14, 1849)

Jesse B. HYATT married Martha C. HORNE, daughter of the late Caswell HORNE, at Tarboro on February 11, 1851, by Jesse Harrell, Esq. (T. P. February 15, 1851)

Jesse B. HYATT married Margaret SHURLEY, daughter of the late Geraldus SHURLEY of Edgecombe County, on April 15, 1847. (T. P. April 17, 1847)

Thomas C. HUSSEY of Tarboro married Edith ROGERS in Pitt County on March 24, 1857, by Allen Bynum, Esq. (S. April 4, 1857)

Arthur HYMAN married Sally HOWARD, daughter of Wilson HOWARD, in Edgecombe County on February 27, 1831, by Theophilus Cherry, Esq. (N. C. F. P. March 1, 1831)

Ebenezer HYMAN married Caroline BURNETT in Martin County on January 15, 1833. (N. C. F. P. January 29, 1833)

George W. HYMAN married Mary T. HARRELL in Martin County on November 22, 1853, by William R. A. Williams, Esq. (S. December 17, 1853)

Henry HYMAN married Martha PORTER, daughter of Ely PORTER, on February 27, 1834, by Rev. Joshua Lawrence. (T. F. P. February 28, 1834)

John H. HYMAN of Palmyra in Halifax County married Leah A. HART, daughter of Elder Robert D. HART, in Nash County on October 10, 1855, by Rev. T. R. Owen. (S. October 13, 1855)

Dr. Francis W. IRBY of Mecklenburg, Virginia, married Susan EVANS, daughter of the late Richard EVANS, Esq., near Greenville in Pitt County on November 30, 1831, by Rev. John H. Norment. (N. C. F. P. December 20, 1832)

Col. John H. IRBY of Mecklenburg County, Virginia, married Margaret A. EVANS from Pitt County, North Carolina, at Plymouth, Mississippi, on December 7, 1833. (T. F. P. March 14, 1834)

Thomas IRWIN of Tarboro married Caroline ARRINGTON, daughter of Arthur ARRINGTON of Nash County, on February 11, 1836. (T. P. March 5, 1836)

Richard N. IVEY married Sarah FULGHUM of Halifax County on October 11, 1827, by William E. Shine, Esq. (F. P. October 27, 1827)

James JACKSON married Mourning SMITH of Nash County "not long since." (The marriage bond was dated December 18, 1843.) (T. P. April 13, 1844)

Micajah JACKSON married Temperance RICKS of Edgecombe County on January 22, 1828. (F. P. February 1, 1828)

Dr. Reuben H. JACKSON of Greenville married Eliza Ann RICKS at Scotland Neck on June 24, 1833, by William R. Smith, Esq. (N. C. F. P. July 6, 1833)

Stephen E. JAKWAY married Elizabeth WILLIFORD, daughter of the late Meedy WILLIFORD, Esq., at Rocky Mount on July 27, 1847. (T. P. July 31, 1847)

Christopher C. JAMES of Tarboro married Susan SWINSON of Duplin County on December 1, 1859, by Rev. J. D. Hufham. (S. December 10, 1859)

Clinton JAMES of Pitt County married Marina TAYLOR, daughter of the late Thomas TAYLOR of Edgecombe County, on February 28, 1843, by Harmon Ward, Esq. (T. P. March 4, 1843)

Rev. C. B. JANNETT, pastor of the Baptist Church at Augusta, Georgia, married Mary Catharine WILLIAMS, daughter of Mrs. A. D. WILLIAMS, at Petersburg on September 5, 1850, by Rev. Dr. Howell. (T. P. September 21, 1850)

James R. JEFFREYS of Franklin County married Ann Eliza LAWRENCE, oldest daughter of John LAWRENCE, Esq., of Edgecombe County, at "Tree Hill" on January 22, 1850, by Rev. Thomas R. Owen. (T. P. January 26, 1850)

Dr. John A. JELKS married Matilda CROWELL in Halifax County on December 16, 1830, by Col. William Wooten, Esq. (N. C. F. P. December 28, 1830)

C. H. JENKINS of Tarboro married Mary Jane DUPREE, daughter of Redmun DUPREE of Edgecombe County on October 20, 1857, by Elisha Cromwell, Esq. (S. October 31, 1857)

Charles H. JENKINS of Edgecombe County married Almira STANCILL, daughter of Jesse STANCILL of Pitt County, on January 16, 1855, by William Cobb, Esq. (S. January 20, 1855)

Frederick H. JENKINS married Hannah STATON, daughter of the late Roderick STATON, in Edgecombe County on September 13, 1855, by Elisha Cromwell, Esq. (S. September 15, 1855)

Joab JENKINS married Mary E. CARNEY in Edgecombe County on July 31, 1851, by Elisha Cromwell, Esq. (T. P. August 2, 1851)

Joseph JENKINS married Rilla HOPKINS, daughter of Frederick HOPKINS, on January 12, 1832, by Joshua Pender, Esq. (N. C. F. P. January 17, 1832)

Thomas JENKINS married Eliza ETHERIDGE in Tarboro on October 8, 1835, by Henry Austin, Esq. (T. P. October 10, 1835)

William A. JENKINS, Esq., married D. M. CLARK, daughter of James S. CLARK, in Greenville on November 18, 1857, by Rev. McDonald. (S. November 21, 1857)

Benjamin JOHNSON, tailor, formerly of Tarboro, married in Halifax County on February 11, 1827, by Valentine Bailey, Esq. (F. P. February 17, 1827) On March 3, 1827, her brother R. READ published a contradiction to the preceding announcement. The Editor added, "The fact was announced in this place by the apparently happy bridegroom." The supposed bride was named Letitia READ.

Henry JOHNSTON married Emily NORFLEET, daughter of I. NORFLEET, on January 12, 1830, by Henry Austin, Esq. (F. P. January 15, 1830)

John JOINER, Esq., married Mrs. Harriet MAY, widow of James MAY, in Pitt County on May 14, 1835, by Rev. Thomas Dupree. (T. P. May 30, 1835)

Rev. Aaron JONES of Edenton Baptist Church married Martha Olivia LAWRENCE daughter of Peter P. LAWRENCE, in Tarboro on December 18, 1850, by Rev. T. R. Owen. (T. P. December 21, 1850)

Calvin JONES married Mary STATON, daughter of the late Bythal STATON, on October 13, 1842. (T. P. October 15, 1842)

James JONES married Anzy CORBETT in Edgecombe County on July 21, 1852, by L. C. Pender, Esq. (S. July 24, 1852)

I. F. JONES married Mary A. CUTCHIN in Edgecombe County on January 21, 1855, by Rev. L. Moore. (S. January 27, 1855)

John JONES married Mary SURMONS in Pitt County on November 29, 1849, by Alfred Moye, Esq. (T. P. December 8, 1849)

Joshua JONES of Franklin County married Susan SORSBY of Nash County on May 29, 1827. (F. P. June 9, 1827)

Orange G. JONES of Asheborough married Susan PAGE, daughter of Mrs. Elizabeth PAGE of Edgecombe County, on April 3, 1849, by Washington Stanton, Esq. (T. P. April 21, 1849)

Thomas JONES, merchant, married Evelina TAYLOR, daughter of Kinchen TAYLOR, in Martin County on December 6, 1832. (N. C. F. P. December 25, 1832)

William A. JONES married Sarah Ann SAVAGE of Edgecombe County on March 16, 1854, by Thomas Norfleet, Esq. (S. March 25, 1854)

William A. JONES married Virginia L. STATON, daughter of the late Col. Simmons B. STATON, in Edgecombe County on May 31, 1855, by Rev. T. R. Owen. (S. June 2, 1855)

Henry JORDAN married Emily GORHAM, daughter of Dr. John C. GORHAM, at Greenville on May 13, 1835, by Rev. John R. Bennett. (T. R. May 30, 1835)

William B. JORDAN of Rocky Mount married Lucy A. DANCY, daughter of Col F. L. DANCY of Buena Vista, Florida, on December 9, 1857, by Rev. Mr. Thackarice. (S. January 2, 1858)

William JOSEY married Mrs. Martha JOSEY in Northampton County on October 30, 1827. (F. P. November 10, 1827)

Dr. Noah JOYNER married Emily A. WILLIAMS, daughter of Dr. Robert WILLIAMS of Pitt County, on April 28, 1841, by Rev. John Singletary. (T. P. May 22, 1841)

Robert JOYNER of Halifax County married Elizabeth DICKEN on February 6, 1840, by Benjamin Batts, Esq. (T. P. February 15, 1840)

Whitmell KEARNEY married Mary D. B. WILLIAMS in Martin County on May 14, 1840, by Rev. George N. Gregory. (T. P. May 23, 1840)

Henry KEEL married Mary HICKS on February 1, 1838, by W. C. Leigh, Esq. (T. P. February 17, 1838)

Charles H. KELLY of Elizabeth City married Miriba A. BABCOCK, of Tarboro, at the Macon House in Portsmouth on March 17, 1861. (S. March 23, 1861)

Mark KELLY married Sarah MOSELY "recently" at the Lovett Atkinson residence in Wilson County, by Simon Barnes, Esq. (S. October 8, 1859)

William KENNEDY married Gracy WINDHAM on April 12, 1837, by Benjamin Sharpe, Esq. (T. P. April 29, 1837)

Churchwell KILLEBREW married Mary JENKINS, daughter of S. P. JENKINS, on January 7, 1840. (T. P. January 18, 1840)

John J. KILPATRICK of Greene County married Sarah TUCKER of Lenoir County on September 8, 1826. (T. P. September 19, 1826)

Drew KING of Halifax County married Elizabeth COTTEN of Edgecombe County at the home of Mrs. Toppin COTTEN on November 20, 1828, by James Biggs, Esq. (F. P. November 28, 1828)

Col. E. KING, formerly of Nash County, married Julia HARRISON, formerly of Edgecombe County, at Captain Charles Harrison's residence near Gonzalez, Texas, on May 20, 1856, by Rev. J. H. Stribling. (S. June 28, 1856)

Edward KING, Jr., married Mary LEWIS of Halifax County on December 9, 1828, by L. Morgan, Esq. (F. P. December 19, 1828)

Enoch KING married Mellissa PEARCE, daughter of Mrs. Mary PEARCE of Dumplin Town in Halifax County on January 13, 1827. (F. P. January 20, 1827)

Henry KING of Tarboro married Rebecca HORNE in Wayne County on November 1, 1848, by Rev. Blount Cooper. (T. P. November 4, 1848)

John KING married Martha JOYNER at Falkland in September of 1855. (S. September 15, 1855)

Kindred KING married Pensey LEWIS on February 28, 1828, by J. H. Simmons, Esq. (F. P. March 7, 1828)

Robert H. KING married Lizzie Ann WEEKS, daughter of Silas WEEKS, Sr., in Edgecombe County on February 27, 1855, by William F. Lewis, Esq. (S. January 20, 1855)

Robert H. KING married Martha J. WELLS in Edgecombe County on August 31, 1859, by William F. Lewis, Esq. (S. September 3, 1859)

William KING of Halifax County married Prudence HOWARD of Edgecombe County on August 9, 1827. (F. P. August 18, 1827)

Russell KINGSBURY, merchant, married Mrs. Mary T. OSBORN of Halifax on October 29, 1827. (F. P. November 10, 1827)

Hezekiah L. KIRTLAND married Sarah PITTMAN in Halifax County at the James H. Parker residence on April 20, 1832. (N. C. F. P. May 8, 1832)

Arthur KNIGHT married Lavina BOOTH on February 13, 1834. (T. F. P. February 21, 1834)

Benjamin W. KNIGHT of Edgecombe County married Emeliza BASS, daughter of Turner BASS, in Halifax County on August 8, 1848. (T. P. August 12, 1848)

Charles C. KNIGHT married Louisiana LAWRENCE, daughter of Rev. Joshua LAWRENCE of Edgecombe County, on December 22, 1828, by Rev. William Hyman. (F. P. January 2, 1829)

Daniel KNIGHT married Mary DAVIS on January 17, 1843, by Henry Austin, Esq. (T. P. January 21, 1843)

Francis Henry KNIGHT married Sally KNIGHT, daughter of Jesse C. KNIGHT, Esq., on September 4, 1834, by Benjamin Wilkinson, Esq. (T. F. P. September 12, 1834)

James W. KNIGHT married Mary A. DANCY, daughter of the late William DANCY, at the Old Church in Tarboro on November 30, 1853, by Rev. T. R. Owen. (S. December 3, 1853)

John KNIGHT married Martha CROMWELL on November 26, 1835, by Benjamin Boykin, Esq. (T. P. November 28, 1835)

John KNIGHT married Sally HARPER at the home of Bythal Staton, Sr., on May 27, 1830, by Joshua Pender, Esq. (F. P. June 2, 1830)

John W. KNIGHT married Elizabeth MCDOWELL, daughter of Patrick MCDOWELL, on December 14, 1847. (T. P. December 18, 1847)

Peter E. KNIGHT married Martha PIPPEN, daughter of the late William PIPPEN, on January 5, 1853, by Robert Norfleet, Esq. (S. January 15, 1853)

William H. KNIGHT married Amelia DUPREE, daughter of Redmun DUPREE, on March 11, 1858, by Elisha Cromwell, Esq. (S. March 13, 1858)

William J. KNIGHT married Adelina FREEMAN, daughter of Josiah FREEMAN of Edgecombe County, on January 3, 1828, by H. Austin, Esq. (F. P. January 11, 1828)

David LANE married Lucretia LAND, daughter of Daniel LAND, in Edgecombe County on November 24, 1844, by Rev. John F. Speight. (T. P. November 30, 1844)

John LANG of Pitt County married Mrs. Elizabeth ROGERS, widow of Stephen ROGERS of Edgecombe County, on November 19, 1826. (F. P. November 28, 1826)

Joseph H. LANGLEY married Mrs. Mary Ann DANIEL, daughter of Daniel HILL, Esq., in Pitt County on October 25, 1849, by Churchill Perkins, Esq. (T. P. November 17, 1849)

William LANIER of Beaufort County married Elytha GRIMES, daughter of William GRIMES, in Edgecombe County on January 24, 1839, by Elder William Hyman. (T. P. February 2, 1839)

Rev. Thomas LANSDELL married Harriet J. LAWRENCE, daughter of the late Peter P. LAWRENCE, at Tarboro on November 21, 1855, by Rev. T. R. Owen. (S. November 24, 1855)

Arthur LAWRENCE of Hertford County married Martha BAKER, daughter of Moses BAKER, Esq., of Edgecombe County, on April 17, 1828. (F. P. May 2, 1828)

David LAWRENCE of Tarboro married Emily G. BOND in Greenville on October 6, 1829, by Rev. Thomas Mason. (F. P. October 9, 1829)

Dr. Ed LAWRENCE of Tarboro married Cecilia D. FOSTER at the home of Leroy Mitchell, Esq., in Louisburg on December 5, 1855, by Rev. F. W. Thomas. (S. December 15, 1855)

James LAWRENCE married Sydney HOWARD, daughter of the late Willie HOWARD of Edgecombe County, on May 23, 1843, by William C. Leigh, Esq. (T. P. May 27, 1843)

James H. LAWRENCE of Scotland Neck married Mary N. BRADDY, daughter of the late Solomon T. BRADDY, in Nash County on May 1, 1856, by Rev. Mr. Finch. (S. May 24, 1856)

Joseph J. LAWRENCE married Frances E. COBB in Edgecombe County on May 23, 1850, by Elisha Cromwell, Esq. (T. P. May 25, 1850)

Dr. Joseph J. LAWRENCE married Josephine EDWARDS in Wilson on May 3, 1859, by Rev. Mr. Tucker. (S. May 7, 1859)

Josephus D. M. LAWRENCE of Northampton County married Elizabeth R. POWELL at the James Powell residence in Halifax County on January 6, 1831, by James J. Pittman, Esq. (N. C. F. P. January 23, 1831)

Joshua LAWRENCE married Lucinda LAWRENCE in Edgecombe County on November 21, 1832, by William C. Leigh, Esq. (N. C. F. P. December 4, 1832)

Joshua L. LAWRENCE married Harriet MAYO on September 28, 1836, by Rev. William Hyman. (T. P. October 1, 1836)

Dr. Josiah LAWRENCE of Tarboro married Mary Eliza TOOLE, daughter of the late H. TOOLE, in Greenville on February 20, 1833. (N. C. F. P. March 5, 1833)

Lemuel LAWRENCE married Grace STATON, daughter of William STATON, on October 3, 1826. (F. P. October 10, 1826)

Peter P. LAWRENCE married Mrs. Mary B. DANCY on April 11, 1833, by Rev. P. W. Dowd. (N. C. F. P. April 13, 1833)

Peter P. LAWRENCE married Abbe MATTHEWSON at Tarboro on December 23, 1838 by Rev. William H. Willis. (T. P. January 5, 1839)

Redding LAWRENCE married Elizabeth LAWRENCE, daughter of John LAWRENCE of Conetoe, on June 3, 1841, by Henry Austin, Esq. (T. P. June 5, 1841)

Thomas D. LAWRENCE married Mary SHERROD, daughter of the late John SHERROD of Edgecombe County, on October 15, 1851, by Rev. R. Post at Charleston, South Carolina. (T. P. October 25, 1851)

Thomas T. LAWRENCE married Sarah DANIEL at Scotland Neck on October 8, 1856. (S. October 18, 1856)

William LAWRENCE of South Quay, Virginia, married Emma L. KING, daughter of Coffield KING of Edgecombe County at her father's home on April 5, 1859, by Rev. T. R. Owen. (S. April 9, 1859)

Dr. William J. LAWRENCE married Laura HARRISON at the John H. Knight residence in Edgecombe County on May 5, 1863, by Elder T. R. Owen. (S. May 9, 1863)

Jonathan LEE married Betsey POPE of Edgecombe County on November 25, 1841, by James George, Esq. (T. P. December 4, 1841)

Lafayette LEGGETT of Beaufort married Laura JOHNSON, daughter of the late Aaron JOHNSON, in Edgecombe County on March 17, 1859, by William F. Lewis, Esq. (S. April 2, 1859)

William R. LEGGETT married Cinderilla NELSON, daughter of Jonas NELSON, on January 11, 1844, by Harmon Ward, Esq. (T. P. January 20, 1844)

John H. LEIGH of Tarboro married Ruth HOUSE, daughter of the late George HOUSE on September 17, 1857, by Elisha Cromwell, Esq. (S. September 19, 1857)

William C. LEIGH, Esq., married Lucy HARRELL, daughter of Christopher HARRELL, in Edgecombe County on August 28, 1839, by W. D. Staton, Esq. (T. P. September 7, 1839)

Thomas J. LEMAY married Eliza A. P. SLEDGE, daughter of Joel SLEDGE, Esq., in Franklin County on May 14, 1828. (F. P. June 6, 1828)

Col. Caleb LEONARD of Nash County married Mrs. Martha RUFFIN of Edgecombe County on May 3, 1829. (F. P. May 22, 1829)

Charles LEWIS of Tyrrell County married Margaret SMITH, daughter of Moses SMITH, in Halifax County on November 1, 1838, by L. B. K. Dicken, Esq. (T. P. November 10, 1838)

Exum LEWIS, Jr., married Jane COTTEN in Edgecombe County on September 29, 1835. (T. P. October 3, 1835)

Ivey F. LEWIS of North Carolina married Kate RHODES, fourth daughter of James RHODES of Bladen Springs, Alabama, on April 15, 1857, by Rev. S. W. Smith. (S. May 2, 1857)

Dr. John W. LEWIS married Catharine BATTLE at the Joel Battle home on February 5, 1829. (F. P. February 13, 1829)

Kenelm Harrison LEWIS of Rocky Mount married Elizabeth Heritage BRYAN, second daughter of the Hon. John H. BRYAN, at Christ Church in Raleigh on April 15, 1857, by Rev. Dr. Mason. (S. April 25, 1857)

Richard Henry LEWIS, Esq., of Greenville but formerly of Edgecombe County married Mary FOREMAN, only daughter of Ivey FOREMAN, in Pitt County on April 24, 1832, by Rev. William N. Hawks. (N. C. F. P. May 8, 1832)

Richard H. LEWIS, Esq., of Greene County, Alabama, married Mrs. Martha E. FOREMAN of "Green Wreath" in Pitt County on June 5, 1849, by Rev. N. Collin Hughes. (T. P. June 9, 1849)

Dr. Richard H. LEWIS of Edgecombe County married Virginia A. CULL, daughter of James CULL, Esq., in Washington City on December 8, 1857, by Rev. G. W. Sampson. (S. December 19, 1857)

Robert H. LEWIS, Esq., of Milton, married Sarah E. HOWARD, daughter of George HOWARD, at Tarboro on November 1, 1854, by Rev. J. B. Cheshire and Robert H. Lewis, Esq. (S. November 4, 1854)

Toby LEWIS of "Dumplin Town" married Mrs. Martha BRANCH of Halifax County "a few days since." (F. P. January 25, 1828)

Lt. Col. W. G. LEWIS of the 43rd Regiment of North Carolina Troops married Mittie PENDER, daughter of J. J. P. PENDER, Esq., on March 15, 1864, by Elder T. R. Owen. (S. March 19, 1864)

Col. John E. LINDSEY married Emma Eliza Jane THORP in Nash County on March 13, 1843. (T. P. April 8, 1843)

John W. LIPSCOMBE married Mrs. Elizabeth A. PEEBLES at Tarboro on March 14, 1858, by Rev. T. R. Owen. (S. March 20, 1858)

William A. LIPSCOMBE of Tarboro married Elizabeth TOLER in Richmond on November 2, 1854. (S. November 11, 1854)

Cullen LITTLE married Lucy ALFORD in Edgecombe County on January 5, 1830, by John F. Hughes, Esq. (F. P. January 8, 1830)

Frederick LITTLE married Harriet KNIGHT, daughter of Willis KNIGHT, on May 27, 1830, by Benjamin Boykin, Esq. (F. P. June 2, 1830)

Col. Lewis G. LITTLE married Eliza EBORN, daughter of Benjamin EBORN, Esq., in Pitt County on May 3, 1838, by Rev. George N. Gregory. (T. P. May 12, 1838)

William LITTLE of Stantonsburg married Temperance SPEIGHT, daughter of William V. SPEIGHT, in Greene County on February 27, 1828. (F. P. March 28, 1828)

Willis LITTLE married Sarah HARDY, daughter of the late Allen HARDY, in Edgecombe County on October 21, 1858, by David Cobb, Esq. (S. October 23, 1858)

Gen. Joseph B. LITTLEJOHN of Franklin County married Sallie Jones FIELDS, daughter of Dr. George FIELD of "Glenwood" in Warren County, on October 13, 1852. (S. October 30, 1852)

Joseph B. LITTLEJOHN, Jr., Esq., married Mary I. TOOLE, daughter of the late Geraldus TOOLE of Edgecombe County, in Franklin County on January 11, 1838, by Rev. William Arendell. (T. P. January 26,1838)

Joseph R. LLOYD, Esq., of Tarboro married Maria A. PUGH of Bertie County at the home of General Bryan in Oxford on July 19, 1827. (F. P. July 28, 1827)

Joseph W. LLOYD married Sarah E. BARLOW, daughter of David BARLOW, on April 9, 1856, near Tarboro, by Rev. T. R. Owen. (S. April 12, 1856)

Whitmel P. LLOYD of Tarboro married Hattie E. HOWARD, daughter of George HOWARD, on January 13, 1858, by Rev. Jos. Blount Cheshire. (S. January 16, 1858)

Richard LODGE married William Delha SESSUMS, daughter of Nathan H. SESSUMS, in Edgecombe County on March 17, 1857, by R. H. Pender, Esq. (S. March 21, 1857)

James LONG married Mary Louisa LAWRENCE, daughter of Rev. Joshua LAWRENCE on January 21, 1836, by Rev. William Hyman. (T. P. January 30, 1836)

James S. LONG married Wealthy Ann HOWELL, daughter of Eli HOWELL, deceased, in Edgecombe County on October 8, 1839. (T. P. October 12, 1839)

John LONG of Martin County married Marian MAYO of Edgecombe County on March 29, 1836, by Rev. William Hyman. (T. P. April 2, 1836)

William S. LONG married Mary BATTS, daughter of Benjamin BATTS, Esq., of Edgecombe County on December 31, 1844, by Rev. William Hyman. (T. P. January 4, 1845)

Jefferson M. LOVEJOY married Virginia A. STEPTOE in Greenville on June 5, 1838. (T. P. June 16, 1838)

Jesse LYNCH married Sarah CAIN of Halifax County in Martin County on August 19, 1830, by Figures Lowe, Esq. (N. C. F. P. August 31,1830)

Bennett T. LYON married Penelope PITTMAN, daughter of Harrison PITTMAN, on May 12, 1836. (T. P. May 21, 1836)

Joshua L. LYON married Martha CHERRY, daughter of Major Lunsford R. CHERRY, on May 18, 1841, by R. Pittman, Esq. (T. P. May 22, 1841)

Thomas LYON married Mary HARTT on November 9, 1826. (F. P. November 14, 1826)

Dr. Baker W. MABREY married Lucy B. LAWRENCE, daughter of John LAWRENCE, in Edgecombe County on October 7, 1856, by Rev. T. R. Owen. (S. October 11, 1856)

Dr. Baker W. MABREY of Tarboro married Mary Eliza FREEMAN, daughter of the late Jos. FREEMAN, on December 20, 1859, by Rev. T. R. Owen. (S. December 24, 1859)

Charles D. MABREY of Edgecombe County married S. A. GIER of Charlotte on April 12, 1860, at Melville in Alamance County. (S. April 28, 1860)

Charles MABRY married Frances STATON on November 2, 1826. (F. P. November 14, 1826)

Col. Charles MABREY married Penny BRYAN, daughter of Drury BRYAN, on January 29, 1839, by Benjamin Batts, Esq. (T. P. February 16, 1839)

William Almarine MABRY married Louisa KNIGHT, daughter of Peter E. KNIGHT in Edgecombe County on October 20, 1847, by Benjamin Batts, Esq. (T. P. November 13, 1847)

Dr. A. H. MACNAIR of Tarboro married Mary Penelope HALSEY, in Perquimans County on November 5, 1850, by Rev. T. R. Owen. (T. P. November 9, 1850)

Dr. A. H. MACNAIR of Tarboro marred Anna Lou HORNE, daughter of D. W. HORNE, at Orange Hill in Washington County, Florida, on March 9, 1853, by Rev. J. H. Wombwell. (S. April 2, 1853)

Colin MACNAIR of Tarboro married M. R. CHURCH near Madison, Florida, on June 2, 1859. (S. June 18, 1859)

Hugh MACNAIR married Margaret Ann BAKER, daughter of Dr. W. S. BAKER, near Tarboro on March 16, 1859, by Rev. T. R. Owen. (S. March 19, 1859)

Henry MACRAE, Principal Assistant Engineer of the Tarboro' Rail Road, married Elizabeth COWLING of Nansemond County, Virginia, on March 22, 1860, by Rev. George T. Williams. (S. April 7, 1860)

Littleberry MANNING married Pennina B. EXUM in Edgecombe County on October 25, 1842, by Joseph Jo. B. Pender, Esq. (T. P. October 29, 1842)

James MARKS married Rosina MCWILLIAMS, daughter of the late George MC-WILLIAMS, in Tarboro on September 6, 1835, by Henry Austin, Esq. (T. P. September 19, 1835)

Jos. J. MARKS married Amanda WEEKS, daughter of Silas WEEKS, in Edgecombe County on March 30, 1842, by Joseph John B. Pender, Esq. (T. P. April 30, 1842)

Napoleon B. MARRINER married Elizabeth MIZELL in Martin County on June 5, 1838, by E. Brenof, Esq. (T. P. June 16, 1838)

Dr. Robert H. MARRIOTT married Temperance A. BATTLE, daughter of the late Joseph S. BATTLE, in Edgecombe County on November 8, 1853, by Rev. J. L. Cotten. (S. November 26, 1853)

Joshua MASON of Beaufort married Fanny BENTON of "Lousy Level" near Falling Creek on May 8, 1856. (S. May 31, 1856)

Nathan MATHEWSON married Mary Jane AUSTIN, daughter of the late Henry Austin, Esq., in Tarboro on May 11, 1847, by Rev. T. R. Owen. (T. P. May 15, 1847)

Allen MAYO married Eliza WILKINSON, daughter of Abner C. WILKINSON, on March 10, 1841, by W. C. Leigh, Esq. (T. P. March 21, 1841)

Amos MAYO married Patsey KELLY in Edgecombe County on December 19, 1833, by William C. Leigh, Esq. (T. F. P. December 27, 1833)

Benjamin C. MAYO married Evelina JONES, daughter of Allen JONES, in Edgecombe County on January 18, 1844, by Rev. William Hyman. (T. P.

January 20, 1844)

Frederick MAYO married Manisia Ganer Menetta Anders Sylvester Malvina Lewellen SHERRARD in Edgecombe County on February 27, 1828, by Rev. William Hyman. (F. P. April 4, 1828)

John MAYO, Jr., married Maria SHELTON on August 3, 1834, by William C. Leigh, Esq. (T. F. P. August 15, 1834)

Kinchen MAYO married Nancy KNIGHT in Edgecombe County on August 24, 1826. (T. P. August 29, 1826)

Lawrence S. MAYO married Mary E. TERRELL, daughter of Nathaniel M. TERRELL of Tarboro on December 28, 1850, at the F. P. Redmond residence in Fayette County, Tennessee, on December 28, 1850, by Rev. Mr. Culp. (T. P. February 8, 1851)

Dr. Peyton H. MAYO of Falkland married Susan E. SAVAGE, daughter of the late Joseph SAVAGE of Halifax County, at Weldon on June 28, 1860, by E. D. Peterson, Esq. (S. July 7, 1860)

Reuben MAYO married Lucinda BEST on December 19, 1832, by William C. Leigh, Esq. (N. C. F. P. January 1, 1833)

Robert W. MAYO of La Grange, Tennessee, married Margaret L. H. LOCKE of Tippah County, Mississippi, on February 6, 1855.

Thomas MAYO married Mary BRYAN, daughter of Dempsey BRYAN on February 19, 1833, by the Rev. Joshua Lawrence. (N. C. F. P. March 5, 1833)

Captain David MCDANIEL of Raleigh married Celeste DORTCH in Nash County on January 22, 1840. (T. P. February 8, 1840)

William MCGEE of Tennessee married Eugenia BELL, daughter of Frederick BELL, in Tarboro on April 2, 1835, by L. D. Wilson, Esq. (T. P. April 4, 1835)

Rev. William MCKINNIE married Ann M. RAGSDALE in Washington City on March 25, 1852. (S. April 24, 1852)

Edward MCPHERSON of Fayetteville married Margaret SUGG, daughter of the late Dr. P. SUGG, near Sparta in Edgecombe County on January 19, 1859. (S. January 22, 1859)

John MEARS married Sarah A. TANNER in Edgecombe County on May 17, 1860, by R. D. Macnair, Esq. (S. May 26, 1860)

James MEHEGAN married Emily BOND, daughter of Lewis BOND, at Tarboro on January 20, 1853, by the Rev. T. R. Owen. (S. January 22, 1853)

Jesse MERCER married Margaret NORFLEET, daughter of Isaac NORFLEET, Esq., of Edgecombe County, on June 19, 1844, by the Rev. Mark Bennett. (T. P. June 22, 1844)

Dr. John R. MERCER of Edgecombe County married Susan VICK, daughter of the late Josiah VICK of Nash County, on November 18, 1849. (T. P. November 24, 1849)

Dr. Thomas N. MERCER of Edgecombe County married Mary Jane OUTTEN, daughter of William OUTTEN, Esq., at Gosport on June 3, 1844, by the Rev. Vernon Eskridge. (T. P. June 15, 1844)

William F. MERCER married Mrs. Emily A. PARKER, daughter of Nathan MATTHEWSON, deceased, on October 12, 1852, by Elder Mark Bennett. (S. October 16, 1852)

E. J. MERRITT of "Dumplin Town" in Halifax County married Margaret GUNTER, daughter of Abner GUNTER of Edgecombe County "a short time since." (F. P. February 6, 1829) (The marriage bond of Ethington J. MERRITT and Margaret M. GUNTER was dated December 29, 1828.)

Joseph MERRITT married Susan HENLEY at the home of James HENLEY of Halifax County on February 1, 1829, by William Doggett, Esq. (F. P. February 13, 1829)

David J. MILLIKEN married Antoinette E. NORFLEET at the William Higgs residence in Halifax County on July 7, 1829, by Laertes Morgan, Esq. (F. P. July 17, 1829)

Abner MILLS, aged seventy years, married Mrs. Martha CARNEY, aged thirty-five, in Tarborough on July 10, 1828, by Robert Joyner, Esq.

(F. P. July 18, 1828)

Cullen MILTON from Georgia married Milbry GAY, daughter of Richard GAY, in Edgecombe County on October 3, 1835, by Henry Austin, Esq. (T. P. October 10, 1835)

Dr. John A. MINNIS married Mrs. Pennina HORNE, daughter of Frederick PHILIPS, in Edgecombe County on June 21, 1837, by the Rev. Amos J. Battle. (T. P. June 24, 1837) (T. S. June 23, 1837)

John MINSHEW married Ann CUTCHEN, daughter of the late Eli CUTCHEN of Edgecombe County, in Nash County on April 19, 1859, by Henry G. Williams, Esq. (S. April 30, 1859)

J. D. MONTAGUE of New Hanover County married Julia A. FARMER of Nansemond County, Virginia, on January 11, 1855, by Elisha Barnes, Esq. (S. February 3, 1855)

Andrew J. MOORE married Della A. COTTEN, daughter of the late John L. COTTEN, in Edgecombe County on February 3, 1859, by John W. Johnston, Esq. (S. February 12, 1859)

B. F. MOORE, Esq., married Lucy BODDIE at the George Boddie residence in Nash County on April 28, 1835, by Rev. Amos J. Battle. (T. P. May 23, 1835)

Bartholomew F. MOORE, attorney at law, married Louisa BODDIE, daughter of George BODDIE, Esq., of Nash County, on December 2, 1828, by Rev. John Armstrong. (F. P. December 19, 1828)

James S. MOORE married Isabella BARNHILL, daughter of Henry BARNHILL, on April 2, 1839, in Pitt County. (T. P. April 20, 1839)

John MOORE married Mrs. Rutha CARNEY on November 26, 1840, by Winfield D. Staton, Esq. (T. P. December 5, 1840)

John O. MOORE married Ann CARLISLE at Tarboro on September 11, 1855, by Thomas Norfleet, Esq. (S. September 15, 1855)

Joseph MOORE married Rebecca HARRELL, daughter of Christopher HARRELL, on December 24, 1839, by Meedy Williford, Esq. (T. P. January 18,1840)

Maurice MOORE married Sarah Ann WATTS, daughter of Maj. William WATTS, at Williamston on November 1, 1832. (N. C. F. P. November 27, 1832)

Miles B. MOORE married Ann Eunice BENNETT of Martin County at Jamestown about July of 1836 by Rev. John A. Miller. (T. P. July 16, 1836)

Samuel MOORE of Pitt County married Mary Ann WILLIFORD, daughter of Media WILLIFORD, Esq., of Edgecombe County, on March 5, 1837, by John Mercer, Esq. (T. P. March 11, 1837)

Samuel E. MOORE married Alice Ann ELLIOTT, only daughter of Elijah ELLIOTT, at Tarboro on January 8, 1845, by Rev. T. R. Owen. (T. P. January 11, 1845)

William A. MOORE married Mary Ann OBERRY in Tarboro on November 11, 1858, by Rev. T. R. Owen. (S. November 13, 1858)

Arthur MOORING married Martha E. MAYO in Martin County on September 5, 1837, by Rev. William Hyman. (T. S. September 15, 1837. T. P. September 23, 1837)

Jesse H. MOORING of Pitt County married Ann N. LAURENCE of Northampton County on January 4, 1827. (F. P. January 27, 1827)

James MORECOCK married Mary Ann MYRICK at the home of Capt. Edmunds Myrick of Halifax County on June 26, 1828, by Thomas Gary, Esq. (F. P. July 11, 1828)

Canady MORGAN married Sarah DANIEL, daughter of Ephraim DANIEL, on November 16, 1830, by Frederick F. Robbins, Esq. (N. C. F. P. November 30, 1830)

Henry MORRIS married Mary CARTER, daughter of John CARTER, Sr., in Halifax County on June 10, 1828, by T. S. Brownlow, Esq. (F. P. June 20, 1828)

Thomas MORRIS of Hamilton married Virginia Ann PARKER in Tarboro on August 2, 1855, by R. H. Pender, Esq. (S. August 4, 1855)

James W. MOYE of Edgecombe County married Henrietta L. ANDERSON of Pitt

County on May 5, 1851, by Rev. John Dunn. (T. P. May 31, 1851)

General Wyatt MOYE from Edgecombe County married the widow of the late Hon. Jesse SPEIGHT "recently, in Lowndes County, Mississippi." (T. P. September 29, 1849)

General Wyatt MOYE of Aberdeen, Mississippi, married Mrs. Mary Mason MCMASTER, daughter of the late Colonel Francis DANCY, at "Dancy" in St. Mary's Parish on September 16, 1858. (S. October 9, 1858)

Dr. Jethro MURPHY of Snow Hill married Elizabeth MUSGRAVE in Wayne County on April 27, 1849. (T. P. May 19, 1849)

William MURRAY of Wilson married Margaret ROUNTREE, daughter of the late N. H. ROUNTREE, on October 18, 1854, by Rev. Mr. Gibbons. He was "recently of Baltimore." (S. October 21, 1854)

Lewis MUSGRAVE of Wayne County married Alice SPEIGHT, daughter of William Fobhead SPEIGHT of Greene County, by Jesse Speight, Esq., on May 15, 1827. (F. P. May 26, 1827)

John G. MYERS of Washington married Susan GRIMES, daughter of Bryan GRIMES, Esq., in Pitt County on July 6, 1853, by Rev. Ed. Geer. (S. July 9, 1853)

Louis B. MYERS, merchant, married Harriet E. WORTHINGTON, daughter of Joseph W. WORTHINGTON, Esq., of Pitt County, on June 30, 1831, at Washington, North Carolina. (N. C. F. P. July 5, 1831)

Charles E. NEAL married Pernetti JENKINS, daughter of S. P. JENKINS, Esq., of Edgecombe County on May 11, 1852, by W. H. Hines, Esq. (S. May 15, 1852)

David NEAL married Della HORNE, daughter of the late Caswell HORNE, at Tarboro on July 3, 1855, by Rev. T. R. Owen. (S. July 7, 1855)

John NELSON married Elizabeth A. GRIMES, only daughter of Thomas GRIMES, in Edgecombe County on December 22, 1857, by James W. Howard, Esq. (S. January 2, 1858)

Allen NETTLES of Edgecombe County married Dicey MOYE in Pitt County on January 28, 1834. (T. F. P. February 7, 1834)

John E. NETTLES, Esq., of Haywood County but formerly of Edgecombe County, married Elizabeth GOODWIN, daughter of Hardy GOODWIN of Chatham County, by Rev. John T. Brame in or prior to April of 1841. (T. P. May 1, 1841)

Henry NEWSOM married Nancy B. COTTEN in Edgecombe County on December 25, 1849, by Hugh B. Bryan, Esq. (T. P. January 5, 1850)

William NICKELS of Scotland Neck, merchant, married Catharine R. LAWRENCE on January 29, 1829, by William R. Smith, Esq. (F. P. February 6, 1829)

Peter NIXON married Mary SIMMONS, daughter of Mrs. BARRINGTON, in Tarboro on August 25, 1839, by Henry Austin, Esq. (T. P. August 31, 1839)

Dr. Allen B. NOBLES married Susan E. GARRETT, daughter of the late James J. GARRETT of Mississippi, in Edgecombe County on May 20, 1855, at the J. C. Knight residence, by Wright W. Barnes, Esq. (S. May 26, 1855)

Robert NORFLEET married Margaret P. WILLIAMS, daughter of the late John WILLIAMS, on December 19, 1849, by Rev. R. J. Carson, in Tarboro. (T. P. December 22, 1849)

Thomas NORFLEET married Azula MEHEGAN, daughter of James MEHEGAN, at Tarboro on September 1, 1858, by Rev. T. R. Owen. (S. September 4, 1858)

Rev. William NORWOOD married Winifred B. HILL at Scotland Neck on April 11, 1833, by Bishop Ives, Methodist Minister. (N. C. F. P. April 20, 1833)

John O. OATES married Martha MERCER, daughter of the late William MERCER in Edgecombe County at the residence of Bennett Pitt, Esq., by Rev. John H. Daniel, on July 20, 1852. (S. August 21, 1852)

Green OBERRY married Elizabeth DAY, daughter of Thomas OBERRY (DAY?), near Tarboro on July 15, 1847. (T. P. July 17, 1847)

Green OBERRY married Elvira PARKER, daughter of the late Arthur PARKER, at the Old Church in Tarboro on March 4, 1852, by Elder Blount Cooper. (S. March 6, 1852)

Joseph O'BERRY married Harriet EDWARDS, eldest daughter of John B. EDWARDS, at Cotton's Meeting House on February 27, 1848, by Benjamin Batts, Esq. (T. P. March 4, 1848)

John O'CAIN, Jr., aged nineteen, married Maniza PHILLPOT, aged fifteen, daughter of John PHILLPOT, in Martin County on November 30, 1830, by William S. Rayner, Esq. (N. C. F. P. December 7, 1830)

John B. ODOM of Norfolk married Susan ARRINGTON of Hilliardston in Nash County on October 18, 1853, by Rev. Thomas G. Lowe. (S. October 29, 1853)

Davie OUTLAW, attorney, married Emily RYAN in Windsor on June 7, 1837, by Solomon Cherry, Esq. (T. S. June 30, 1837)

Rev. Thomas R. OWEN married Mary B. MCCOTTOR at Tarboro on October 8, 1839, by Rev. Mr. Stratton. (T. P. October 12, 1839)

Rufus PAGE married Cynthia C. HILL, youngest daughter of the Hon. William HILL, at Raleigh on July 23, 1845. (T. P. August 6, 1845)

Isaac B. PALAMOUNTAIN of Tarboro married Elizabeth MATTHEWS of Wales in New York on July 30, 1854. (S. September 2, 1854) He operated a smithy "near the bridge" in Tarboro.

William R. PALMER of Tyrrell County married Cornelia BURROUGHS in Martin County on August 23, 1832, by W. B. Bennett, Esq. (N. C. F. P. September 4, 1832)

Edward C. PARKER married Mrs. Celia PRICE at Tarboro on September 12, 1837, by James George, Esq. (T. S. September 15, 1837. T. P. September 30, 1837)

Col. Francis M. PARKER married Sarah Tartt PHILIPS, daughter of Dr. James J. PHILIPS, at Mount Moriah in Edgecombe County on December 17, 1851, by Rev. Jos. B. Cheshire. (T. P. December 20, 1851)

James H. PARKER married Mrs. Sarah DAWSON in Halifax County on March 26, 1827. (F. P. March 31, 1827)

John PARKER, Sheriff of Edgecombe County, married Martha TARTT on September 23, 1829. (F. P. September 25, 1829)

John PARKER of Mobile married Eliza J. PHILIPS at Mt. Moriah in Edgecombe County on October 15, 1851, by Rev. J. B. Cheshire. (T. P. October 18, 1851)

John Haywood PARKER, late of Tarboro, married Martha T. LAWRENCE, daughter of Haywood LAWRENCE, at Greensborough, Alabama, on April 14, 1836. (T. P. May 14, 1836)

Simmons B. PARKER married Emily MATTHEWSON, daughter of the late Nathan MATTHEWSON, in Tarboro on June 28, 1838, by Rev. Amos J. Battle. (T. P. June 30, 1838)

William Weeks PARKER married Sarah P. EDWARDS at the home of Mrs. EDWARDS on February 12, 1857, by Henry T. Clark, Esq. (S. February 21,1857)

Frank PARROTT of Lenoir County married Pattie MAY "a few days since" at her home in Pitt County, by Rev. Peter E. Hines. (S. October 23, 1858)

Joshua PEEL married Lucinda BRAKE, daughter of Daniel BRAKE, Esq., of Nash County, at Tarboro on February 18, 1857. (S. February 21, 1857)

Andrew Jackson PENDER married Ann Eliza JOINER, daughter of Wright W. JOINER, at Tarboro on March 4, 1841, by Henry Austin, Esq. (T. P. March 13, 1841)

Cullen PENDER married Lucy BRADLEY, daughter of Willis BRADLEY of Edgecombe County, on January 6, 1836, by Benjamin Batts, Esq. (T. P. January 16, 1836)

David PENDER married Mary C. JOHNSTON, daughter of the late Henry JOHN-
STON, at the R. R. Bridges residence near Tarboro on July 27, 1859,
by Rev. R. S. Moran. (S. July 30, 1859)

James PENDER married Polly RAWLS in Scotland Neck on December 24, 1834.
(T. P. January 2, 1835)

John PENDER married Sylva HARRELL in Edgecombe County "a few days since"
by R. Harrison, Esq. (F. P. February 1, 1828)

Joseph John B. PENDER married Elizabeth MASON, granddaughter of Benjamin
COFFIELD, in Edgecombe County on June 29, 1836. (T. P. July 2,
1836)

Colonel Joshua PENDER married Mrs. Margaret HYMAN, widow of Kenneth
HYMAN, on November 29, 1838. (T. P. December 8, 1838)

Captain Josiah S. PENDER of Beaufort married Laura M. PENDER, daughter
of Louis C. PENDER of Edgecombe County, on September 23, 1862, by
Elder T. R. Owen. (S. September 27, 1862)

Josiah S. PENDER of Tarboro married Maria Louisa WILLIAMS, daughter of
Mrs. A. D. WILLIAMS, at Petersburg, Virginia, on January 25, 1842,
by Rev. A. B. Smith. (T. P. January 29, 1842)

L. D. PENDER married Martha L. HOWARD, daughter of George HOWARD, in
Tarboro on October 20, 1852, by Rev. Robert J. Carson. (S. October
23, 1852)

Lawrence PENDER of Halifax County married Elizabeth POWELL, daughter of
the late Kader POWELL, in Bertie County on December 23, 1845, by
Jeremiah Harrell, Esq. (T. P. January 7, 1846)

Lewis PENDER married Mary HYMAN, daughter of Kenneth HYMAN, deceased, on
October 3, 1839, by J. J. Pippen, Esq. (T. P. October 12, 1839)

Robert H. PENDER married Amarilla James PENDER, daughter of William
PENDER, in Edgecombe County on October 31, 1843, by Rev. Mark
Bennett. (T. P. November 4, 1843)

Solomon PENDER, "tavern keeper of this place," married Elizabeth HINES
on December 20, 1827, by Exum Lowe, Esq. (F. P. December 28, 1827)

Lt. Solomon M. PENDER married Mary J. WARD, daughter of the late Harmon
WARD of Edgecombe County, on January 28, 1864, by Elder T. R. Owen.
(S. March 5, 1864)

Thomas PENDER of Plymouth married Sarah CARSTAPHEN of Edgecombe County
at the Willie Powell residence on December 10, 1835, by Rev. Amos
J. Battle. (T. P. January 9, 1836)

Lieut. William Dorsey PENDER, U. S. A., "a native of this [Edgecombe,
now Wilson] county," married Mary Frances SHEPPERD, daughter of the
Hon. A. H. SHEPPERD of Salisbury, at the SHEPPERD home on the morning of March 3, 1859, by the Rev. Mr. Haughton, Episcopal Minister.
(S. March 12, 1859)

John PEOPLES of Pitt County married Caroline WORSLEY, daughter of Mayo
WORSLEY, in Edgecombe County on February 18, 1851, by Elisha
Cromwell, Esq. (T. P. February 22, 1851)

Churchill PERKINS married Margaret E. JORDAN, daughter of Valentine
JORDAN of Pitt County, on October 13, 1830. (N. C. F. P. October
26, 1830)

James D. PERKINS married Harriet DANIEL at the Willis Daniel, Esq., home
in Halifax County on January 15, 1828, by Valentine Bailey, Esq.
(F. P. January 25, 1828)

Julian V. PERKINS of Pitt County married Lucy F. ALSTON, daughter of
Thomas N. F. ALSTON, Esq., of Warren County on November 9, 1859,
by the Rev. R. G. Barrett. (S. November 19, 1859)

Abner J. PERRY of Hertford County married Julia Ann POWELL at the James
Powell residence in Halifax County on January 6, 1831. (N. C. F.
P. January 23, 1831)

Micajah PETWAY, "a revolutionary officer," married Mrs. Elizabeth
SKINNER "a few days since" in Edgecombe County by Reddick Barnes,
Esq. (F. P. February 1, 1828)

William L. PETWAY married Lucy KNIGHT, daughter of Peter E. KNIGHT of Edgecombe County on May 22, 1849, by Henry T. Clark, Esq. (T. P. May 26, 1849)

Captain Frederick PHILIPS married Mattie S. HYMAN, daughter of the late Henry HYMAN, at Tarboro on January 27, 1864, by Elder T. R. Owen. (S. March 5, 1864)

Dr. James J. PHILIPS married Harriet BURT, daughter of William Burt, Esq., of Nash County, on April 23, 1834, by M. R. Garrett, Esq. He was from Edgecombe County. (T. F. P. May 2, 1834)

Richard T. PHILIPS married Elizabeth WARREN, daughter of Ollen WARREN, in Edgecombe County on March 2, 1857. (S. March 6, 1857)

John PHILLIPS married Elizabeth GREEN in Halifax County "a short time since" by J. H. Simmons, Esq. (F. P. January 18, 1828)

Noah PHILLPOT married Mrs. Sally BOYETT on December 22, 1831, by Arthur S. Cotten, Esq. (N. C. F. P. December 27, 1831)

James Spencer PIPPEN married Sue F. MABREY, daughter of the late Colonel Charles MABREY, in Edgecombe County on February 26, 1861, by Rev. T. R. Owen. (S. March 9, 1861)

Joseph PIPPEN, "an officer of the Revolution," aged seventy-three, married Mrs. Temperance LEE, aged forty-three, in Edgecombe County on February 15, 1827, by Daniel Hopkins, Esq. (F. P. February 17, 1827)

Joseph H. PIPPEN married Sarah CHERRY, daughter of Maj. Lunsford R. CHERRY, in Edgecombe County on October 25, 1854, by Rev. John F. Speight. (S. October 28, 1854)

Joseph John PIPPEN married Sarah Eliza HARPER, daughter of Joseph HARPER, in Tarboro on July 20, 1852, by Henry T. Clark, Esq. (S. July 24, 1852)

Silas M. PIPPEN married Sarah Ann MADDREY, daughter of the late Micajah MADDREY, in Edgecombe County on July 11, 1860, by John W. Johnson, Esq. (S. July 21, 1860)

William M. PIPPEN married Mary H. POWELL, daughter of Jesse POWELL, at Tarboro on March 21, 1855, by the Rev. J. B. Cheshire. (S. March 24, 1855)

Dr. F. G. PITT married Susan E. KNIGHT, daughter of Jordan KNIGHT, on November 4, 1855, by James Carney, Esq. (S. November 24, 1855)

Dr. Franklin G. PITT married Sally Ann KNIGHT, daughter of Jordan KNIGHT in Edgecombe County on October 9, 1849, by Kenneth Thigpen, Esq. (T. P. October 13, 1849)

Colonel Joab P. PITT married Mrs. Winnifred G. WARREN in Edgecombe County on March 2, 1843. (T. P. March 4, 1843)

Nathan PITT married Emily WEAVER, daughter of the late Richard WEAVER, in Edgecombe County on October 21, 1841. (T. P. October 23, 1841)

Nathan PITT married Mary SPIVEY, daughter of John SPIVEY, in Edgecombe County on December 11, 1845, by David Barlow, Esq. (T. P. December 17, 1845)

Beverly T. PITTMAN married Elizabeth JOHNSON, daughter of Joseph J. JOHNSON of Edgecombe County, on January 25, 1859, by Rev. John F. Speight. (S. February 5, 1859)

Elisha PITTMAN married Caroline G. PITTMAN of Halifax County on December 16, 1830, by Wilson C. Whitaker, Esq. (N. C. F. P. December 28, 1830)

John R. PITTMAN married Annis PRIDGEN of Nash County "not long since." (T. P. April 13, 1844) (The marriage bond was dated December 31, 1843.)

Laertes M. PITTMAN married Rowena WHITEHEAD in Halifax County on October 13, 1859, at the residence of Jacob Higgs, Esq. (S. October 22, 1859)

Lunsford G. H. PITTMAN married Zelpha BRADLEY at the Jacob Pope residence in Halifax County on March 15, 1827. (F. P. March 24, 1827)

Dr. N. J. PITTMAN married Mary PITTMAN, daughter of the late Reddin PITTMAN, at Calvary Church on April 29, 1858, by Rev. Jos. Blount Cheshire. (S. May 1, 1858)

Redding PITTMAN married Martha BRYAN, daughter of Dempsey BRYAN, in Edgecombe County on March 10, 1831, by L. D. Wilson, Esq. (N. C. F. P. March 15, 1831)

Spier PITTMAN married Harriet Wiley HIGGS, daughter of the late Wiley HIGGS, at the Jacob Higgs residence in Halifax County on September 25, 1844. (T. P. October 5, 1844)

Warren PITTMAN married Gatsey PROCTOR at Tarboro on March 10, 1853, by R. H. Pender, Esq. (S. March 12, 1853)

William H. PITTMAN of Halifax County married Martha Ann KNIGHT, daughter of James C. KNIGHT, on August 24, 1841, by J. J. B. Pender, Esq. (T. P. August 28, 1841)

Rev. William S. PLUMMER married Mrs. Eliza G. HASEL at Hillsborough on June 11, 1829. (F. P. June 26, 1829)

Henderson POLING married Sarah E. WOMBLE of Edgecombe County at Rocky Mount on December 23, 1855, by G. W. Hammond, Esq. (S. January 12, 1856)

Colonel George W. POLK of Raleigh married Sarah HILLIARD, daughter of the late Isaac HILLIARD, Esq., formerly of Nash County, at her mother's residence in Franklin County, Tennessee, on December 24, 1840, by Right Reverend Bishop Polk. (T. P. January 9, 1841)

Jacob R. POPE of Halifax County married Martha Frances PARKER, daughter of Richard PARKER, in Edgecombe County on August 8, 1844, by Rev. John F. Speight. (T. P. August 10, 1844)

Dr. John T. POPE married Mary Jane HIGGS, daughter of Jacob HIGGS, on April 26, 1848, in Halifax County, by W. J. Hill, Esq. (T. P. May 6, 1848)

John W. POPE married Eliza TAYLOR, daughter of Allen TAYLOR, in Edgecombe County on January 31, 1840, by D. W. Maner, Esq. (T. P. February 8, 1840)

W. A. POPE of Rocky Mount married Mary L. DORTCH, daughter of the late William DORTCH, in Nash County on November 9, 1847. (T. P. November 13, 1847)

Benjamin PORTER married Eliza KING, daughter of William C. KING, deceased, on January 17, 1833, by L. R. Cherry, Esq. (N. C. F. P. January 22, 1833)

Joseph John PORTER married Susan WILKINS, daughter of Willis WILKINS, on February 16, 1837, by Rev. Thomas Dupree. (T. P. February 25, 1837)

Robert POTTER, Esq., formerly of Halifax but now of Oxford married Isabella A. TAYLOR of Granville County on April 9, 1828. (F. P. April 25, 1828)

Dr. John W. POTTS of Edgecombe County married Lucy Nelson BOYD in Mecklenburg County, Virginia, on November 4, 1834. (T. F. P. November 14, 1834)

Cullen POWELL of Nash County married Susan PEEBLES, daughter of George PEEBLES, on February 28, 1828, by Thomas Ousby, Esq. (F. P. March 7, 1828)

Jesse POWELL of Edgecombe County married Eliza PITTMAN, daughter of Robert J. PITTMAN, in Halifax County on December 21, 1837. (T. P. January 5, 1838)

Jesse H. POWELL, Esq., married Mrs. Mary Ann BATTLE in Edgecombe County on December 15, 1857, by William F. Lewis, Esq. (S. January 2, 1858)

Dr. Joseph J. W. POWELL married Martha B. WHITAKER, daughter of L. H. B. WHITAKER, Esq., at Whitaker's Chapel in Halifax County on January 7, 1845. (T. P. January 11, 1845)

Willie POWELL of Nash County married Mrs. Mary CARSTAPHEN of Halifax County on December 18, 1827, by Thomas Ousby, Esq. (F. P. December

28, 1827)

William H. POWELL married Ann Blount LAWRENCE, daughter of Dr. Josiah
LAWRENCE, in Tarboro on November 24, 1852, by Rev. T. R. Owen. (S.
November 27, 1852)

John H. PRICE married Martha WEEKS, daughter of W. A. J. WEEKS, in Edgecombe County on November 10, 1859, by W. F. Lewis, Esq. (S. November 19, 1859)

William PRIER, aged eighty, married Nancy ELMORE, aged about seventy-
five, in Halifax County on May 23, 1829. (F. P. June 5, 1829)

Thomas M. C. PRINCE of Chatham County married Lucilla CARR of Edgecombe
County "a few days ago." (F. P. September 11, 1829) (The marriage
bond was dated August 20, 1829.)

Thomas PUGH married Gennett CLOMAN of Martin County on January 19, 1836.
(T. P. January 30, 1836)

William W. PUGH of Louisiana married William Ann THOMPSON of Woodville
in Bertie County on August 16, 1831, by Thomas J. Pugh, Esq. (N.
C. F. P. August 30, 1831)

Micajah T. PURNELL, merchant of Halifax, married Eunice READ on December
26, 1826, by M. T. Ponton, Esq. (F. P. January 9, 1827)

John H. PURRINGTON, Jr., married Maria Ann MONK of Martin County at
Scotland Neck on November 10, 1828, by Samuel M. Nichols, Esq. (F.
P. November 14, 1828)

Elder John W. PURVIS married Mrs. Gracy SOREY at the Archibald Staton
residence in Martin County on December 9, 1858, by Elder John H.
Daniel. (S. December 18, 1858)

William L. QUALLS married Sarah W. EDMUNDSON, daughter of Wright EDMUND-
SON, Esq., on August 7, 1853, by Rev. Gibbons. (S. August 20,1853)

A. M. QUARLES married Josephine DANIEL at Mrs. Battle's Hotel in Wilson
on February 27, 1861, by Rev. Mr. Hudson. Both were from Halifax.
(S. March 9, 1861)

William H. RANDOLPH, formerly of Tarboro, married Mary L. MERRITT at the
Shadrach Merritt home in Halifax County on November 30, 1832, by
William Doggett, Esq. (N. F. C. P. December 11, 1832)

Thomas W. RASCOE married Penina HYMAN, daughter of Rev. William HYMAN,
in Edgecombe County "a few days since." (N. C. F. P. December 11,
1832) (The marriage bond was dated November 27, 1832.)

James G. RAYNER married E. B. SMITHWICK in Martin County on August 20,
1832, by D. Latham, Esq. (N. C. F. P. September 4, 1832)

Francis P. REDMOND, formerly of Tarboro, married Catharine MAYO, daughter of James MAYO, in Martin County on November 25, 1834. (T. F.
P. November 28, 1834)

James M. REDMOND married Catharine STILMAN in Tarboro on February 7,
1839, by Rev. William H. Wills. (T. P. February 9, 1839)

Henry REEVES of Northampton County married Mrs. Lucy BELL of Halifax
County on January 22, 1829. (F. P. February 6, 1829)

Archibald G. RHODES married Martha Louisa BATTLE, daughter of Elder A.
J. BATTLE, at Wilson on November 14, 1854, by Elder Thomas J. Latham. (S. November 26, 1854)

Danford RICHARDS married Mary R. HEARN, daughter of Michael HEARN, at
Tarboro on January 3, 1833. (N. C. F. P. January 8, 1833)

Richard R. RICHARDS of Northampton County married Margaret PEARCE, daughter of Nathaniel PEARCE of Halifax County, on January 17, 1828, by
Rev. Curtis Hooks. (F. P. January 25, 1828)

Richard RICHARDSON married Caroline LANDING, daughter of Elisha LANDING
of Edgecombe County, on December 24, 1858, by J. H. Hyman, Esq.
(S. January 8, 1859)

Dr. Addison E. RICKS of Tarboro married Emily TAFT in Pitt County on
January 26, 1859, by Elder C. B. Hassell. (S. January 29, 1859)

D. A. S. RICKS married Frances Ann HARRISON, daughter of Nathaniel
    HARRISON, in Nash County on October 8, 1845. (T. P. October 29,
    1845)

Isaac W. RICKS married Mary PENDER, daughter of James PENDER, in Edge-
    combe County on December 26, 1849. (T. P. January 26, 1850)

John C. RICKS of New Orleans married Mary Ann WARREN in Edgecombe County
    on February 29, 1857, by Rev. L. S. Burkhead. (S. March 6, 1857)

Dr. William B. RICKS married Helen BATTLE, daughter of B. D. BATTLE,
    Esq., in Nash County on July 6, 1853, by Rev. Mr. Tobey. (S. July
    9, 1853)

John E. RIDLEY of Granville County married Amelia M. TOOLE, daughter of
    Geraldus TOOLE, Esq., of Edgecombe County, on September 15, 1829,
    by Rev. Thomas P. Hunt. (F. P. October 12, 1829)

Dr. John G. RIVES married Lucy D. FOXHALL, daughter of the late William
    FOXHALL, near Tarboro on September 20, 1848, by Rev. J. B. Cheshire.
    (T. P. September 23, 1848)

Richard W. RIVES married Elmirah JOHNSON, daughter of the late Jordan
    JOHNSON, in Pitt County on March 24, 1852, by S. F. Johnson, Esq.
    (S. April 10, 1852)

William H. ROBARDS of Granville County married Ann Eliza TOOLE, daughter
    of Geraldus TOOLE, in Edgecombe County on October 11, 1827. (F. P.
    December 15, 1827)

William P. ROBERTS married Clara Ann ADAMS at Tarboro on December 5,
    1832, by L. R. Cherry, Esq. (N. C. F. P. December 11, 1832)

A. Sidney ROBERTSON of New Orleans married Mrs. Maria A. LLOYD, formerly
    of Tarboro, at the residence of Noah L. Thompson, Esq., near
    Tallahassee, Florida, on May 4, 1845. (T. P. June 4, 1845)

Elijah ROBERTSON married Sally BRITT in Edgecombe County on December 19,
    1839, by Spencer L. Hart, Esq. (T. P. December 21, 1839)

Joseph ROBERTSON married Deborah SMITHWICK, daughter of Joel SMITHWICK,
    Esq., in Martin County on February 14, 1832, by James B. Slade, Esq.
    (N. C. F. P. February 28, 1832)

Joshua ROBERTSON, Esq., married Elizabeth HAWKINS of Washington at
    Jameston in Martin County on June 5, 1838, by E. Brenas, Esq. (T.
    P. June 16, 1838)

Rev. William ROBINSON married Eliza Ann DAVIS, daughter of Col. James
    DAVIS, all being of Lenoir County, on August 28, 1845, by Rev. Henry
    Swinson. (T. P. September 10, 1845)

John P. ROGERS of Edgecombe County married E. M. J. ASKEW of Pitt County
    on January 12, 1854, by Elder Ichabod Moore. (S. January 21, 1854)

Joseph ROGERS married Hannah SHORT of Halifax County on April 8, 1827.
    (F. P. April 28, 1827)

Peleg ROGERS of Wake County married Mary A. EXUM in Edgecombe County on
    September 29, 1852, by L. R. Cherry, Esq. (S. October 9, 1852)

Nathan H. ROUNTREE married Emeliza BELL at Tarboro on December 11, 1832,
    by Benjamin Boykin, Esq. (N. C. F. P. December 18, 1832)

George ROUSE of Snow Hill married Mrs. Ann Eliza THIGPEN, daughter of
    Rev. John H. DANIEL, in Edgecombe County on December 18, 1855, by
    Elisha Cromwell, Esq. (S. December 22, 1855)

Robert H. ROWE of Richmond, Virginia, married Mary S. C. BOND, daughter
    of Lewis BOND, in the Taboro Church on December 23, 1852, by Rev.
    T. R. Owen. (S. January 1, 1853)

A. G. RUFFIN married Sarah J. STEVENS at Wilson on September 1, 1859, by
    Rev. N. A. H. Goddin. (S. September 17, 1859)

Etheldred RUFFIN of Wilson County married Elizabeth Lee KENNEDY, daugh-
    ter of Colonel William L. KENNEDY of Washington, on October 13,
    1858, by Rev. Mr. Geer. (S. October 23, 1858)

William H. RUFFIN married Martha J. RUFFIN at "The Edgecombe House" in
    Tarboro on December 18, 1856, by Thomas Norfleet, Esq. (S. Decem-

ber 20, 1856)

Linn Banks SANDERS, Esq., Senator from Johnston County, married Susan
Frances DRAKE, daughter of Senator Dr. John H. DRAKE of Nash County,
at Nashville on August 22, 1855, by Rev. Dr. Charles F. Deems. (S.
September 1, 1855)

John W. SAUNDERS married Leonora C. HARDY, daughter of Humphrey H. HARDY,
Esq., of Bertie County, on August 20, 1854, by Rev. Mr. Bronson.
(S. August 26, 1854)

Rev. Joseph H. SAUNDERS married Laura BAKER at the Dr. Simmons J. BAKER
home in Martin County on April 25, 1833. (N. C. F. P. May 15, 1833)

Frederick SAVAGE married Martha DOWNING, daughter of James DOWNING, in
Edgecombe County on May 13, 1857, by Kenneth Thigpen, Esq. (S.
June 6, 1857)

James SAVAGE married Pheribee LAWRENCE, daughter of the late Rev. Joshua
LAWRENCE of Edgecombe County, on July 18, 1844. (T. P. August 3,
1844)

James D. SAVAGE married Jane F. JOHNSON, daughter of the late Aaron
JOHNSON, in Edgecombe County on October 6, 1853, by Jordan Thigpen,
Esq. (S. October 15, 1853)

James H. SAVAGE married Catharine BARFIELD on August 14, 1834, by William
E. Bellamy, Esq. (T. F. P. September 5, 1834)

Joseph John SAVAGE married Martha JIGGETTS at Roseneath in Halifax County on November 21, 1839, by L. B. K. Dicken, Esq. (T. P. November
30, 1839) He was of Edgecombe County.

Lemuel SAVAGE married Tabitha LONG, daughter of William R. LONG, on
January 10, 1833, by J. J. Pippen, Esq. (N. C. F. P. January 15,
1833)

Richard A. SAVAGE of Tarboro married James Murphy KILLEBREW, daughter of
George Washington KILLEBREW, on May 18, 1848, by William H. Hines,
Esq. (T. P. May 20, 1848)

Richard A. SAVAGE married Martha LITTLE, daughter of James LITTLE of
Edgecombe County, on November 10, 1853. (S. November 12, 1853) In
the issue of November 19, 1853, the Editor stated that he has been
"misinformed . . . no such occurrence having taken place."

Richard A. SAVAGE married Mrs. S. L. MABREY, widow of Almorine MABREY
and daughter of Peter E. KNIGHT, in Edgecombe County on March 6,
1860. (S. March 10, 1860)

Caleb SAVIDGE married Louisa SMITH of Halifax County on December 4,
1827, by S. M. Nickels, Esq. He was from Virginia. (F. P. December 8, 1827)

Isaac SAWYER married Winifred GRIFFIN of Edgecombe County on May 13,
1830, by Benjamin Wilkinson, Esq. (F. P. May 28, 1830)

George W. SCAY of Petersburg married Mrs. Julia WILKINSON in Tarboro on
November 16, 1859, by Rev. T. R. Owen. (S. November 19, 1859)

Major Lunsford W. SCOTT married Mary Ann SIMMONS, youngest daughter of
James SIMMONS, Sr., on February 7, 1828. (F. P. February 15, 1828)

Dr. Theophilus H. SCOTT of Raleigh married Mary E. BATTLE, daughter of
the late Lawrence BATTLE of Nashville on May 8, 1845. (T. P. May
24, 1845)

Benjamin SCREWS married Mourning DRAKE, daughter of the late Captain
James DRAKE, in Nash County on August 18, 1836. (T. P. September
10, 1836)

Charles E. SEARS of Nashville married Delphia DRAUGHN, daughter of the
late William DRAUGHN, in Edgecombe County on February 20, 1856, by
Rev. Jeremiah Johnson. (S. March 8, 1856)

Jacob SESSOMS of Halifax County married Emma MORRISS of Martin County
on August 8, 1830, by William S. Rayner, Esq. (F. P. August 20,
1830)

Blake SESSOMS married Lucinda BASS in Halifax County on April 17, 1828, by John Young, Esq. (F. P. May 16, 1828)

Nathan H. SESSUMS married Martha HARRIS of Edgecombe County on June 12, 1857, by Thomas Norfleet, Esq. (S. June 13, 1857)

Solomon D. SESSUMS of Nash County married Lucy SILLS, daughter of the late David SILLS, in Franklin County on December 13, 1842, by Rev. Mr. Hudgins. (T. P. December 17, 1842)

Wilson SESSUMS married Mary FOXHALL, daughter of Robert FOXHALL, on August 26, 1834, by William Savage, Esq. (T. F. P. September 5, 1834)

Dr. William E. J. SHALLINGTON married Sarah BARNES, daughter of the late Jesse BARNES, on November 30, 1843, by John G. Williams, Esq. (T. P. December 16, 1843)

Colonel Benjamin SHARP married Mary Ann Susan EDWARDS on November 22, 1838, by Jesse C. Knight, Esq. (T. P. December 1, 1838)

Van Buren SHARP married Sally COBB, daughter of Edward COBB of Edgecombe County on December 24, 1857. (S. January 2, 1858)

John SHARPE married Margaret TAYLOR, daughter of Stephen TAYLOR, on January 6, 1829, by David Williams, Esq. (F. P. January 16, 1829)

John P. SHARPE married Nancy BYNUM, daughter of Turner BYNUM, Esq., on June 4, 1844, in Edgecombe County. (T. P. June 8, 1844)

Burwell SHELTON married Sally BOOTH of Edgecombe County on July 12, 1829, by Elijah Price, Esq. (F. P. July 31, 1829)

Captain William R. SHERROD married Mary TAYLOR in Martin County on November 18, 1830, by William Rayner, Esq. (N. C. F. P. November 23, 1830)

William W. SHERROD married Margaret E. HYMAN, daughter of the late Kenneth HYMAN, at Hickory Fork on November 18, 1858, by Rev. H. H. Gibbons. (S. November 20, 1858)

Thomas SHIELDS, Jr., of Halifax married Sarah WHITING on June 27, 1827, by S. M. Nickels, Esq. (F. P. July 7, 1827)

Robert SHORT married Catharine ROGERS in Halifax County on April 18, 1827. (F. P. April 28, 1827)

Garret SHURLEY married Temperance AMASON of Edgecombe County on February 15, 1827. (F. P. February 24, 1827)

Geraldus SHURLEY married Susan BRIDGERS at the Colonel Joab P. Pitt residence on January 19, 1841, by John F. Hughes, Esq. (T. P. January 23, 1841)

Henry A. SHURLEY married Louisa HORNE, daughter of the late Caswell HORNE, in Tarboro on June 3, 1858, by Henry T. Clark, Esq. (S. June 5, 1858)

Bazel SIKES married Mary Ann EDWARDS on September 26, 1830, by Howell Hearn, Esq. (N. C. F. P. October 5, 1830)

Solomon SILLS married Lucinda WILLFORD in Leon County, Florida, on March 28, 1844. (T. P. April 20, 1844)

James SIMMONS, Sheriff of Halifax County, married Martha A. COOK at the George W. Gary home in Halifax County, on November 2, 1830, by Thomas Ousby, Esq. (N. C. F. P. November 9, 1830)

Jos. L. SIMMONS, Post Master of Halifax, married Lydia M. READ at the home of Mrs. Mary R. Read on November 11, 1828, by Henry Garrett, Esq. (F. P. November 21, 1828)

Andrew J. SIMMS of Edgecombe County married Ellen M. BARHAM, youngest daughter of Dr. C. D. BARHAM of Southampton County, at Boykins Depot, Virginia, on May 11, 1859, by Rev. J. M. Arnold. (S. June 4, 1859)

Gen. G. E. B. SINGLETARY of Nashville married Cora MANLY, daughter of Governor Charles MANLY, at Raleigh on October 28, 1850, by Rev. Albert Smedes. (T. P. November 2, 1850)

Robert A. SIZER married Caroline BELL, daughter of the late Lorenzo D. BELL, at Tarboro on September 23, 1857, by Rev. L. S. Burkhead.

(S. September 26, 1857)

Andrew Jackson SKINNER of Tennessee married Arcene FLEMING, daughter of Willis L. FLEMING, in Edgecombe County on April 1, 1841, by Benjamin Sharpe, Esq. (T. P. April 3, 1841)

John SKINNER married Emily WEAVER in Edgecombe County on August 22, 1860, by E. D. Macnair, Esq. (S. September 1, 1860)

Uriah W. SKINNER married Priscilla LEWIS in Halifax County on April 26, 1829, by William Doggett, Esq. (F. P. May 29, 1829)

William SKINNER married Rebecca GILL in Edgecombe County on February 19, 1829, by Joab P. Pitt, Esq. (F. P. February 20, 1829)

Thomas SLADE of Martin County married Eliza R. GORDON, daughter of James GORDON, Esq., of Norfolk, in Warren County on October 28, 1830, by M. T. Hawkins, Esq. (N. C. F. P. November 9, 1830)

William SLADE married Penelope WILLIAMS, daughter of the late Richard WILLIAMS, in Martin County on October 13, 1829, by James L. G. Baker, Esq. (F. P. October 23, 1829)

Dr. Charles SMALLWOOD married Harriet J. CLARK at Woodville in Bertie County on March 20, 1850, by Rev. J. B. Cheshire. (T. P. April 6, 1850)

Orestes R. SMALLWOOD married Mrs. Rebecca EURE at the Laertes Morgan, Esq., residence in Halifax County on November 18, 1830. (N. C. F. P. December 7, 1830)

Arthur SMITH of New Hanover County married Frances B. SUGG, daughter of Dr. P. SUGG, in Edgecombe County on December 5, 1854, by Rev. Mr. Brent. (S. December 9, 1854)

George A. SMITH of Scotland Neck married Rozella WIGGINS in Nash County on June 10, 1856, by Rev. Joseph Blount Cheshire. (S. June 14, 1856)

Marshall SMITH of Illinois married Temperance SORREL, daughter of James SORREL "of this county," on April 1, 1832, at Sparta, Georgia. (N. C. F. P. April 17, 1832)

Peter SMITH married Rebecca N. HILL of Halifax County on December 22, 1853, by Rev. Joseph B. Cheshire. (S. January 8, 1853)

William SMITH married Phenetta THIGPEN, daughter of Lemuel THIGPEN of Edgecombe County, on January 27, 1835, by William C. Leigh, Esq. (T. P. February 7, 1835)

Captain William B. SMITH, recently Editor of The Tarboro' Mercury, married Pennie CHURCHILL of Goldsboro at her mother's home on April 3, 1862, by Rev. Mr. Hunter. (S. April 12, 1862)

William R. SMITH, Jr., of Scotland Neck, married Susan EVANS, daughter of Peter EVANS of Edgecombe County, on January 22, 1828. (F. P. January 25, 1828)

Eli SOREY of Halifax County married Nancy HARRIS, daughter of Eli HARRIS, in Edgecombe County on December 20, 1838. (T. P. January 5, 1839)

Robert SOREY married Anne WIGGINS in Edgecombe County on June 18, 1849, by Elder S. I. Chandler. (T. P. June 30, 1849)

Robert SOREY of Edgecombe County married Gracy COOPER at Hamilton on November 23, 1854, by Jos. Waldo, Esq. (S. December 2, 1854)

Stephen W. SOUTHALL of Smithfield, Virginia, married Martha F. MALLORY, formerly of Norfolk, at Mrs. M. E. Lewis's home near Tarboro on January 9, 1861, by Rev. Joseph Blount Cheshire. (S. January 19, 1861)

Dr. Samuel L. SOUTHERLAND of Warrenton married Mary Ann Evans, daughter of Peter EVANS of Edgecombe County, on January 12, 1830, by Rev. T. Dupree. (F. P. January 15, 1830)

Thomas SOUTHERLAND of Edgecombe County married Mrs. Harriet COKELY at Plymouth on February 1, 1827. (F. P. February 10, 1827)

General Jesse SPEIGHT of Greene County married Louisa MAY, daughter of the late Benjamin MAY, Esq., at the residence of Mrs. Penelope May of Pitt County on May 3, 1827. (F. P. May 12, 1827)

Rev. John F. SPEIGHT married Emma LEWIS, daughter of the late Exum LEWIS, on September 29, 1840, by Rev. William Bellamy. (T. P. October 10, 1840)

James M. SPRAGGINS married Martha Ann WILLIAMS, daughter of Benjamin WILLIAMS, at Tarboro on January 31, 1856, by Rev. T. R. Owen. (S. February 2, 1856)

Benjamin J. SPRUILL of Scotland Neck married Margaret ROSS near Tarboro on December 4, 1830, by Rev. Philip Wiley. (N. C. F. P. December 21, 1830)

Thelphilus STALLINGS from Edgecombe County married Martha BRAME, daughter of Anderson F. BRAME, Esq., of Warren County on September 8, 1852, by Rev. Robert O. Burton. (S. September 25, 1852)

John M. STANDIN of Edenton married Rosa PELTIER at Halifax on January 25, 1829, by John T. Clanton, Esq. (F. P. February 6, 1829)

Jesse STANSELL married Harriet HOPKINS, daughter of Colonel Daniel HOPKINS, on January 9, 1834, by William C. Leigh, Esq. (T. F. P. January 24, 1834)

Benjamin F. STANTON of Edgecombe County married Rebecca STANTON, daughter of the late Frederick STANTON of Northampton County, on November 7, 1826. (F. P. November 21, 1826)

Baker STATON married Jeanette YOUNG in Edgecombe County on December 20, 1827. (F. P. January 18, 1828)

Bythal STATON, Jr., married Elizabeth CLOMAN on March 1, 1827, in Edgecombe County, by Rev. William Hyman. (F. P. March 10, 1827)

H. La Fayette STATON married Margaret BATTS, daughter of Benjamin BATTS, Esq., on January 12, 1848. (T. P. January 15, 1848)

James Burt STATON married Nancy Jane PIPPEN, daughter of the late Joseph John PIPPEN, in Edgecombe County on February 14, 1854, by Rev. J. H. Daniel. (S. February 18, 1854)

Leweling STATON married Mrs. Susan HOPKINS in Edgecombe County on November 7, 1837. (T. S. November 17, 1837. T. P. November 25, 1837)

Dr. Robert STATON married Barbara HADLEY in Tarboro on October 13, 1847. (T. P. October 23, 1847)

Simmons B. STATON married Drucilla L. KNIGHT, daughter of James KNIGHT, on July 2, 1835, by Joshua Pender, Esq. (T. P. July 11, 1835)

William John STATON married Gatsey DANIEL, daughter of Rev. John H. DANIEL, in Edgecombe County on February 13, 1851, by Elisha Cromwell, Esq. (T. P. February 22, 1851)

William John STATON married Huldah Virginia STANTON, daughter of the late W. M. STANTON, near Stantonsburg on March 18, 1858, by Joshua Barnes, Esq. (S. March 27, 1858)

William N. STEPTOE of Scotland Neck married Euginia M. DANIEL of Sussex, Virginia, at the James S. Battle residence near Tarboro on December 1, 1857, by Rev. J. B. Cheshire. (S. December 9, 1857)

Joseph C. STEWART married Mrs. Jeanette HURSEY in Tarboro on January 14, 1850, by Robert Norfleet, Esq. (T. P. January 19, 1850)

William STEWART married Mary Ann TARTT in Edgecombe County on October 18, 1831, by Rev. Josiah R. Horn. (N. C. F. P. October 25, 1831)

David STRICKLAND married Nancy HOWELL of Edgecombe County on January 22, 1829. (F. P. February 6, 1829)

John STUBBS of Pitt County married Jane Elizabeth LEGGETT, daughter of the late Levin LEGGETT, in Edgecombe County on March 16, 1856, by Rev. Mr. Cox. (S. March 29, 1856)

George C. SUGG married Mrs. Nancy SHARPE, daughter of Turner BYNUM, Esq., in Edgecombe County on June 10, 1851, by Rev. Blount Cooper. (T. P. June 21, 1851)

Dr. Pheasanton S. SUGG married Lucinda PENDER, daughter of Solomon PENDER at Tarboro on January 9, 1827, by Henry Bryan, J. P. (F. P. January

16, 1827)

William C. R. SUMMERRELL of Tarboro married Mary JOHNSTON, daughter of the late James JOHNSTON, in Pitt County on February 19, 1835. (T. P. February 28, 1835)

William SUTTON, Esq., married Martha HEARN, daughter of Michael HEARN, at Tarboro on December 1, 1829, by Benjamin Boykin, Esq. He was from Williamston. (F. P. December 4, 1829)

William TAFT married Louisa Van NOORDEN in Pitt County on February 15, 1844, by Benjamin F. Eborn, Esq. (T. P. February 24, 1844)

William TANNAHILL, merchant of Washington, married Susan M. MACNAIR, eldest daughter of E. D. MACNAIR, Esq., at Hope Lodge near Tarboro on January 4, 1832, by Rev. Mr. Goodman. (N. C. F. P. January 10, 1832)

James TANNER married Susan BILBREY of Edgecombe County on June 7, 1860, by E. D. Macnair, Esq. (S. June 16, 1860)

John TATE of Bertie County married Rebecca PITTS of Nash County on June 21, 1827, by Joseph Arrington, Esq. (F. P. July 21, 1827)

Benjamin L. TAYLOR married Lydia E. SHERROD in Martin County on September 26, 1833, by J. L. G. Baker, Esq. (T. F. P. October 4, 1833)

John F. TAYLOR married Penelope Caroline MANER, daughter of Thomas L. MANER, Esq., in Edgecombe County on April 12, 1855, by C. C. Bonner, Esq. (S. April 21, 1855)

Johnson TAYLOR married Lucy MEDFORD on September 22, 1831, by Theophilus Cherry, Esq. (N. C. F. P. October 11, 1831)

Kindred TAYLOR of Nash County married Lucy CLARK, daughter of William CLARK of Edgecombe County, on December 12, 1833, by Richard Harrison, Esq. (T. F. P. December 20, 1833)

McGilbray TAYLOR of Martin County married Sally BEST, daughter of William BEST, in Edgecombe County on May 22, 1860, by F. H. Jenkins, Esq. (S. May 26, 1860)

Nelson TAYLOR of Martin County married Charlotte JONES at Scotland Neck on March 3, 1830, by J. L. G. Baker, Esq. (F. P. March 12, 1830)

Partick TAYLOR married Mary PROCTOR, daughter of Absalom PROCTOR, Esq., in Edgecombe County on May 18, 1848, by B. D. Battle, Esq. (T. P. June 3, 1848)

Thomas TAYLOR married Elizabeth EDWARDS on December 21, 1826, by David Williams, Esq. (F. P. December 26, 1826)

Thomas TAYLOR of Haywood County, Tennessee, married Jane MOORING, youngest daughter of John MOORING of Edgecombe County, on November 14, 1844, by Joseph John Pippen, Esq. (T. P. November 16, 1844)

Thomas TAYLOR married Priscilla BRADY at Falkland on November 30, 1852, by H. C. Jordan, Esq. (S. December 4, 1852)

William TAYLOR married Elizabeth TAYLOR on October 4, 1836, by J. J. Pippen, Esq. (T. P. October 8, 1836)

Green TEAT married Sally Ann MOORE in Edgecombe County on May 10, 1846, by W. D. Bryan, Esq. (T. P. May 20, 1846)

O. W. TELFAIR of Washington married Pauline D. MACNAIR, daughter of the late Edward D. MACNAIR, in the Tarboro Episcopal Church on March 23, 1853, by Rev. J. B. Cheshire. (S. March 26, 1853)

Nathaniel M. TERRELL, late of Raleigh, married Alicia A. REDMOND of Tarboro on December 26, 1832, by Rev. John A. Miller. (N. C. F. P. January 1, 1833)

Nathaniel M. TERRELL of Tarboro married Mrs. Eliza A. ELLIS at Washington on September 22, 1836, by Rev. George N. Gregory. (T. P. October 1, 1836)

James THIGPEN married Gatsey A. PITT, daughter of Colonel Joab P. PITT on August 12, 1851, by Elisha Cromwell, Esq. (T. P. August 16, 1851)

James THIGPEN, Sr., married Patsey BROWN on July 24, 1834, by William C. Leigh, Esq. (T. F. P. August 8, 1834)

Kenneth THIGPEN married Ann LANE, daughter of Lamon LANE of Nash County, in Edgecombe County on July 11, 1849, by Joab P. Pitt, Esq. (T. P. July 14, 1849)

Littleberry THIGPEN married Ann LITTLE, daughter of the late Jesse LITTLE on August 2, 1827. (F. P. August 11, 1827)

Rufus C. THIGPEN, Esq., married Ann E. T. DANIEL, daughter of the Rev. John H. DANIEL, on March 20, 1851, by the Rev. William Hyman. (T. P. March 29, 1851)

Jacob THOMAS married Amanda R. BRIDGERS of Edgecombe County at the Mark H. Bennett residence on July 17, 1830, by John Mercer, Esq. (F. P. July 30, 1830)

N. H. THOMAS married Laney HILLMAN near Enfield on January 17, 1828, by J. H. Simmons, Esq. (F. P. January 25, 1828)

Wade R. THOMAS married Millisent HORN, daughter of Jacob HORN of Edgecombe County on January 10, 1827. (F. P. June 16, 1827)

Dr. William George THOMAS married Mary Sumner CLARK, daughter of Major James W. CLARK, at Tarboro on November 1, 1843, by Rev. Jos. B. Cheshire. (T. P. November 4, 1843)

William H. THOMAS of Edgecombe County married Dianna HORN of Virginia at Rocky Mount on December 10, 1857, by Rev. R. D. Hart. (S. January 2, 1858)

Henry THOMPSON of Edgecombe County married Louisa JOYNER, daughter of the late Benjamin JOYNER of Pitt County, in Grimmersburg on March 30, 1852, by Rev. Peter E. Hines. (S. April 17, 1852)

Lewis THOMPSON, Esq., married Margaret W. CLARK, daughter of William M. CLARK, Esq., in Bertie County on January 22, 1833, by Rev. William Norwood. (N. C. F. P. January 29, 1833)

Noah THOMPSON of Bertie County married Eliza W. COTTEN, daughter of Spencer D. COTTEN, at Tarboro on February 15, 1832, by Rev. William Norwood. (N. C. F. P. February 21, 1832)

Noel THOMPSON married Mrs. Harriet Eliza WRIGHT on October 18, 1838, by Rev. J. Singletary. (T. P. October 20, 1838)

Thomas B. THOMPSON married Temperance WILLIAMS, daughter of Lewis WILLIAMS, Esq., on August 1, 1832, in Martin County. (N. C. F. P. August 14, 1832)

Z. W. THOMPSON of Wayne County married Annie Sharpe BARNES, daughter of Elias BARNES, Esq., of "Dunlora" in Edgecombe County on February 12, 1850. (T. P. February 15, 1850)

James T. THORNE married Milly BATTS, youngest daughter of the late John BATTS, Sr., in Wilson County at the home of David W. BATTS, on April 3, 1859, by William W. Batts, Esq. (S. April 16, 1859)

William D. THORNE married Sarah ROBBINS in Edgecombe County on October 15, 1846, by Larry Dew, Esq. (T. P. October 21, 1846)

John B. TILLERY married Martha J. DUNN, daughter of Colonel B. DUNN, in Halifax County on February 13, 1851, by Thomas Ousby, Esq. (T. P. March 1, 1851)

William H. TILLORY of Halifax County married Mary A. BATTLE, niece of the late Colonel L. D. WILSON, in Edgecombe County on February 13, 1849, by the Rev. Stephen I. Chandler. (T. P. February 17, 1849)

William D. TISDEL married Adelia WHITFIELD in Nash County at Nashville on August 21, 1832. (N. C. F. P. August 28, 1832)

James TOMLINSON married Eliza A. NANCE of Johnston County on March 25, 1824. (F. P. April 2, 1824)

Thomas TOMLINSON married Elizabeth WILKINSON in Wilson on May 25, 1856, by Rev. Hope Bain. (S. June 7, 1856)

Henry TOOLE of Tarborough married Margaret TELFAIR, daughter of Hugh TELFAIR, at the home of John Singletary, Esq., in Pitt County on

October 20, 1829, by the Rev. Mr. Goodman. (F. P. November 6, 1829)

Jonathan TOOTLE married _____ KERNER on January 29, 1829, by John Young, Esq. (F. P. February 6, 1829)

William C. TREVATHAN married Sarah Jane PRICE in Edgecombe County on May 11, 1854, by C. C. Bonner, Esq. (S. May 27, 1854)

Alexander D. TUMBRO, Senior Editor of The Wilson Ledger, married Elizabeth S. KNIGHT, daughter of F. H. KNIGHT, in Edgecombe County on September 1, 1859, by Elder John H. Daniel. (S. September 3, 1859)

Samuel TUNE married Eliza LANHAM in Halifax County on March 23, 1827. (F. P. March 31, 1827)

Bird B. TUNNEL of Nash County married Mrs. Drucilla BARKER of Edgecombe County at Rocky Mount on June 22, 1854, by C. C. Bonner, Esq. (S. July 1, 1854)

Alfred TURNER married Taxsey Ann Sena JOINER of Edgecombe County "not long since." (T. P. April 13, 1844) (Their marriage bond was dated March 23, 1844.)

Jacob TURNER married Patsey LEE "not long since" in Edgecombe County. (T. P. April 13, 1844)

John E. TURNER of Enfield married Penelope KING of Edgecombe County on December 1, 1852, by Rev. John F. Speight. (S. December 4, 1852)

John UPTON married Ann DEAVERAUX, daughter of John DEAVREAUX, on December 9, 1830, by F. Lowe, Esq. (N. C. F. P. December 21, 1830)

Gilbert VALENTINE of Nash County married Sally JENKINS of Edgecombe County "some time past." (F. P. November 7, 1828)

Rev. Maurice H. VAUPIN, Chaplain of the 3rd N. C. Regiment, C. S. A., married Camilla H. COOK, daughter of the late Colonel William G. COOK of Baltimore, at Calvary Church in Tarboro on May 13, 1862, by Rev. Joseph W. Murphy, Chaplain of the 43rd N. C. Regiment, C. S. A. (S. May 17, 1862)

M. L. VENABLE married V. L. PEEBLES in Scotland Neck on June 9, 1863, by Rev. J. Blount Cheshire. (S. June 20, 1863)

James VICK married Polly SOREY at Tarboro on April 14, 1842, by Henry Austin, Esq. (T. P. April 23, 1842)

Charles L. VINES married Martha Ann WILLIAMS, daughter of William Williams, Esq., in Pitt County on July 7, 1846, by Rev. Thomas Dupree. (T. P. July 15, 1846)

William WADFORD of Franklin County married Martha C. P. NOBLES, daughter of the Rev. Willis NOBLES, in Pitt County on May 20, 1857, by W. A. Manning, Esq. (S. June 6, 1857)

Major Jordan WALKER of Washington County married Martha Ann NICHOLSON, daughter of John NICHOLSON, Esq., of Halifax County on December 6, 1827. (F. P. December 15, 1827)

Dr. J. R. WALKER of Virginia married Martha A. HART, eldest daughter of Spencer L. HART, on December 9, 1851, by Richard Harrison, Esq. (T. P. December 13, 1851)

James W. WALLER married Margaret L. LAWRENCE in Edgecombe County on May 27, 1859, by Henry T. Clark, Esq. (S. May 28, 1859)

John WALSTON married Margaret CHERRY, daughter of Eason CHERRY, in Edgecombe County on March 11, 1838, by J. J. Pitt, Esq. (T. P. March 17, 1838)

Captain Wiley WALSTON married Mary COBB, daughter of Eaton COBB, on October 26, 1854, by Jesse Harrell, Esq. (S. October 28, 1854)

Armistead M. WARD of Smith County, Tennessee, married Mary P. PENDER, first daughter of J. J. B. PENDER, Esq., at Tarboro on May 27, 1857, by Rev. Thomas R. Owen. (S. May 30, 1857)

Dr. D. G. W. WARD of Greene County married E. A. MOYE, only daughter of Colonel Macon MOYE, in Wilson County on June 7, 1859, by Rev. George W. Keene. (S. June 11, 1859)

Harmon WARD married Catharine E. PIPPEN, daughter of J. J. PIPPEN, on January 9, 1834, by Rev. William Hyman. (T. F. P. January 17,1834)

John F. WARD married Lucy TYLER in Tarboro on August 26, 1858, by Rev. T. R. Owen. (S. September 11, 1858)

Luke WARD of Pitt County married Mahala LEGGETT, daughter of Levin LEGGETT of Edgecombe County, on June 17, 1834, by Rev. William Hyman. (T. F. P. June 20, 1834)

Timothy W. WARD of Hamilton married Mary PENDER, daughter of the late Colonel Joshua PENDER, in Tarboro on March 22, 1859, by Rev. R. S. Moran. (S. March 26, 1859)

William W. WARD married Lucy BRYAN, daughter of John BRYAN, in Martin County on January 10, 1832, by William S. Rayner, Esq. (N. C. F. P. January 17, 1832)

Willie WARD of Greene County married Louisa LEGGETT, daughter of Levin LEGGETT of Edgecombe County, on March 8, 1837, by Rev. William Hyman. (T. P. March 18, 1837)

Eli WARREN married Margaret A. LITTLE, daughter of the late John LITTLE, in Edgecombe County on January 27, 1858, by David Cobb, Esq. (S. February 6, 1858)

Richard WARREN of Pitt County married Elizabeth THIGPEN, daughter of Lemuel THIGPEN, in Edgecombe County on October 8, 1835, by William C. Leigh, Esq. (T. P. October 24, 1835)

James WATKINS married Loes CUTCHINS on August 29, 1832, by Lunsford R. Cherry, Esq. (N. C. F. P. September 4, 1832)

Dr. Barron C. WATSON of Wilson married Julia Whitman WILLIS, daughter of William WILLIS, Esq., at Portland, Maine, on February 26, 1852, by Right Reverend Bishop Southgate, assisted by the Rev. Dr. Nichols. (S. March 6, 1852)

Dr. John T. WATSON married Sallie A. ARRINGTON, only daughter of Dr. John ARRINGTON, on June 10, 1847, at the residence of the Hon. A. H. Arrington near Hilliardston, by the Rev. William H. Wills. (T. P. June 19, 1847)

Joshua WATSON, merchant and Post Master of Palmyra, married Alice B. JOYNER, daughter of Blount JOYNER, Esq., of Halifax County, on September 19, 1826. (T. P. September 26, 1826)

Thomas WATSON of Windsor married Agnes BRADDY, daughter of Mr. Isaac B. BRADDY, at Hamilton on February 4, 1853, by Elder Spivey. (S. February 19, 1853)

Thomas W. WATTS, Esq., of Martin County married Susan A. WILCOX, daughter of Major Littleberry WILCOX of Halifax County, on September 6, 1831, by Rev. Joseph H. Saunders. (N. C. F. P. September 20, 1831)

William WATTS, aged seventy-three, married Ann ROBERTSON, aged about forty, in Williamston on March 30, 1854, by Rev. Mr. Duvall. (S. April 15, 1854)

Brigadier-General John WAYNES of Duplin County married Mary MERRIT of Sampson County on April 15, 1828, "after a tedious courtship of 29 minutes and 7 seconds." (F. P. May 9, 1828)

Willis WEATHERSBEE of Halifax County married Della BELLAMY, daughter of the late William E. BELLAMY, in Edgecombe County on November 11, 1856, by Kenneth Thigpen, Esq. (S. November 29, 1856)

Charles N. WEBB married Frances C. E. THURSTON at Halifax on December 4, 1833. (T. F. P. December 13, 1833)

James WEDDELL married Margaret WARD, daughter of the late Dr. John F. WARD, at Tarboro on February 26, 1835, by Rev. J. Singletary. (T. P. February 28, 1835)

Matthew WEDDELL of New York City married Maria T. CLARK, daughter of the late James W. CLARK, in Calvary Church at Tarboro on October 20, 1852, by the Rev. J. B. Cheshire. (S. October 23, 1852)

Henry WEST married Rebecca ROBERTSON of Edgecombe County on January 28, 1830, by Henry Austin, Esq. (F. P. February 5, 1830)

Wade WEST married Elizabeth H. GEE in Halifax County on September 17, 1829, by Jesse N. Faulcon, Esq. (F. P. October 2, 1829)

Henry WHEATLEY married Nancy HYMAN, daughter of John P. HYMAN, Esq., on March 13, 1831. (N. C. F. P. March 29, 1831)

Isham WHEELER married Emilia SUMMERLIN for a second time at the home of James Pitt, Sr., on January 15, 1828, by Ralph Pitt, Esq. (F. P. January 18, 1828) (The first marriage apparently took place on or after September 21, 1826, according to the marriage bond.)

James C. WHITAKER married Delphia LYON, daughter of Thomas LYON, at Fishing Creek on October 9, 1827. (F. P. October 13, 1827)

John H. WHITAKER, Esq., married Mary E. ANTHONY, daughter of Colonel Whitmill J. ANTHONY, in Halifax County on June 17, 1851, by Rev. J. B. Cheshire. (T. P. June 21, 1851)

Burton WHITE of Halifax County married Isabel LEGGETT, daughter of Levin LEGGETT of Edgecombe County, on January 9, 1849, by William Cherry, Esq. (T. P. January 20, 1849)

Jarrett WHITE married Mary Ann Pitt, daughter of James PITT, in Edgecombe County on February 27, 1855, by William F. Lewis, Esq. (S. January 20, 1855)

John W. WHITE married Martha HUNTER, daughter of Weldon S. HUNTER, at Tarboro on March 1, 1860, by Rev. T. R. Owen. (S. March 3, 1860)

Henry A. WHITEHEAD married Lucy JOYNER on December 8, 1836, by Benjamin Batts, Esq. (T. P. December 17, 1836)

Jacob H. WHITEHEAD married Mary E. WHITE in Halifax County at the Robert White home on December 16, 1845, by John Young, Esq. (T. P. January 7, 1846)

Thomas WHITEHEAD married Mary MANGUM of Halifax County in Edgecombe County "a short time since" by James Biggs, Esq. (N. C. F. P. August 23, 1831) (The marriage bond was dated July 30, 1831.)

W. A. J. WHITEHEAD married Caroline PETWAY, daughter of William D. PET-WAY, on January 15, 1850, in Edgecombe County by John S. Dancy, Esq. (T. P. January 19, 1850)

James WHITEHURST married Nancy STATON, daughter of Winfield D. STATON, Esq., on February 17, 1842, by William S. Baker, Esq. (T. P. February 19, 1842)

George W. WHITFIELD married Catharine W. HART "formerly of Edgecombe County" in Johnston County on February 7, 1828, by Pharaoh Richerson, Esq. (F. P. February 29, 1828)

George W. WHITFIELD of Alabama married Mory Louisa WIMBERLEY, daughter of Robert D. WIMBERLEY, on December 13, 1849, by John S. Dancy, Esq. (T. P. December 15, 1849)

Rev. J. G. WHITFIELD of Norfolk married Martha C. COFIELD at "The Oaks" in Edgecombe County on January 29, 1856, by Rev. G. A. T. Whitaker. (S. February 16, 1856)

P. Lawson WHITFIELD of Nash County married Mary BURGESS from Halifax County at Rocky Mount on July 20, 1852, by D. Ferguson, Esq. (S. July 24, 1852)

Alexander S. WHITLEY married Emily E. PHILPOTT of Martin County on Janu-arey 14, 1836, by Rev. William Hyman. (T. P. January 30, 1836)

John WHITLEY of Warren County married Nancy DANIEL, daughter of the Rev. John H. DANIEL, in Edgecombe County on November 11, 1851, by Elisha Cromwell, Esq. (T. P. November 15, 1851)

Samuel S. WHITLEY married Elizabeth MOORING at the home of Mrs. Gracie Mooring in Pitt County on November 3, 1831. (N. C. F. P. November 8, 1831)

Thomas R. WIGGINS, Esq., married Mary ARRINGTON in Nash County on April 11, 1833. (N. C. F. P. April 27, 1833)

Amos G. WILKINS of Crockett, Texas, and formerly of Edgecombe County, married Louisa HEFLEY from northern Alabama on April 4, 1847. (T. P. July 17, 1847)

Captain Willis WILLCOX married Mrs. Mary MITCHELL in Halifax County on May 26, 1829, by Jesse Faulcon, Esq. (F. P. June 12, 1829)

Abner WILKINSON married Nancy BYNUM, daughter of Joseph BYNUM, on August 16, 1835, by Benjamin Moore, Esq. (T. P. August 29, 1835)

Benoni M. WILKINSON of Martin County married Sarah Caroline JONES, daughter of Frederick JONES, deceased, on February 18, 1840, by Joshua Pender, Esq. (T. P. February 29, 1840)

Israel B. WILKINSON married Elizabeth BELL, daughter of the late Marmaduke BELL of Edgecombe County, at Greenville on November 1, 1831, by Rev. William Clark. (N. C. F. P. November 8, 1831)

James WILKINSON married Julia A. E. SNEADER at Petersburg on June 26, 1844, by the Rev. Mr. Scott. (T. P. July 6, 1844)

William L. WILKINSON of Alabama married Melinda WILKINSON in Edgecombe County on January 9, 1837, by Daniel Hopkins, Esq. (T. P. January 21, 1837)

Dr. B. Brown WILLIAMS of Philadelphia but formerly of Pitt County married at Milford Delaware, on July 27, 1857, Mollie E. ANDERSON, daughter of B. D. Anderson. (S. August 1, 1857)

Colonel David WILLIAMS married Mrs. Catharine ROUTH daughter of Redding SUGG, on February 1, 1831, by John Mercer, Esq. (N. C. F. P. February 8, 1831)

Henry WILLIAMS married Elvira E. K. WILLIAMS, daughter of the late Louis A. WILLIAMS, at the William K. A. Williams home at Rose Hill in Martin County on February 26, 1840, by William Slade, Esq. (T. P. March 7, 1840)

John WILLIAMS, merchant of Tarboro, married Caroline MATHEWSON, daughter of County Clerk Nathan MATHEWSON, on May 26, 1829, by Rev. John Armstrong. (F. P. May 29, 1829)

John G. WILLIAMS married Nancy BARNES, daughter of Burrell BARNES, on January 8, 1829, by David Williams, Esq. (F. P. January 16, 1829)

John H. WILLIAMS, Esq., of Warren County, married Mrs. C. L. IRWIN, daughter of Arthur ARRINGTON of Nash County, on July 2, 1853, by Rev. Thomas G. Lowe. (S. September 3, 1853)

Joseph John WILLIAMS married Eliza Helen THOMPSON, only daughter of Noah L. THOMPSON, at Glenwood, Florida, on April 4, 1854, by the Right Reverend Bishop Rutledge. (S. April 15, 1854)

Joshua WILLIAMS, aged about sixty, married Cherry LANGLEY, aged twenty-five, in Edgecombe County on June 23, 1829, by Henry Austin, Esq. (F. P. July 3, 1829)

Michael WILLIAMS married Mary BRINKLEY of Brake's District in Edgecombe County on June 24, 1852, by Duncan Ferguson assisted by Theophilus Thomas, Esq. (S. June 26, 1852)

Orren WILLIAMS married Alice A. HOWARD, daughter of George HOWARD at Tarboro on March 8, 1859, by Rev. Joseph Blount Cheshire. (S. March 12, 1859)

Reddin S. WILLIAMS of Edgecombe County married Kate EDWARDS in Greene County on March 7, 1861, by Rev. Mr. Mahoney. (S. March 16, 1861)

Richard F. J. H. WILLIAMS married Caroline PRICE, daughter of the late Nymphas PRICE, in Pitt County on June 25, 1853. (S. July 9, 1853)

Colonel Robert W. WILLIAMS married Susan BRANCH in Tallahassee, Florida, on March 28, 1844. (T. P. April 20, 1844)

Dr. Robert WILLIAMS of Pitt County married Caroline H. M. DRAKE, daughter of Major John H. DRAKE of Nash County, on February 28, 1832. (N. C. F. P. March 13, 1832)

Thomas WILLIAMS, saddler of Stantonsburg, married Harriet LEWIS of Pitt County in Greene County on April 22, 1827, by Jesse Speight, Esq. (F. P. May 5, 1827)

William WILLIAMS married Laura Jane SELBY, daughter of B. M. SELBY, Esq., of Pitt County, in Greenville on September 13, 1849, by the Rev. N. Collins Hughes. (T. P. September 22, 1849)

William Dancy WILLIAMS, son of Elijah WILLIAMS, and a clerk in the factory store of Battle & Son, married Margaret Elizabeth JONES, daughter of the late Davis JONES, on October 12, 1854, by C. B. Bonner, Esq., assisted by W. B. Jordan. "The bride and groom are spending their honeymoon at the picturesque Falls of Tar River."

William R. T. WILLIAMS of Northampton County married Martha Indiana HIGGS, daughter of the late Wiley HIGGS, at the Jacob Higgs home in Halifax County on May 26, 1847. (T. P. June 5, 1847)

Reverend William W. WILLIAMS married Elizabeth B. HARVEY at Palmyra on August 9, 1836, by the Rev. G. N. Gregory. (T. P. August 20, 1836)

Elijah WILLIFORD married Julia A. BATCHELOR of Nash County in Edgecombe County "a few weeks since," by William F. Lewis, Esq. (S. December 18, 1852) (They were actually married on November 14, 1852.)

Jesse WILLIS married Nancy BRYAN, daughter of the late Dempsey BRYAN, in Edgecombe County recently at the home of Mr. Thomas B. Mayo by the Rev. J. F. Speight. (S. December 25, 1858)

William H. WILLS married Ann Maria WHITAKER in Halifax County at Dr. C. Whitaker's home on May 13, 1835, by the Rev. Miles Nash. (T. P. May 23, 1835)

John WILSON married Susan DUNN in Tarboro on May 8, 1834. (T. F. P. May 16, 1834)

Colonel Robert WILSON married Lucinda HOUZE of Franklin County, "after a courtship of only five days," on May 4, 1837, by Thomas D. Wright, Esq. (T. P. July 1, 1837)

George L. WIMBERLY married Fannie J. WHITFIELD of Edgecombe County at Richmond on October 8, 1857, by the Rev. Basil Manly, Jr. (S. October 24, 1857)

Joseph W. WIMBERLY married Pattie LAWRENCE, daughter of John LAWRENCE of Edgecombe County, on December 1, 1859, by the Rev. T. R. Owen. (S. December 3, 1859)

Robert WIMBERLY of Tennessee married Margaret Ann POWELL of Halifax County on May 22, 1828, by Rev. Joshua Lawrence. (F. P. May 30, 1828)

G. Lawrence WINBURN married Martha A. PARKER, daughter of the late Arthur PARKER, at Tarboro, on January 15, 1852. (S. January 17, 1852)

William WOMACK married Lucinda PITTMAN at "Strawberry" on September 24, 1840, by P. McDowell, Esq. (T. P. October 3, 1840)

Aquilla WOMBLE married Mrs. Diana SNEADER at Halifax on June 24, 1827, by James Simmons, Esq. (F. P. June 30, 1827)

Enos WOMBLE married Elizabeth SKINNER at Tarboro on August 30, 1837, by Henry Austin, Esq. (T. P. September 9, 1837)

Elisha WOODARD, aged seventy, married Terese DEBERRY, aged eighteen, on Sunday evening, May 27, 1828. (F. P. May 30, 1828) (Sunday did not fall on May 25 as stated, since that was a Friday.)

James B. WOODARD married Sarah B. KING, daughter of the late William C. KING, at Tarboro on April 7, 1841, by the Reverend Joshua Lawrence. (T. P. April 10, 1841)

James S. WOODARD, Esq., of Wilson married Penelope WOODARD near Black Creek on July 12, 1858, by Dr. Brooks, Esq. (S. July 24, 1858)

John WOOTEN married Mary DAWSON in Pitt County on January 29, 1835, by John L. Foreman, Esq. (T. P. February 28, 1835)

Nathan WOOTTEN of Northampton County married Ann STEWART in Norfolk on April 15, 1828. (F. P. April 25, 1828)

E. G. WORSLEY of Edgecombe County married Martha PEEBLES, daughter of the late Howell PEEBLES of Pitt County, on January 10, 1859, by the Rev. Peter E. Hines. (S. January 15, 1859)

Littleberry WORSLEY married Reanny CHERRY of Edgecombe County on March 5, 1832, by William C. Leigh, Esq. (N. C. F. P. March 13, 1832)

Mayo WORSLEY married Mary L. STATON, daughter of Windield D. STATON, Esq. in Edgecombe County on February 22, 1842, by J. J. Pippen, Esq. (T. P. March 5, 1842)

Redding WORSLEY married Ann Eliza ARMSTRONG, daughter of Gray ARMSTRONG, on August 28, 1842, by Moses Price, Esq. (T. P. September 3, 1842)

Jordan C. WRIGHT, Esq., of Bettner & Wright, Commission Merchants of New York, married Harriet Eliza PUGH, daughter of Dr. Whitmel H. PUGH of Louisiana, at Tarboro on July 17, 1832, by the Reverend Mr. Norwood. (N. C. F. P. July 24, 1832)

Charlton W. YELLOWLEY, Esq., of Greenville, married in Calvary Church at Tarboro on February 11, 1858, Caroline TOOLE, daughter of the late Henry I. TOOLE, by the Reverend Joseph Blount Cheshire. (S. February 13, 1858)

INDEX TO THE BRIDES

IN

TARBORO NEWSPAPERS

1824-1865

By

Hugh Buckner Johnston

Wilson, North Carolina

1983

Elizabeth B. ABBOTT married Joseph H. BOWDITCH on April 2, 1845.

Clara Ann ADMAS married William P. ROBERTS on December 5, 1832.

Nancy J. ADAMS married Dr. Lewis J. DORTCH on October 10, 1844.

Rachael ALEXANDER married Jacob FELDENHEIMER on December 8, 1859.

Lucy ALFORD married Cullen LITTLE on January 5, 1830.

Mary F. ALLEXON married Joshua HARRINGTON on December 1, 1859.

Mary Ann ALSOBROOK married James DUGGAN on January 20, 1835.

Adella ALSTON married James B. HAWKINS on December 16, 1835.

Eliza Ann ALSTON married William B. BODDIE on December 20, 1831.

Lucy F. ALSTON married Julian V. PERKINS on November 9, 1859.

Temperance AMASON married Garret SHURLEY on February 24, 1827.

Henrietta L. ANDERSON married James W. MOYE on May 5, 1851.

Mollie E. ANDERSON married Dr. B. Brown WILLIAMS on July 27, 1857.

Martha E. ANDREWS married Asa BIGGS on June 26, 1832.

Unity P. ANDREWS married Spencer L. HART on November 2, 1857.

Mary E. ANTHONY married John H. WHITAKER on June 17, 1851.

Ann Eliza ARMSTRONG married Redding WORSLEY on August 28, 1842.

Arabella ARRINGTON married Frederick EVANS on February 13, 1834.

Caroline ARRINGTON married Thomas IRWIN on February 11, 1836.

Elizabeth ARRINGTON married James R. BATTLE on November 14, 1826.

Martha A. E. ARRINGTON married Col. Robert H. D. L. HART on September 10, 1829.

Mary ARRINGTON married Thomas R. WIGGINS on April 11, 1833.

Sallie A. ARRINGTON married Dr. John T. WATSON on June 10, 1847.

Susan ARRINGTON married John B. ODOM on October 18, 1853.

Susan S. ARRINGTON married Joseph D. W. COMANN on March 8, 1849.

E. M. J. ASKEW married John P. ROGERS on January 12, 1854.

Mary C. ATKINSON married Simon BARNES on April 21, 1859.

Rhoda A. ATKINSON married Ralph P. BRIDGERS on August 17, 1852.

William Rebecca Frances ATKINSON married Thaddeus E. DILLARD on October 27, 1845.

Winifred ATKINSON married Arthur K. BARLOW on February 25, 1830.

Catharine E. AUSTIN married William M. CRENSHAW on February 12, 1839.

Martha Ann Austin married Rev. Patrick W. DOWD on October 21, 1830.

Mary Jane AUSTIN married Nathan MATHEWSON on May 11, 1847.

Miriba A. BABCOCK married Charles H. KELLY on March 17, 1861.

Mrs. Catharine BAKER married William J. ARMSTRONG on January 29, 1846.

Laura BAKER married Rev. Joseph H. SAUNDERS on April 25, 1833.

Laura E. BAKER married Henry A. DOWD on January 20, 1859.

Margaret Ann BAKER married Hugh MACNAIR on March 16, 1859.

Martha BAKER married Arthur LAWRENCE on April 17, 1828.

Mary BALLARD married Bennet BRILEY on March 29, 1838.

Nancy BARBEE married W. P. FITZGERALD on September 1, 1859.

Catharine BARFIELD married James H. SAVAGE on August 14, 1834.

Martha BARFIELD married Thomas H. CHRISTIE on January 27, 1859.

Mary Ann BARFIELD married William T. CUTCHIN on January 11, 1855.

Ellen M. BARHAM married Andrew J. SIMMS on May 11, 1859.

Mrs. Drucilla BARKER married Bird B. TUNNEL on June 22, 1854.

Sarah E. BARLOW married Joseph W. LLOYD on April 9, 1856.

Annie Sharpe BARNES married Z. W. THOMPSON on February 12, 1850.

Charity BARNES married Maj. Whitmel H. ANTHONY on August 2, 1831.

Delaney BARNES married Jordan BELL on August 23, 1855.

Frances BARNES married Solomon DREW on May 1, 1832.

Lavinia D. BARNES married Whitmel J. HILL on November 24, 1829.

Mrs. Maria BARNES married Lovet GRIFFIN on December 9, 1830.

Mary BARNES married James BARNES on May 10, 1851.

Mrs. Mary A. S. BARNES married J. J. HARPER on August 6, 1857.

Nancy BARNES married Andrew A. CALHOUN on December 27, 1836.

Nancy BARNES married John G. WILLIAMS on January 8, 1829.

Sarah BARNES married Dr. William E. J. SHALLINGTON on November 30, 1843.

Isabella BARNHILL married James S. MOORE on April 2, 1839.

Rosalie BARROW married Charles G. HUNTER on May 6, 1845.

Elvy BARTEE married James COBB on December 7, 1826.

Emeliza BASS married Benjamin W. KNIGHT on August 8, 1848.

Lucinda BASS married Blake SESSOMS on April 17, 1828.

Julia A. BATCHELOR married Elijah WILLIFORD on November 14, 1852.

Bettie B. BATTLE married Capt. John B. DRAKE on October 11, 1853.

Catharine BATTLE married John W. LEWIS on February 5, 1829.

Cornelia V. BATTLE married John S. DANCY on December 12, 1843.

Helen BATTLE married Dr. William B. RICKS on July 6, 1853.

Kate BATTLE married Joseph H. FOY on March 19, 1860.

Margaret BATTLE married H. LaFayette STATON on January 12, 1848.

Martha E. BATTLE married Kemp BATTLE on November 28, 1855.

Martha Louisa BATTLE married Archibald G. RHODES on November 14, 1854.

Mary A. BATTLE married William H. TILLORY on February 13, 1849.

Mary E. BATTLE married Dr. Theophilus H. SCOTT on May 8, 1845.

Mrs. Mary Ann BATTLE married Jesse H. POWELL on December 15, 1857.

Mary Eliza BATTLE married William F. DANCY on January 14, 1858.

Penelope B. BATTLE married William R. COX on November 27, 1856.

Temperance A. BATTLE married Dr. Robert H. MARRIOTT on November 8, 1853.

(Cynthia) Eliza BATTS married William GARDNER on January 22, 1828.

Emma L. BATTS married Thomas F. CHERRY on April 2, 1863.

Mary BATTS married William S. LONG on December 31, 1844.

Milly BATTS married James T. THORNE on April 3, 1859.

Margaret Ann BECKWITH married Rev. Edwin GEER on December 2, 1840.

Margaret BEDFORD married John COGGIN on September 19, 1830.

Caroline BELL married Robert A. SIZER on September 23, 1857.

Elizabeth BELL married William D. BELL on October 17, 1839.

Elizabeth BELL married Charles HARRISON on July 5, 1832.

Elizabeth BELL married Israel B. WILKINSON on November 1, 1831.

Mrs. Elizabeth BELL married Stephen BENNETT on November 19, 1829.

Emeliza BELL married Nathan H. ROUNTREE on December 11, 1832.

Emily BELL married Thomas CHERRY on March 4, 1830.

Eugenia BELL married William McGEE on April 2, 1835.

Julia BELL married Lorenzo D. BELL on June 4, 1840.

Lavinia BELL married McGilbry BELL in January of 1846.

Mrs. Lucy BELL married Henry REEVES on January 22, 1829.

Margaret BELL married Ethington BARFIELD on September 20, 1831.

Margaret Ann BELL married Lawrence Henry HEARN on May 16, 1836.

Margaret H. BELL married David BARLOW on June 7, 1863.

Mary BELL married Cador CHERRY on November 16, 1828.

Mary P. BELL married Henry BRYAN on October 11, 1827.

Della BELLAMY married Willis WEATHERSBEE on November 11, 1856.

Ann Eunice BENNETT married Miles B. MOORE about July 1836.

Elizabeth BENSON married Patrick BOYT on May 27, 1828.

Sarah E. BENSON married Baker HOWERTON on December 15, 1853.

Fanny BENTON married Joshua MASON on May 8, 1856.

Peggy BENTON married William D. BRYAN on August 13, 1835.

Julia BEST married Capt. William D. HOPKINS on May 27, 1830.

Lucinda BEST married Reuben MAYO on December 19, 1832.

Nancy BEST married Thomas GRIMES on August 4, 1835.

Sally BEST married McGilbray TAYLOR on May 22, 1860.

Elizabeth BIGGS married Hardiman ABINGTON on February 8, 1830.

Susan BILBREY married James TANNER on June 16, 1860.

Lucy BLOUNT married William B. GULICK on January 15, 1852.

Catharine BODDIE married Marmaduke N. BELL on January 23, 1827.

Louisa BODDIE married Bartholomew Flow MOORE on December 2, 1828.

Lucy BODDIE married B. F. MOORE on April 28, 1835.

Emily BOND married James MEHEGAN on January 20, 1853.

Emily G. BOND married David LAWRENCE on October 6, 1829.

Mrs. Mary E. BOND married John BRANCH on November 9, 1853.

Mary S. C. BOND married Robert H. ROWE on December 23, 1852.

Lavina BOOTH married Arthur KNIGHT on February 13, 1834.

Sally BOOTH married Burwell SHELTON on July 12, 1829.

Nancy BOTTOMS married Caswell Hines BARNES "not long" after May 16, 1842.

Mary BOYCE married Cullen CASPER on December 22, 1831.

Frances Ann BOYD married William H. HODGE on December 30, 1828.

Lucy Nelson BOYD married Dr. John W. POTTS on November 4, 1834.

Sarah BOYETT married Alvin BALLANCE on September 25, 1859.

Mrs. Sally BOYETT married Noah PHILLPOT on December 22, 1831.

Jincie BOYKIN married S. D. BOYKIN on September 22, 1858.

Sally BOYKIN married Alexander S. BELLAMY on December 15, 1829.

Rhoda BRACEWELL married William HYLES on May 16, 1836.

Agnes BRADDY married Thomas WATSON on February 4, 1853.

Julia Ann BRADDY married John C. BLOCKER on December 31, 1839.

Mary N. BRADDY married James H. LAWRENCE on May 1, 1856.

Sarah Eliza BRADDY married Jesse HAWLEY on July 30, 1844.

Catharine BRADLEY married Joshua L. ANDERSON on December 25, 1828.

Lucy BRADLEY married Cullen PENDER on January 6, 1836.

Mary BRADLEY married Elias BRADLEY on June 23, 1836.

Zelpha BRADLEY married Lunsford G. H. PITTMAN on March 15, 1827.

Mary BRADY married Allen HODGE on November 7, 1826.

Priscilla BRADY married Thomas TAYLOR on November 30, 1852.

Lucinda BRAKE married Joshua PEEL on February 18, 1857.

Martha BRAME married Theophilus STALLINGS on September 8, 1852.

Martha BRANCH married Toby LEWIS in January 1828.

Sarah BRANCH married Dr. James HUNTER on July 16, 1833.

Susan BRANCH married Col. Robert W. WILLIAMS on March 28, 1844.

Arretta BRASWELL married James H. DRAUGHAN on March 11, 1858.

Martha BRASWELL married Robert S. BRASWELL on March 11, 1858.

Mrs. Susan BRASWELL married Hansel CROSS on January 10, 1839.

Mrs. Emeline BRAY married Jesse A. BYNUM on May 28, 1839.

Rebecca BRAZZIL married John HARRELL on December 9, 1830.

Amanda R. BRIDGERS married Jacob THOMAS on July 17, 1830.

Susan BRIDGERS married Geraldus SHURLEY on January 19, 1841.

Mary BRINKLEY married Michael WILLIAMS on June 24, 1852.

Sally BRITT married Elijah ROBERTSON on December 19, 1839.

Sarah BROOKER married Charles HATHCOCK on June 21, 1829.

Julia Ann BROTHERS married Joseph B. FARMER on May 24, 1853.

Patsey BROWN married James THIGPEN, Sr., on July 24, 1834.

Susan BROWN married Levi BLOUNT on May 6, 1839.

_____ BROWNING married John ALLEN about September 1828.

Maria BROWNRIGG married Arnold BORDEN on October 30, 1824.

Elizabeth Heritage BRYAN married Kenelm Harrison LEWIS on April 15, 1857.

Lucy BRYAN married William W. WARD on January 10, 1832.

Martha BRYAN married Redding PITTMAN on March 10, 1831.

Mary BRYAN married Redmun BUNN on March 20, 1832.

Mary BRYAN married Thomas MAYO on February 19, 1833.

Nancy BRYAN married Jesse WILLIS about December 1858.

Penny BRYAN married Col. Charles MABRY on January 29, 1839.

Sarah BRYAN married Dr. Franklin HART on November 5, 1845.

Polly BULLOCK married Willie BRASWELL on July 16, 1829.

Sallie BURGES married William F. GARVAY on November 6, 1858.

Mary BURGESS married P. Lawson WHITFIELD on July 20, 1852.

Caroline BURNETT married Ebenezer HYMAN on January 15, 1833.

Cornelia BURROUGHS married William R. PALMER on August 23, 1832.

Eliza Jane BURT married John R. HORNE on October 24, 1833.

Harriet BURT married Dr. James J. PHILIPS on April 23, 1834.

Sally Ann BURT married Peter ARRINGTON, Jr., on June 23, 1831.

Caroline A. BUSH married Joseph L. DICKEN on July 29, 1858.

A. C. BYNUM married R. BEST on September 11, 1855.

Julia BYNUM married Justice G. DANIEL on June 29, 1848.

Louisa BYNUM married William BEST on October 20, 1859.

Margaret BYNUM married Nathan P. DANIEL on April 9, 1846.

Nancy BYNUM married John P. SHARPE on June 4, 1844.

Nancy BYNUM married Abner WILKINSON on August 16, 1835.

Sue M. BYNUM married J. J. BYNUM on May 7, 1857.

Sarah CAIN married Jesse LYNCH on August 19, 1830.

Jemima CANNON married George L. BLOUNT on April 24, 1833.

Ann CARLISLE married John O. MOORE on September 11, 1855.

Mrs. Martha CARNEY married Abner MILLS on July 10, 1828.

Mary E. CARNEY married Joab JENKINS on July 31, 1851.

Mrs. Rutha CARNEY married John MOORE on November 26, 1840.

Lucilla CARR married Thomas M. C. PRINCE about September 1829.

Mary B. CARR married David HINTON on March 31, 1852.

Mrs. Mary CARSTAPHEN married Willie POWELL on December 18, 1827.

Sarah CARSTAPHEN married Thomas PENDER on December 10, 1835.

Mary CARTER married Henry MORRIS on June 10, 1828.

Isabella A. CHAPMAN married Benjamin A. DICKENS on February 15, 1853.

Elizabeth CHERRY married Thomas HOWELL on January 3, 1833.

Emma E. CHERRY married William H. CLARKE, Jr., in September 1856.

Margaret CHERRY married Blount BRYAN on December 16, 1847.

Margaret CHERRY married John WALSTON on March 11, 1838.

Martha CHERRY married Joshua L. LYON on May 18, 1841.

Mary Frances CHERRY married Bennet CARLISLE on December 11, 1851.

Penelope E. CHERRY married George A. DANCY on November 23, 1847.

Reanny CHERRY married Littleberry WORSLEY on March 5, 1832.

Sarah CHERRY married Joseph H. PIPPEN on October 25, 1854.

M. R. CHURCH married Colin MACNAIR on June 2, 1859.

Pennie CHURCHILL married Capt. William B. SMITH on April 3, 1862.

D. M. CLARK married William A. JENKINS on November 18, 1857.

Harriet J. CLARK married Dr. Charles SMALLWOOD on March 20, 1850.

Laura P. CLARK married John W. COTTEN on December 19, 1832.

Louisa Ann CLARK married Archibald FORBES on January 21, 1833.

Louisa J. CLARK married Dr. Alexander HALL on November 10, 1831.

Lucy CLARK married Kindred TAYLOR on December 12, 1833.

Margaret W. CLARK married Lewis THOMPSON on January 28, 1833.

Maria T. CLARK married Matthew WEDDELL on October 20, 1852.

Mrs. Mary Ann CLARK married William R. BOWERS on October 9, 1851.

Mary Sumner CLARK married Dr. William George THOMAS on November 1, 1843.

Hannah CLEMENTS married Henry A. GILLIAM on May 24, 1859.

Elizabeth CLOMAN married Bythal STATON on March 1, 1827.

Gennett CLOMAN married Thomas PUGH on January 19, 1836.

Mrs. Fanny COBB married Eli GAY on December 18, 1828.

Frances E. COBB married Joseph J. LAWRENCE on May 23, 1850.

Louisa COBB married Ezekiel CRISP on March 5, 1835.

Mary COBB married Capt. Wiley WALSTON on October 26, 1854.

Mary E. COBB married Richard BYNUM on February 17, 1857.

Sally COBB married Van Buren SHARP on December 24, 1857.

Nancy COFFEY married William GRAGG on July 9, 1837.

Elizabeth W. COFFIELD married Frederick R. COTTEN on October 7, 1846.

Martha C. COFFIELD married Rev. J. G. WHITFIELD on January 29, 1856.

Mrs. Sarah COFFIELD married Dr. John F. BELLAMY on March 23, 1836.

Sarah S. W. COFFIELD married Dr. John T. BELLAMY on November 8, 1858.

Mrs. Harriet COKELY married Thomas SOUTHERLAND on February 1, 1827.

Patsey CONE married Thomas BANKS on January 22, 1828.

Camilla H. COOK married Rev. Maurice H. VAUPIN on May 13, 1862.

Martha A. COOK married James SIMMONS on November 2, 1830.

Eliza COOPER married William HOWELL on April 23, 1835.

Gracy COOPER married Robert SOREY on November 23, 1854.

Anzy CORBETT married James JONES on July 21, 1852.

Della A. COTTEN married Andrew J. MOORE on February 3, 1859.

Eliza W. COTTEN married Noah THOMPSON on February 15, 1832.

Elizabeth COTTEN married Drew KING on November 20, 1828.

Emily COTTEN married Robert BELCHER on February 5, 1837.

Jane COTTEN married Exum LEWIS, Jr., on September 29, 1835.

Margaret E. COTTEN married J. A. ENGELHARD on September 26, 1855.

Mary COTTEN married Henry DOWNING on January 24, 1839.

Nancy B. COTTEN married Henry NEWSOM on December 25, 1849.

Mrs. Charity COWEY married Hardy H. BROWN on January 14, 1836.

Mary Eliza COWEY married Thomas GRIMES on October 27, 1831.

Elizabeth COWLING married Henry MACRAE on May 22, 1860.

Elizabeth CRICKMAN married Daniel BATCHELOR on August 27, 1839.

Margaret CROMWELL married Elisha CROMWELL on February 1, 1848.

Martha CROMWELL married John KNIGHT on November 26, 1835.

Mrs. Martha CROMWELL married James ELLINOR on June 23, 1844.

Martha P. CROMWELL married James P. HOWARD about March 1852.

Sally Ann CROMWELL married Capt. Charles BLOCKER on May 13, 1863.

Ann B. CROOM married Edward C. BELLAMY on December 8, 1829.

Elizabeth Jane CROOM married Dr. Samuel C. BELLAMY on June 26, 1834.

Matilda CROWELL married Dr. John A. JELKS on December 16, 1830.

Virginia A. CULL married Dr. Richard H. LEWIS on December 8, 1857.

Ann D. CULPEPPER married Edmund P. FINCH on December 12, 1826.

Louisa CURRY married Jesse BREWER on December 19, 1837.

Ann CUTCHEN married John MINSHEW on April 19, 1859.

Louisa J. CUTCHIN married Lawrence J. ELLINOR on December 21, 1859.

Margaret CUTCHIN married Archelus BRASWELL on February 24, 1848.

Mary A. CUTCHIN married I.F. JONES on January 21, 1855.

Loes CUTCHINS married James WATKINS on August 29, 1832.

Elizabeth DAFFIN married L. F. FOSTER on January 31, 1850.

Delha DANCY married Agesilaus S. FOREMAN on November 10, 1836.

Elizabeth M. DANCY married William S. BATTLE on June 25, 1845.

Lucy A. DANCY married William B. JORDAN on December 9, 1857.

Martha E. DANCY married Francis L. BOND on November 20, 1849.

Mary A. DANCY married James W. KNIGHT on November 30, 1853.

Mrs. Mary B. DANCY married Peter P. LAWRENCE on April 11, 1833.

Ann E. T. DANIEL married Rufus C. THIGPEN on March 20, 1851.

Eugenia M. DANIEL married William N. STEPTOE on December 1, 1857.

Gatsey DANIEL married William John STATON on February 13, 1851.

Harriet DANIEL married James D. PERKINS on January 15, 1828.

Huldah T. DANIEL married Thomas J. DAWSON on October 20, 1846.

Josephine DANIEL married A. M. QUARLES on February 27, 1861.

Martha P. DANIEL married Dr. John J. DANIEL on November 15, 1838.

Mrs. Martha P. DANIEL married Duncan FERGUSON on April 18, 1840.

Mrs. Mary Ann DANIEL married Joseph H. LANGLEY on October 25, 1849.

Lavinia B. DANIEL married T. W. BATTLE on May 1, 1850.

Mary DANIEL married Robert C. BROWN on December 4, 1860.

Nancy DANIEL married John WHITLEY on November 11, 1851.

Sarah DANIEL married Thomas T. LAWRENCE on October 8, 1856.

Sarah DANIEL married Canady MORGAN on November 16, 1830.

Eliza Ann DAVIS married Rev. William ROBINSON on August 28, 1845.

Mary DAVIS married C. B. HASSELL on May 17, 1832.

Mary DAVIS married Daniel KNIGHT on January 17, 1843.

Mary DAWSON married John WOOTEN on January 29, 1835.

Mrs. Sarah DAWSON married James H. PARKER on March 26, 1827.

Elizabeth DAY married Green OBERRY on July 15, 1847.

Terese DEBERRY married Elisha WOODARD on May 27, 1828.

Absilla A. DENTON married Micajah ANDERSON, Jr., on January 31, 1861.

Sally DERRING married Holman GARDNER on November 21, 1826.

Ann DEAVREAUX married John UPTON on December 9, 1830.

Elizabeth DEW (not DUNN) married Stephen DUNN on January 18, 1852.

Elizabeth DICKEN married Robert JOYNER on February 6, 1840.

Rebecca Louisa DICKEN married John L. BRIDGERS on April 27, 1847.

Mrs. Susan DICKEN married Turner BASS on January 11, 1827.

Elizabeth DILDA married Richard HOCOTT about April 1852.

Sally Ann DONALDSON married Dr. John J. DANIEL on January 7, 1832.

Celeste DORTCH married Capt. David MCDANIEL on January 22, 1840.

Frances A. D. DORTCH married Dr. James GORHAM on April 15, 1851.

Mary L. DORTCH married Maj. W. A. POPE on November 9, 1847.

Martha DOWNING married Frederick SAVAGE on May 13, 1857.

Caroline H. M. DRAKE married Dr. Robert WILLIAMS on February 28, 1832.

Lucinda J. DRAKE married William DOZIER on February 3, 1829.

Mourning DRAKE married Benjamin SCREWS on August 18, 1836.

Susan Frances DRAKE married Linn Banks SANDERS on August 22, 1855.

Delphia DRAUGHN married Charles E. SEARS on February 20, 1856.

Drucilla DRAUGHN married Burrell DUNN on January 22, 1828.

Harriet E. DUGGER married Capt. Henry H. BRYAN on July 12, 1849.

Elizabeth DUNCAN married William BRANCH on May 14, 1829.

Susan DUNN married John WILSON on May 8, 1834.

Martha J. DUNN married John B. TILLERY on February 13, 1851.

Amelia DUPREE married William H. KNIGHT on March 11, 1858.

Mary F. DUPREE married Corp. Elisha ABRAMS on August 24, 1848.

Mary Jane DUPREE married C. H. JENKINS on October 20, 1857.

Elizabeth EASON married Jos. FORBES on August 29, 1839.

Nancy EASON married Joseph HARVEY on March 22, 1842.

Eliza EASTON married Dr. William BERNARD on June 28, 1853.

Mary H. EATON married Alexander H. FALCONER on September 11, 1828.

Eliza EBORN married Col. Lewis G. LITTLE on May 3, 1838.

Mary L. EBORN married John ADAMS on September 16, 1856.

Elizabeth EDMONDSON married Alexander BRADLEY on January 28, 1834.

Winnefred EDMONDSON married Littleberry BRADLEY on January 30, 1834.

Sarah W. EDMUNDSON married William L. QUALLS on August 7, 1853.

Elizabeth EDWARDS married Thomas TAYLOR on December 21, 1826.

Harriet EDWARDS married Joseph O'BERRY on February 27, 1848.

Josephine EDWARDS married Dr. Joseph J. LAWRENCE on May 3, 1859.

Kate EDWARDS married Reddin S. WILLIAMS on March 7, 1861.

Mary Ann EDWARDS married Bazel SIKES on September 26, 1830.

Mary Ann Susan EDWARDS married Col. Benjamin SHARP on November 22, 1838.

Sarah P. EDWARDS married William Weeks PARKER on February 12, 1857.

Elizabeth ELLINOR married William BILLUPS on June 20, 1833.

Alice Ann ELLIOTT married Samuel E. MOORE on January 8, 1845.

Mrs. Eliza A. ELLIS married Nathaniel M. TERRELL on September 22, 1836.

Mrs. Queen Esther ELLIS married Hickman ELLIS on January 4, 1838.

Nancy ELMORE married William PRIER on May 23, 1829.

Mary Eliza EPPES married Michael FERRALL on October 31, 1831.

Eliza ETHERIDGE married Thomas JENKINS on October 8, 1835.

Mrs. Rebecca EURE married Orestes R. SMALLWOOD on November 18, 1830.

Eliza Imogen EVANS married Dr. Isaac HALL on May 15, 1834.

Margaret A. EVANS married Col. John H. IRBY on December 7, 1833.

Mary Ann EVANS married Dr. Samuel L. SOUTHERLAND on January 12, 1830.

Susan EVANS married Dr. Francis W. IRBY on November 30, 1831.

Susan EVANS married William R. SMITH, Jr., on January 22, 1828.

Catharine EXUM married Peter FORBES on March 17, 1850.

Elizabeth EXUM married Joseph BARNES on December 4, 1850.

Mary A. EXUM married Peleg ROGERS on September 29, 1852.

Pennina B. EXUM married Littleberry MANNING on October 25, 1842.

Julia A. FARMER married J. D. MONTAGUE on January 11, 1855.

Mary R. FARMER married Levi BRYAN on May 27, 1828.

Arcene FLEMING married Andrew Jackson SKINNER on April 1, 1841.

Mildreth FLEMING married John CANADY on February 7, 1854.

Eliza FLORA married Coffield ELLIS on April 5, 1859.

Nancy FLOWERS married John CLARK on November 27, 1856.

Mrs. Margaret FORD married Elijah ELLIOTT on October 1, 1837.

Mrs. Elizabeth FOREMAN married Edmund B. FREEMAN on November 14, 1837.

Mrs. Martha E. FOREMAN married Richard H. LEWIS on June 5, 1849.

Mary FOREMAN married Richard Henry LEWIS on April 24, 1832.

Florida FORSYTH married Lt. Francis L. DANCY on October 17, 1833.

Diana FORT married James W. BATTLE on January 22, 1852.

Nancy FORT married Richard H. BRADFORD on November 15, 1827.

Cecilia D. FOSTER married Dr. Ed. LAWRENCE on December 5, 1855.

Lou F. FOSTER married Thomas D. GAY about January 1858.

Elizabeth FOUNTAIN married George W. ANDERSON on May 29, 1845.

Lucy D. FOXHALL married Dr. John G. RIVES on September 20, 1848.

Mary FOXHALL married Wilson SESSUMS on August 26, 1834.

Susan A. FOXHALL married Dr. Joseph H. BAKER on May 15, 1855.

Adelina FREEMAN married William J. KNIGHT on January 3, 1828.

Mary Eliza FREEMAN married Dr. Baker W. MABREY on December 20, 1859.

Mrs. Sarah FREEMAN married Dr. Samuel CARSON on November 26, 1841.

Susan FULCHER married Henry HAYWOOD on July 23, 1829.

Sarah FULGHUM married Richard N. IVEY on October 11, 1827.

Elizabeth GARDNER married James W. BRIDGERS on January 4, 1853.

Evelina GARDNER married Zadock BRASWELL on March 14, 1854.

Mrs. Martha A. GARDNER married Gray L. HARGRAVES on March 31, 1853.

Matilda GARDNER married Benjamin B. BATTS on June 1, 1848.

Susan E. GARRETT married Dr. Allen B. NOBLES on May 20, 1855.

Mary E. GRAY married Alexander P. ALSOBROOK on September 11, 1838.

Caroline E. GATLIN married Dr. Joseph J. ANTHONY on May 30, 1854.

Georgiana GATLIN married Dr. Lemon S. DUNN on May 13, 1851.

Esther GAY married Lawrence L. BOON "not long" before April 13, 1844.

Milbry GAY married Cullen MILTON on October 3, 1835.

Piety GAY married Charles BARNES on February 20, 1838.

Rachel GAY married Commodore Stephen Decatur DAVIS not long before April 13, 1844.

Susan M. GAY married James DAVIS on July 9, 1855.

Elizabeth H. GEE married Wade WEST on September 17, 1829.

Mary GEORGE married Maj. Lunsford R. CHERRY on July 5, 1832.

S. A. GIER married Charles D. MABREY on April 12, 1860.

Rebecca GILL married William SKINNER on February 19, 1829.

N. J. GLOVER married John H. FINCH on February 4, 1849.

Mrs. _____ GODLEY married Dr. S. Cooper BENJAMIN about February 1845.

B. GOODMAN married Moses FRANKFORT on May 29, 1857.

Elizabeth GOODWIN married John E. NETTLES about April 1841.

Eliza R. GORDON married Thomas SLADE on October 28, 1830.

Emily GORHAM married Henry JORDAN on May 13, 1835.

Martha GRAHAM married Thomas S. BURT on March 6, 1838.

Matilda GRANBERRY married Zebidee BAILEY on January 22, 1829.

Caroline GRAY married Charles C. BONNER on November 20, 1850.

Helen GRAY married James CHAPMAN on October 6, 1858.

Martha E. GRAY married James D. HOWELL on July 29, 1847.

Elizabeth GREEN married John PHILLIPS about January 1828.

Jane GREENE married Dr. W. M. B. BROWN on November 1, 1854.

Sabra GRIFFIN married Bennett BRADLEY on March 22, 1827.

Winifred GRIFFIN married Isaac SAWYER on May 13, 1830.

Nancy GRIFFITHS married Weldon S. HUNTER on February 14, 1844.

Elizabeth A. GRIMES married John NELSON on December 22, 1857.

Elytha GRIMES married William LANIER on January 24, 1839.

Susan GRIMES married John G. MYERS on July 6, 1853.

Margaret GUNTER married E. J. MERRIT about January 1829.

Barbara HADLEY married Dr. Robert STATON on October 13, 1847.

Mary Penelope HALSEY married Dr. A. H. MACNAIR on November 5, 1850.

Deborah M. HARDISON married William B. BENNETT on July 20, 1830.

Leonora C. HARDY married John W. SAUNDERS on August 20, 1854.

Sarah HARDY married Willis LITTLE on October 21, 1858.

Mrs. Caroline HARGRAVE married Rev. Dr. DRANE on December 3, 1850.

Mrs. Mary Weeks HARGRAVE married Col. Henry T. CLARK on February 11,1850.

Sally HARPER married John KNIGHT on May 27, 1830.

Sarah Eliza HARPER married Joseph John PIPPEN on July 20, 1852.

Louisa HARRELL married Asa BROWN on January 5, 1845.

Lucy HARRELL married William C. LEIGH on August 28, 1839.

Margaret J. HARRELL married Seth S. HICKS on December 22, 1857.

Mary T. HARRELL married George W. HYMAN on November 22, 1853.

Rebecca HARRELL married Joseph MOORE on December 24, 1839.

Sylva HARRELL married John PENDER about January 1828.

Martha HARRIS married Nathan H. SESSUMS on June 12, 1857.

Mary HARRIS married Andrew GUNTER on October 26, 1843.

Nancy HARRIS married Eli SOREY on December 20, 1838.

Sally HARRISS married James EVANS on December 2, 1839.

Elizabeth Ann HARRISON married Col. Robert BYNUM on February 21, 1843.

Frances Ann HARRISON married D. A. S. RICKS on October 8, 1845.

Julia HARRISON married Col. E. KING on May 20, 1856.

Louisa HARRISON married Dr. William J. LAWRENCE on May 5, 1863.

Louisa V. HARRISON married William W. HOLDEN on March 7, 1854.

Rebecca HARRISON married Southern HIGGS on January 12, 1830.

Catharine W. HART married George W. WHITFIELD on February 7, 1828.

Eden HART married Joseph H. CUTCHEN on November 25, 1858.

Frances A. HART married James J. HINTON on June 17, 1830.

Leah A. HART married John H. HYMAN on October 10, 1855.

Margaret HART married L. M. CONYERS on October 22, 1856.

Martha A. HART married Dr. J. R. WALKER on December 9, 1851.

Mary HARTT married Thomas LYON on November 9, 1826.

Elizabeth B. HARVEY married Rev. William W. WILLIAMS on August 9, 1836.

Ann P. HARWELL married Dixie C. FENNER on November 1, 1827.

Mrs. Eliza G. HASEL married Rev. William S. PLUMMER on June 11, 1829.

Elizabeth HAWKINS married Joshua ROBERTSON on June 5, 1838.

Lucinda HAWKINS married Alfred EDMONDSON on March 22, 1832.

Virginia HAWKINS married William J. ANDREWS on May 8, 1833.

Martha HEARN married William SUTTON on December 1, 1829.

Mary R. HEARN married Danford RICHARDS on January 3, 1833.

Louisa HEFLEY married Amos G. WILKINS on April 4, 1847.

Susan HENLEY married Joseph MERRITT on February 1, 1829.

Mary HICKS married Henry KEEL on February 1, 1838.

Martha Indiana HIGGS married William R. T. WILLIAMS on May 26, 1847.

Mary Jane HIGGS married Dr. John T. POPE on April 26, 1848.

Mary Louisa HIGGS married Joseph BRYAN on November 14, 1839.

Winifred HIGGS married William CLARK on May 28, 1835.

Mrs. Martha HIGH married William BUNTING on September 3, 1833.

Cynthia C. HILL married Rufus PAGE on July 23, 1845.

Rebecca N. HILL married Peter SMITH on December 22, 1853.

Winifred B. HILL married Rev. William NORWOOD on April 11, 1833.

Elizabeth K. HILLIARD married James CARR on September 19, 1832.

Elizabeth Kearney HILLIARD married Maj. Robert A. BURTON on March 18, 1840.

Sarah HILLIARD married Col. George W. POLK on December 24, 1840.

Laney HILLMAN married N. H. THOMAS on January 17, 1828.

Elizabeth HINES married Solomon PENDER on December 20, 1827.

Lucy B. HINES married Daniel A. DUGGER on August 8, 1832.

Martha A. HINES married Nathaniel B. BRAKE on July 28, 1831.

Elizabeth HINNANT married Josiah BARNES on November 3, 1859.

Jinsey HOBGOOD married Richard CAIN on January 10, 1839.

Harriet HOPKINS married Jesse STANSELL on January 9, 1834.

Litha HOPKINS married William T. ELLINOR on January 10, 1834.

Mrs. Mary HOPKINS married James CARNEY on January 15, 1850.

Nancy HOPKINS married Joseph ELLINOR on August 28, 1833.

Rilla HOPKINS married Joseph JENKINS on January 12, 1832.

Mrs. Susan HOPKINS married Leweling STATON on November 7, 1837.

Dianna HORN married William H. THOMAS on December 10, 1857.

Millisent HORN married Wade R. THOMAS on January 10, 1827.

Anna Lou HORNE married Dr. A. H. MACNAIR on March 9, 1853.

Della HORNE married David NEAL on July 3, 1855.

Katie Ruth HORNE married Dr. James P. BATTLE on January 12, 1858.

Louisa HORNE married Henry A. SHURLEY on June 3, 1858.

Martha C. HORNE married Jesse B. HYATT on February 11, 1851.

Mrs. Paulina HORNE married Dr. John A. MINNIS on June 21, 1837.

Mrs. Pennina HORNE married Dr. John A. MINNIS on June 21, 1837.
    (Pennina rather than Pauline seems to be correct.)

Rebecca HORNE married Henry KING on November 1, 1848.

Martha E. HOSKINS married John L. FOREMAN on February 25, 1836.

Lucinda HOUZE married Col. Robert WILSON on May 4, 1837.

Ruth HOUSE married John H. LEIGH on September 17, 1857.

Alice A. HOWARD married Orren WILLIAMS on March 8, 1859.

Hattie E. HOWARD married Whitmel P. LLOYD on January 13, 1858.

Jannette HOWARD married Bynum COOPER on April 29, 1858.

Martha L. HOWARD married L. D. PENDER on October 20, 1852.

Mary HOWARD married Horace BARFIELD on February 5, 1857.

Prudence HOWARD married William KING on August 9, 1827.

Sally HOWARD married Arthur HYMAN on February 27, 1831.

Sarah E. HOWARD married Robert H. LEWIS on November 1, 1854.

Sydney HOWARD married James LAWRENCE on May 23, 1843.

Susan HOWARD married Pollard EDMONDSON on October 3, 1839.

Jane E. HOWELL married William J. EDWARDS on January 11, 1857.

Mary L. HOWELL married Dr. William E. BELLAMY on March 12, 1857.

Nancy HOWELL married David STRICKLAND on January 22, 1829.

Wealthy Ann HOWELL married James S. LONG on October 8, 1839.

Virginia HOWERTON married William BURNETT on September 21, 1837.

Anna I. HOWZE married Elias BRYAN on February 1, 1836.

Martha HUNTER married John W. WHITE on March 1, 1860.

Mrs. Jeanette HURSEY married Joseph C. STEWART on January 14, 1850.

Annie E. HYMAN married John S. DANCY on November 11, 1858.

Ellen HYMAN married William R. BROWN on December 7, 1835.

Lucy A. HYMAN married William D. GURGANUS on August 17, 1859.

Mrs. Margaret HYMAN married Col. Joshua PENDER on November 29, 1838.

Margaret E. HYMAN married William W. SHERROD on November 18, 1858.

Marina HYMAN married Seth EVANS on January 19, 1836.

Mary HYMAN married Lewis PENDER on October 3, 1839.

Mattie S. HYMAN married Capt. Frederick PHILIPS on January 27, 1864.

Nancy HYMAN married Henry WHEATLEY on March 13, 1831.

Penina HYMAN married Thomas W. RASCOE about December 1832.

Winnefred HYMAN married Alford ANDREWS on March 12, 1829.

Zilpha HYMAN married Peyton T. BOYETT on December 26, 1830.

Mrs. C. L. IRWIN married John H. WILLIAMS on July 2, 1853.

Elizabeth H. IRVIN married William B. CARR on June 10, 1856.

Elizabeth IRWIN married Arthur ARRINGTON on December 7, 1830.

Mary IVEY married John GARY on July 29, 1828.

Mrs. Sarah JAMES married Franklin HATHAWAY on May 16, 1848.

Janett JEFFRIES married Robert H. AUSTIN on January 29, 1840.

Mrs._____ JENKINS married Daniel HOPKINS on December 28, 1827.

Elizabeth JENKINS married Andrew J. COTTEN on August 12, 1856.

Louisa JENKINS married Richard M. GARRETT on November 20, 1852.

Mary JENKINS married Churchwell KILLEBREW on January 7, 1840.

Mary Eliza JENKINS married William F. BATTLY on July 17, 1839.

Mary P. JENKINS married Hugh BRYAN on September 5, 1848.

Pernetti JENKINS married Charles E. NEAL on May 11, 1852.

Sally JENKINS married Gilbert VALENTINE about October 1828.

Mrs. Maria M. JEWETT married Elder C. B. HASSELL on March 20, 1849.

Martha JIGGETTS married Joseph John SAVAGE on November 21, 1839.

Elizabeth JOHNSON married Beverly T. PITTMAN on January 25, 1859.

Elmirah JOHNSON married Richard W. RIVES on March 24, 1852.

Jane F. JOHNSON married James D. SAVAGE on October 6, 1853.

Laura JOHNSON married Lafayette LEGGETT on March 17, 1859.

Lucy JOHNSON married Rev. William F. GRAY on October 5, 1858.

Nancy JOHNSON married John L. COTTEN on January 4, 1838.

Sally Ann JOHNSON married T. R. CHERRY on November 1, 1853.

Eliza M. JOHNSTON married James V. ALLEN on May 6, 1829.

Margaret E. JOHNSTON married Robert R. BRIDGERS on December 11, 1849.

Martha C. JOHNSTON married Capt. D. D. BRYAN on September 18, 1856.

Mary JOHNSTON married William C. R. SUMMERRELL on February 19, 1835.

Mrs. Mary JOHNSTON married Henry FREEAR on March 5, 1829.

Mary C. JOHNSTON married David PENDER on July 27, 1859.

Sarah F. JOHNSTON married Battle BRYAN on October 16, 1856.

Catherine JONES married James H. DOZIER on January 24, 1855.

Charlotte JONES married Nelson TAYLOR on March 3, 1830.

Eliza JONES married Joseph J. FREEMAN on February 5, 1839.

Elizabeth JONES married Elisha CAIN on November 1, 1838.

Evelina JONES married Benjamin C. MAYO on January 18, 1844.

Margaret Elizabeth JONES married William Dancy WILLIAMS on October 12, 1854.

Sallie JONES married Gen. Joseph B. LITTLEJOHN on October 13, 1852.

Sally JONES married Richard BELL on August 18, 1836.

Sarah Caroline JONES married Benoni M. WILKINSON on February 18, 1840.

Ann Eliza JOINER married Andrew Jackson PENDER on March 4, 1841.

Marny JOINER married Hugh P. HARPER on August 19, 1835.

Rhoda JOINER married Moses DAUGHTRIDGE on or soon after January 4, 1844.

Tassey Ann Sena JOINER married Alfred TURNER on or soon after March 23, 1844.

Claudia JORDAN married Louis HILLIARD on June 6, 1860.

Margaret E. JORDAN married Churchill PERKINS on October 13, 1830.

Harriet JOSEY married Henry GUNTER on January 8, 1828.

Mrs. Martha JOSEY married William JOSEY on October 30, 1827.

Alice B. JOYNER married Joshua WATSON on September 19, 1826.

Charity A. JOYNER married Henry BURGES on March 18, 1834.

Louisa JOYNER married Henry THOMPSON on March 30, 1852.

Lucy JOYNER married Henry A. WHITEHEAD on December 8, 1836.

Martha JOYNER married John KING about September 1855.

Mary JOYNER married William H. DAY on December 24, 1833.

W. E. KEARNEY married Elias CARR on May 24, 1859.

Patsey KELLY married Amos MAYO on December 19, 1833.

_____ KERNER married Jonathan TOOTLE on January 29, 1829.

James Murphy KILLEBREW married Richard A. SAVAGE on May 18, 1848.

Eliza KING married Benjamin PORTER on January 17, 1833.

Emma L. KING married William LAWRENCE on April 5, 1859.

Martha KING married Thomas BENSON on May 24, 1832.

Mary Frances KING married William B. FIELDS on June 5, 1855.

Nannie R. KING married John M. BOND on December 29, 1857.

Penelope KING married John E. TURNER on December 1, 1852.

Sally Ann KING married Elisha CROMWELL on December 8, 1842.

Sarah B. KING married James B. WOODARD on April 7, 1841.

Drucilla L. KNIGHT married Simmons B. STATON on July 2, 1835.

Elizabeth S. KNIGHT married Alexander D. TUMBRO on September 1, 1859.

Mrs. Emeliza KNIGHT married William BRASWELL on December 10, 1856.

Harriet KNIGHT married Frederick LITTLE on May 27, 1830.

Louisa KNIGHT married William Almarine MABRY on October 20, 1847.

Mrs. Louisiana KNIGHT married Harmon H. BURKE on May 16, 1841.

Martha Ann KNIGHT married William H. PITTMAN on August 24, 1841.

Nancy KNIGHT married Kinchen MAYO on August 24, 1826.

Sally KNIGHT married Francis Henry KNIGHT on September 4, 1834.

Sally Ann KNIGHT married Dr. Franklin G. PITT on October 9, 1849.

Susan KNIGHT married James J. GARRETT on February 11, 1830.

Susan E. KNIGHT married Dr. F. G. PITT on November 4, 1855.

William Ann KNIGHT married William L. DOZIER on August 6, 1850.

Lucretia LAND married David LANE on November 24, 1844.

Caroline LANDING married Richard RICHARDSON on December 24, 1858.

Ann LANE married Kenneth THIGPEN on July 11, 1849.

Cherry LANGLEY married Joshua WILLIAMS on June 23, 1829.

Eliza LANHAM married Samuel TUNE on March 23, 1827.

Ann Blount LAWRENCE married William H. POWELL on November 24, 1852.

Ann Eliza LAWRENCE married James R. JEFFREYS on January 22, 1850.

Ann N. LAWRENCE married Jesse H. MOORING on January 4, 1827.

Catharine R. LAWRENCE married William NICKELS on January 29, 1829.

Elizabeth LAWRENCE married Redding LAWRENCE on June 3, 1841.

Elizabeth A. LAWRENCE married Richard T. HOSKINS on October 6, 1846.

Harriet J. LAWRENCE married Rev. Thomas LANSDELL on November 21, 1855.

Louisiana LAWRENCE married Charles C. KNIGHT on December 22, 1828.

Lucinda LAWRENCE married Joshua LAWRENCE on November 21, 1832.

Lucy LAWRENCE married Dr. W. A. DUGGAN on June 18, 1861.

Lucy B. LAWRENCE married Dr. Baker W. MABREY on October 7, 1856.

Margaret L. LAWRENCE married James W. WALLER on May 27, 1859.

Maria T. LAWRENCE married John Haywood PARKER on April 14, 1836.

Martha Olivia LAWRENCE married Rev. Aaron JONES on December 18, 1850.

Mary Amelia Ann LAWRENCE married Duke William HORNE on September 29, 1829.

Mary Louisa LAWRENCE married James LONG on January 21, 1836.

Nancy LAWRENCE married John GARRETT on January 12, 1854.

Pattie LAWRENCE married Joseph W. WIMBERLY on December 1, 1859.

Pheribee LAWRENCE married James SAVAGE on July 18, 1844.

Mary T. LEA married Dr. Richard W. GARRETT on May 21, 1833.

Elizabeth LEE married Etheldred RUFFIN on October 13, 1858.

Lizzie LEE married Capt. J. A. FUQUA on January 27, 1863.

Myra E. LEE married Charles N. CIVALIER on August 23, 1864.

Patsey LEE married Jacob TURNER about March of 1844.

Mrs. Temperance LEE married Joseph PIPPEN on February 15, 1827.

Isabel LEGGETT married Burton WHITE on January 9, 1849.

Jane Elizabeth LEGGETT married John STUBBS on March 16, 1856.

Louisa LEGGETT married Willie WARD on March 8, 1837.

Mahala LEGGETT married Luke WARD on June 17, 1834.

Temperance LEGGETT married William HARRELL on February 16, 1845.

Emma LEWIS married Rev. John F. SPEIGHT on September 29, 1840.

Harriet LEWIS married Thomas WILLIAMS on April 22, 1827.

Mary LEWIS married Edward KING, Jr., on December 9, 1828.

Pensey LEWIS married Kindred KING on February 28, 1828.

Priscilla LEWIS married Uriah W. SKINNER on April 26, 1829.

Ann LITTLE married Littleberry THIGPEN on August 2, 1827.

Delia Ann LITTLE married Benjamin F. EBORN on July 13, 1858.

Fannie O. LITTLE married I. F. BATTS on February 2, 1864.

Felicia LITTLE married Gray L. HARGROVE on January 27, 1859.

Margaret A. LITTLE married Eli WARREN on January 27, 1858.

Martha LITTLE married Capt. Gray COBB on July 16, 1856.

Martha LITTLE married Richard A. SAVAGE on November 10, 1853.

Mrs. Maria A. LLOYD married A. Sidney ROBERTSON on May 4, 1845.
Margaret L. H. LOCKE married Robert W. MAYO on February 6, 1855.
Henrietta LONG married Bythal HOWELL on January 10, 1833.
Louisa LONG married Reading S. BLOUNT on October 29, 1828.
Tabitha LONG married Lemuel SAVAGE on January 10, 1833.
Susan Ann LUNDY married John M. DICKIN on September 19, 1839.
Hester Ann LYNCH married Thomas H. CUTCHINS on August 18, 1836.
Mrs. Nancy LYNCH married Willie BRADLEY on January 22, 1828.
Delphia LYON married James C. WHITAKER on October 13, 1827.

Mrs. S. L. MABREY married Richard A. SAVAGE on March 6, 1860.
Sue F. MABREY married James Spencer PIPPEN on February 26, 1861.
Rebecca MABRY married William CLOMAN on November 20, 1851.
Pauline D. MACNAIR married O. W. TELFAIR on March 23, 1853.
Sarah MACNAIR married Peter E. HINES on February 17, 1834.
Susan M. MACNAIR married William TANNAHILL on January 4, 1832.
Margaret MADDERA married John ADKINS on December 19, 1837.
Sarah Ann MADDREY married Silas M. PIPPEN on July 11, 1860.
Martha F. MALLORY married Stephen W. SOUTHALL on January 9, 1861.
Joana MANER married Arthur BARNES on February 26, 1860.
Penelope Caroline MANER married John F. TAYLOR on April 12, 1855.
Mary MANGUM married Thomas WHITEHEAD on August __, 1831.
Cora MANLY married Gen. G. E. B. SINGLETARY on October 28, 1850.
Martha MANNING married Pollard EDMONDSON on January 8, 1845.
Esther MARINER married Capt. Jesse COOPER on March 3, 1831.
Frances Penelope MARTIN married William HOWARD on October 4, 1855.
Elizabeth MASON married Joseph John B. PENDER on June 29, 1836.
Caroline MATHEWSON married John WILLIAMS on May 26, 1829.
Elizabeth MATTHEWS married Isaac B. PALAMOUNTAIN on July 30, 1854.
Abbe MATTHEWSON married Peter P. LAWRENCE on December 23, 1838.
Emily MATTHEWSON married Simmons B. PARKER on June 28, 1838.
Mrs. Harriet MAY married John JOINER on May 14, 1835.
Hattie D. MAY married Dr. S. G. BENJAMIN on December 10, 1857.
Louisa MAY married Gen. Jesse SPEIGHT on May 3, 1827.
Mary MAY married Peter E. HINES on February 18, 1836.
Pattie MAY married Frank PARROTT about October 1858.
Penina MAY married Thomas B. DUPREE on February 15, 1842.
Catharine MAYO married Francis P. REDMOND on November 25, 1834.
Harriet MAYO married Joshua L. LAWRENCE on September 28, 1836.
Louisa MAYO married Arthur COTTEN on May 10, 1827.
Lydia Ann MAYO married Joshua HICKS on January 25, 1838.
Marian MAYO married John LONG on March 29, 1836.
Martha E. MAYO married Arthur MOORING on September 5, 1837.
Mary E. H. MAYO married Robert BELCHER on December 21, 1853.
Sally MAYO married Lacy ALFORD on February 4, 1838.
Mary B. MCCOTTOR married Rev. Thomas R. OWEN on October 8, 1839.
Elizabeth MCDOWELL married John W. KNIGHT on December 14, 1847.
Ann MCKAY married Dr. Henry DOCKERY about November 1830.

Charity MCKINNEY married Charles EDWARDS on May 20, 1832.

Mrs. Mary Masos MCMASTER married Gen. Wyatt MOYE on September 16, 1858.

Rosina MCWILLIAMS married James MARKS on September 6, 1835.

Lucy MEDFORD married Johnson TAYLOR on September 22, 1831.

Sarah MEDFORD married Imri BLAND on January 21, 1836.

Azula MEHEGAN married Thomas NORFLEET on September 1, 1858.

Elizabeth MERCER married Lawrence HORNE on November 6, 1832.

Henrietta MERCER married Dr. Joseph J. GARRETT on September 15, 1851.

Malvina MERCER married William H. HINES on October 1, 1839.

Martha MERCER married John O. OATES on July 20, 1852.

Nancy MERCER married Dr. Joseph GARRETT on May 13, 1840.

Mary MERRIT married Brig. Gen. John WAYNES on April 15, 1828.

Mary L. MERRITT married William H. RANDOLPH on December 31, 1832.

Sarah Susan Elizabeth MILLS married Sennor Don Alonzo Edgar HOWARD on February 25, 1853.

Margaret MITCHELL married John DAY on February 14, 1832.

Mrs. Nancy MITCHELL married Capt. Willis WILLCOX on May 26, 1829.

Elizabeth MIZELL married Napoleon B. MARRINER on June 5, 1838.

Maria Ann MONK married John H. PURRINGTON, Jr., on November 10, 1828.

Elizabeth MOORE married Capt. William BRINKLEY on May 1, 1827.

Elizabeth MOORE married Ransom ETHERAGE on December 16, 1846.

Sally Ann MOORE married Green TEAT on May 10, 1846.

Sarah MOORE married Robert HOWARD on November 21, 1857.

Elizabeth MOORING married Samuel S. WHITLEY on November 3, 1831.

Harriet Louisa MOORING married Richard EVANS on April 2, 1839.

Jane MOORING married Thomas TAYLOR on November 14, 1844.

Catherine MORGAN married Isaac BRINN on July 24, 1855.

Emma MORRISS married Jacob SESSOMS on August 8, 1830.

Sarah MOSELY married Mark KELLY about September 1859.

Dicey MOYE married Allen NETTLES on January 28, 1834.

E. A. MOYE married Dr. D. G. W. WARD on June 7, 1859.

Elizabeth MOYE married Willis DUPREE about March 1845.

Martha C. MOYE married William F. DANCY on May 7, 1850.

Elizabeth MUSGRAVE married Dr. Jethro MURPHY on April 27, 1849.

Mrs. Mary Ann MYRICK married James MORECOCK on June 26, 1828.

Elizabeth A. NANCE married James TOMLINSON on March 25, 1824.

Charlotte NEAL married William COKER on June 22, 1837.

Adeline NELMES married Lt. John G. HARVEY on November 3, 1831.

Aneliza Drupeny NELSON married Elihu BRILEY on December 3, 1848.

Cinderilla NELSON married William R. LEGGETT on January 11, 1844.

Martha Ann NELSON married John FRIZZLE on March 6, 1839.

Russia Ann NETTLE married Robert DAVIS on January 13, 1841.

Elizabeth NETTLES married John GARRETT on April 14, 1836.

Disha NEWTON married Lafayette DUPREE on March 14, 1839.

Eliza NICHOLSON married Samuel ARRINGTON on December 19, 1826.

Martha Ann NICHOLSON married Maj. Jordan WALKER on December 6, 1827.

Martha C. P. NOBLES married William WADFORD on May 20, 1857.

Mary Biddle NORCOTT married Henry R. BRYAN on November 12, 1859.
Antoinette E. NORFLEET married David J. MILLIKEN on July 7, 1829.
Emily NORFLEET married Henry JOHNSTON on January 12, 1830.
Margaret NORFLEET married Jesse MERCER on June 19, 1844.
Polly NORMAN married Lewis BOND on June 20, 1833.
Mary Ann OBERRY married William A. MOORE on November 11, 1858.
Mrs. Mary T. OSBORN married Russell KINGSBURY on October 29, 1827.
Frances OUTLAW married James H. HARTMUS on January 19, 1830.
Mary Jane OUTTEN married Dr. Thomas N. MERCER on June 3, 1844.

Susan PAGE married Orange G. JONES on April 3, 1849.
Emily PALAMOUNTAIN married Charles E. BENNETT on April 26, 1860.
Mrs. James A. PARKER married Newsom ALSOBROOK on June 20, 1855.
Amanda M. PARKER married James DORTCH on December 21, 1837.
Ann PARKER married John EDMONSTON on December 4, 1828.
Canzady PARKER married Elijah CUTCHIN on December 24, 1848.
Caroline C. S. PARKER married John L. HARGRAVE on February 22, 1837.
Elizabeth PARKER married Rev. Joseph B. CHESHIRE on February 8, 1843.
Elvira PARKER married Green OBERRY on March 4, 1852.
Mrs. Emily A. PARKER married William F. MERCER on October 12, 1852.
Margaret H. PARKER married Amos J. BATTLE on January 7, 1830.
Martha A. PARKER married G. Lawrence WINBURN on January 15, 1852.
Martha Frances PARKER married Jacob R. POPE on August 8, 1844.
Mary Eliza PARKER married Jesse HEDGEPETH on January 3, 1849.
Mary W. PARKER married Franklin HARGRAVE on February 24, 1841.
Virginia Ann PARKER married Thomas MORRIS on August 2, 1855.
Mrs. Charlotte PATTERSON married Elijah ELLIOTT on August 15, 1847.
Eliza PATTERSON married Lewis ETHERIDGE on December 24, 1834.
Sallie Martin PEACOCK married William ELLIS on December 29, 1853.
Margaret PEARCE married Richard R. RICHARDS on January 17, 1828.
Melissa PEARCE married Enoch KING on January 13, 1827.
Mrs. Elizabeth A. PEEBLES married John W. LIPSCOMBE on March 14, 1858.
Louisa PEEBLES married James L. BATTLE on November 26, 1856.
Martha PEEBLES married E. G. WORSLEY on January 10, 1859.
Susan PEEBLES married Cullen POWELL on February 28, 1828.
V. L. PEEBLES married M. L. VENABLE on June 9, 1863.
Rosa PELTIER married John M. STANDIN on January 25, 1829.
Amarilla James PENDER married Robert H. PENDER on October 31, 1843.
Julia PENDER married Thomas GATLIN on June 18, 1829.
Louisiana PENDER married Spencer L. HART on January 18, 1829.
Lucinda PENDER married Dr. Pheasanton S. SUGG on January 9, 1827.
Lucinda R. PENDER married Conway W. BURTON on October 10, 1855.
Mary PENDER married Timothy W. WARD on March 22, 1859.
Mary PENDER married Isaac W. RICKS on December 26, 1849.
Mary P. PENDER married Armistead M. WARD on May 27, 1857.
Mittie PENDER married Lt. Col. W. G. LEWIS on March 15, 1864.
William Ann PENDER married William T. GRAY on April 11, 1857.
Caroline PETWAY married W. A. J. WHITEHEAD on January 15, 1850.

Margaret PETWAY married David B. BELL on October 12, 1848.

Eliza J. PHILIPS married John PARKER on October 15, 1851.

Sarah Tartt PHILIPS married Col Francis M. PARKER on December 17, 1851.

Sarah L. PHILIPS married Norman CROFTON on September 1, 1846.

Susan S. PHILIPS married John J. BATTLE on February 19, 1861.

Emily E. PHILPOTT married Alexander S. WHITLEY on January 14, 1836.

Maniza PHILLPOT married John O'CAIN, Jr., on November 30, 1830.

Bethia PIPPEN married Lunsford BROWN on March 6, 1834.

Catharine E. PIPPEN married Harman WARD on January 9, 1834.

Elizabeth PIPPEN married David COBB on March 28, 1850.

Martha PIPPEN married Peter E. KNIGHT on January 5, 1853.

Nancy Jane PIPPEN married James Burt STATON on February 14, 1854.

Gatsey A. PITT married James THIGPEN on August 12, 1851.

Mary Ann PITT married Jarrett WHITE on February 27, 1855.

Rebecca S. PITT married Lewis BELCHER about August 1843.

Adeline PITTMAN married Jacob HIGGS on May 5, 1831.

Caroline G. PITTMAN married Elisha PITTMAN on December 16, 1830.

Eliza PITTMAN married Jesse POWELL on December 21, 1837.

Lucinda PITTMAN married William WOMACK on September 24, 1840.

Mrs. Lucy PITTMAN married Benjamin B. BATTS on November 9, 1848.

Mary PITTMAN married Jesse FLEMING on October 19, 1841.

Mary PITTMAN married Dr. N. J. PITTMAN on April 29, 1858.

Mary Elizabeth PITTMAN married William T. DORTCH on March 17, 1846.

Mary Frances W. PITTMAN married Thomas L. B. GREGORY on October 7, 1828.

Penelope C. PITTMAN married Bennett T. LYON on May 12, 1836.

Rosa A. PITTMAN married Thomas N. GAUTIER on June 24, 1852.

Sarah PITTMAN married Hezekiah L. KIRTLAND on April 20, 1832.

Rebecca PITTS married John TATE on June 21, 1827.

Ann L. POPE married Rev. Mark BENNETT on June 30, 1855.

Betsey POPE married Jonathan LEE on November 25, 1841.

Lucretia POPE married Rev. Philemon BENNETT on April 5, 1837.

Martha Carter POPE married John W. EARLS on August 11, 1846.

Mary POPE married Joseph HIGGS on February 5, 1828.

Martha PORTER married Henry HYMAN on February 27, 1834.

Nancy PORTER married Asa EDMONDSON on or after October 30, 1832.

Rosela POSSUM married John FOX about August of 1837.

Elizabeth POWELL married Benjamin BURNETT on October 11, 1849.

Elizabeth POWELL married Lawrence PENDER on December 23, 1845.

Elizabeth R. POWELL married Josephus D. M. LAWRENCE on January 6, 1831.

Julia Ann POWELL married Abner J. PERRY on January 6, 1831.

Margaret Ann POWELL married Robert WIMBERLY on May 22, 1828.

Mary H. POWELL married William M. PIPPEN on March 21, 1855.

Sarah R. POWELL married Dr. William S. BAKER on July 9, 1848.

Caroline PPICE married Richard F. J. H. WILLIAMS on June 25, 1853.

Mrs. Celia PRICE married Edward C. PARKER on September 12, 1837.

P. E. PRICE married Richard H. GATLIN on July 19, 1859.

Sarah Jane PRICE married William C. TREVATHAN on May 11, 1854.

Annis PRIDGEN married John R. PITTMAN on or after December 31, 1843.

Gatsey PROCTOR married Warren PITTMAN on March 10, 1853.

Kitturah PROCTOR married Phesanton S. HICKS on December 25, 1856.

Mary PROCTOR married Patrick TAYLOR on May 18, 1848.

Lyde PROUDFIT married B. B. BARNES on September 9, 1858.

Harriet Eliza PUGH married Jordan C. WRIGHT on July 17, 1832.

Mrs. Janet Louisa PUGH married Dr. P. P. CLEMENTS on October 25, 1842.

Maria PUGH married Joseph R. LLOYD on July 19, 1827.

Mary L. PURRINGTON married Britton DUKE on May 28, 1829.

Ann M. RAGSDALE married Rev. William MCKINNIE on March 25, 1852.

Fanny A. C. RANDOLPH married Francis R. ELY on April 9, 1835.

Mrs. Mary T. RAWLS married B. F. FOSTER on February 24, 1850.

Polly RAWLS married James PENDER on December 24, 1834.

Ann Eliza RAYNER married Elisha HARRELL on August 1, 1854.

Eunice READ married Micajah T. PURNELL on December 26, 1827.

Letitia READ married Benjamin JOHNSON on February 11, 1827.

Lydia M. READ married Jos. L. SIMMONS on November 11, 1828.

Alicia A. REDMOND married Nathaniel M. TERRELL on December 26, 1832.

Martha REED married Thomas H. HAWKINS on May 10, 1831.

Elvira P. REID married Col. A. K. BARLOW on May 11, 1851.

Kate RHODES married Ivey F. LEWIS on April 15, 1857.

Milley RICHARDSON married Thomas HADLEY on May 16, 1824.

Eliza Ann RICKS married Dr. Reuben H. JACKSON on June 24, 1833.

Temperance RICKS married Micajah JACKSON on January 22, 1828.

Sally Ann ROBASON married William DANIEL on May 31, 1832.

Mary ROBBINS married William ADAMS, Sr., about January 1839.

Sarah ROBBINS married William D. THORNE on October 15, 1846.

Ann ROBERTSON married William WATTS on March 30, 1854.

Rebecca ROBERTSON married Henry WEST on January 28, 1830.

Catharine ROGERS married Robert SHORT on April 18, 1827.

Edith ROGERS married Thomas C. HUSSEY on March 24: 1857.

Mrs. Elizabeth ROGERS married John LANG on November 19, 1826.

Eleanor P. ROSS married John P. CHESSON on May 1, 1839.

Margaret ROSS married Benjamin J. SPRUILL on December 14, 1830.

Mrs. Emeliza ROUNTREE married Thomas HURSEY on July 8, 1849.

Harriet S. ROUNTREE married Ira Gray ELLIS on February 2, 1848.

Margaret ROUNTREE married William MURRAY on October 18, 1854.

Margaret RUFFIN married John R. BARNES on February 13, 1831.

Mrs. Martha RUFFIN married Col. Caleb LEONARD on May 3, 1829.

Martha J. RUFFIN married William H. RUFFIN on December 18, 1856.

Mary RUFFIN married James HILLIARD on February 10, 1835.

Mrs. Catharine RUTH married Col. David WILLIAMS on February 1, 1831.

Margaret RUTH married David BULLUCK on December 15, 1841.

Emily RYAN married David OUTLAW on June 7, 1837.

Harriet SANBORN married John DAFFIN on January 15, 1853.

Sarah SASNETT married Henry W. GARRETT on October 26, 1826.

Delha SAVAGE married Erastus CHERRY on February 24, 1859.

Emily SAVAGE married John L. COTTEN on February 11, 1836.

Frances SAVAGE married William R. CHERRY on April 22, 1857.

Lucy SAVAGE married Henry BRYAN on December 12, 1844.

Margaret SAVAGE married Dr. Reuben COBB on January 17, 1861.

Sarah Ann SAVAGE married William A. JONES on March 16. 1854.

Susan E. SAVAGE married Dr. Peyton H. MAYO on June 28, 1860.

Willie Ann SAVAGE married Willie J. HIGGS on February 5, 1861.

Gatsey SCARBOROUGH married Hugh HARPER. Jr., on April 17, 1828.

Frances E. SELBY married George F. GORHAM on April 4. 1839.

Laura Jane SELBY married William WILLIAMS on September 13, 1849.

Susan Z. SELBY married Thomas A. GORHAM on January 28. 1844.

Emiliza SESSUMS married Asberry HILL on August 2, 1860.

William Delha SESSUMS married Richard LODGE on March 17, 1857.

Mahala F. SHARPE married Elias BARNES on March 16. 1830.

Mrs. Mary A. S. SHARPE married Wright BARNES on February 13, 1844.

Mrs. Nancy SHARPE married George C. SUGG on June 10, 1851.

Zylphia SHARPE married George BARNES on May 10, 1851.

Elizabeth SHAW married Samuel CARRAWAY on September 27. 1852.

Maria SHELTON married John MAYO. Jr., on August 3, 1834.

Martha SHELTON married Jonas G. COBB on December 19. 1849.

Mary Frances SHEPPERD married Lt. William Dorsey PENDER on March 3, 1859.

M. G. M. A. S. M. L. SHERRARD married Frederick MAYO on February 27, 1828.

Jane SHERROD married Epenetus CROMWELL on December 12. 1839.

Lydia E. SHERROD married Benjamin L. TAYLOR on September 26, 1833.

Mary SHERROD married Thomas D. LAWRENCE on October 15, 1851.

Parthena SHERROD married Isaac B. BRADY on November 21. 1833.

Peninah SHIRLEY married David BARLOW on January 30, 1834.

Hannah SHORT married Joseph ROGERS on April 8. 1827.

Julia SHURLEY married William S. BAKER on January 11, 1831.

Margaret SHURLEY married Jesse B. HYATT on April 15. 1847.

Martha E. SHURLEY married Henry BELCHER on April 18, 1844.

Mary Eliza SHURLEY married Lewis DUPREE on June 9. 1846.

Lucy SILLS married Solomon D. SESSUMS on December 13, 1842.

Mary SIMMONS married Peter NIXON on August 25, 1839.

Mary Ann SIMMONS married Maj. Lunsford W. SCOTT on February 7, 1828.

Maria SIMMS married Adam HEATH on February 14. 1854.

Sarah Eliza SIMMS married Bennett BUNN. Jr., on August 8, 1837.

Charlotte SKINNER married Joseph FELTON on April 21, 1859.

Elizabeth SKINNER married Enos WOMBLE on August 30, 1837.

Mrs. Elizabeth SKINNER married Micajah PETWAY about January of 1828.

Mary Ann SLADE married Dr. Thomas DAVIS on September 4, 1832.

Eliza A. P. SLEDGE married Thomas J. LEMAY on May 14, 1828.

Elizabeth SLEDGE married Lemuel B. BENNETT on January 21, 1827.

Ann SMITH married Willie EDMONDSON on December 20, 1853.

Anna N. B. SMITH married William FENNER on October 28. 1851.

Eva Sallie SMITH married Robert GREENE on April 18. 1860.

Louisa SMITH married Caleb SAVIDGE on December 4, 1827.

Margaret SMITH married Charles LEWIS on November 1. 1838.

Mary A. H. SMITH married Dr. William A. BERNARD on August 17, 1859.

Mourning SMITH married James JACKSON on or not long after December 18, 1843.

Mrs. Pamelia SMITH married Dr. Richard BELL on January 25. 1832.

Deborah SMITHWICK married Joseph ROBERTSON on February 14, 1832.

E. B. SMITHWICK married James G. RAYNER on August 20. 1832.

Caroline SNEAD married Richard HINES on December 18, 1834.

Mrs. Diana SNEADER married Aquilla WOMBLE on June 24, 1827.

Julia A. E. SNEADER married James WILKINSON on June 26, 1844.

Emma J. SNOW married Peter R. HINES on March 22. 1842.

Mrs. Gracy SOREY married Elder John W. PURVIS on December 9, 1858.

Polly SOREY married James VICK on April 14, 1842.

Temperance SORREL married Marshall SMITH on April 1, 1832.

Susan SORSBY married Joshua JONES on May 29, 1827.

Elizabeth Ann SPARKS married James M. BREWER on December 9. 1847.

Alice SPEIGHT married Lewis MUSGRAVE on May 15. 1827.

Mrs. Louisa SPEIGHT married Gen. Wyatt MOYE in September of 1849.

Temperance SPEIGHT married William LITTLE on February 27, 1828.

Mary SPIVEY married Nathan PITT on December 11, 1845.

Margaret E. STALLINGS married Josiah EDMONDSON on August 23, 1860.

Mary Eliza STALLINGS married Kindred HARPER on May 6, 1852.

Almira STANCILL married Charles H. JENKINS on January 16, 1855.

Louisa STANSELL married Edwin BROWN on February 25, 1830.

Mary STANSELL married Jarrett HOPKINS on February 2, 1832.

Huldah Virginia STANTON married William John STATON on March 18, 1858.

Rebecca STANTON married Benjamin F. STANTON on November 7, 1826.

Alavana STATON married Henry S. CLARK on May 20, 1835.

Frances STATON married Charles MABRY on November 2. 1826.

Grace STATON married Lemuel LAWRENCE on October 3. 1826.

Hannah STATON married Frederick H. JENKINS on September 13, 1855.

Harriet STATON married Robert S. BEST on May 20, 1841.

Mary STATON married Calvin JONES on October 13, 1842.

Mary L. STATON married Mayo WORSLEY on February 22, 1842.

Nancy STATON married James WHITEHURST on February 17, 1842.

Phenetta STATON married Joseph HIGGS on March 24, 1835.

Virginia L. STATON married William A. JONES on May 31. 1855.

Martha C. STEPTOE married Eli C. BRIGGS on November 26. 1856.

Virginia A. STEPTOE married Jefferson M. LOVEJOY on June 5, 1838.

Sarah J. STEVENS married A. G. RUFFIN on September 1, 1859.

Ann STEWART married Nathan WOOTTEN on April 15, 1828.

Catharine STILMAN married James M. REDMOND on February 7, 1839.

Fannie STITH married Alfred J. BROWN on October 11. 1859.

Virginia STITH married Thomas C. DAVIS on April 23. 1857.

Susan Virginia STREETER married Peyton A. ATKINSON on July 27, 1843.

Mary STRICKLAND married Jonathan DEW on October 8, 1844.

Frances B. SUGG married Arthur SMITH on December 5. 1854.

Margaret SUGG married Edward MCPHERSON on January 19. 1859.

Marv SUGG married Charles W. GARRETT on June 12. 1851.

Emilia "Milly" SUMMERLIN married Isham WHEELER on January 15, 1828.
(She appears to have married him for the <u>first</u> time on or after
September 21, 1826.)

Mary SUMNER married William E. EDWARDS on February 17. 1846.

Mary SURMONS married John JONES on November 29. 1849.

Mary W. SUTTON married Col. Isidore V. GARNIE about April of 1859.

Tabitha SWANNER married Jesse HARRELL on November 18. 1830.

Susan SWINSON married Christopher C. JAMES on December 1. 1859.

Emily TAFT married Dr. Addison E. RICKS on January 26, 1859.

Sarah A. TANNER married John MEARS on May 17, 1860.

Martha TARTT married John PARKER on September 23, 1829.

Mary Ann TARTT married William STEWART on October 18. 1831.

Blaney TAYLOR married G. BUNTING on December 29, 1852.

Charlotte TAYLOR married Josiah COUNCIL on November 1, 1838.

Eliza TAYLOR married Solomon BRADY on February 6, 1834.

Eliza TAYLOR married John W. POPE on January 31. 1840.

Elizabeth TAYLOR married William TAYLOR on October 4. 1836.

Evelina TAYLOR married Thomas JONES on December 6. 1832.

Isabella A. TAYLOR married Robert POTTER on April 9, 1828.

Margaret TAYLOR married Spencer S. HARRIS on May 20, 1830.

Margaret TAYLOR married John SHARPE on January 6, 1829.

Maria TAYLOR married David GWITHER on April 10. 1832.

Marina TAYLOR married Clinton JAMES on February 28 1843.

Mary TAYLOR married Josiah ELLINOR on October 20, 1841.

Mary TAYLOR married Capt. William R. SHERROD on November 18 1830.

Mary Ann TAYLOR married George DAVENPORT on March 6, 1845.

Penina TAYLOR married Amos CLARK on July 24, 1832.

Margaret TELFAIR married Henry TOOLE on October 20. 1829.

Marv E. TELFAIR married Whitmel HORNE on December 23, 1834.

Mary E. TERRELL married Lawrence S. MAYO on December 28. 1850.

Mrs. Ann Eliza THIGPEN married George ROUSE on December 18, 1855.

Elizabeth THIGPEN married Richard WARREN on October 8, 1835.

Mary THIGPEN married Allen DUPREE on August 15, 1843.

Phenetta THIGPEN married William SMITH on January 27, 1835.

Sally THIGPEN married Jesse HARRELL on March 9, 1834.

Mary A. E. THOMAS married Col. Bolin B. BARRON on July 8, 1851.

Eliza Helen THOMPSON married Joseph John WILLIAMS on April 4, 1854.

William Ann THOMPSON married William W. PUGH on August 16, 1831.

Mrs. Eliza THORNE married Dr. N. J. DRAKE about November of 1828.

Jane THORNE married W. J. BULLUCK on April 19, 1859.

Emma Eliza Jane THORP married Col. John E. LINDSEY on April 13. 1843.

Frances C. E. THURSTON married Charles N. WEBB on December 4, 1833.

Lucy THURSTON married William H. DICKEN on March 20, 1834.

Julia Ann TILLERY married Leartis MORGAN on January 1, 1829.

Elizabeth TOLER married William O. LIPSCOMBE on November 2, 1854.
Amelia M. TOOLE married John E. RIDLEY on September 15, 1829.
Ann Eliza TOOLE married William H. ROBARDS on October 11, 1827.
Caroline TOOLE married Charlton W. YELLOWLEY on February 11, 1858.
Mary Eliza TOOLE married Dr. Josiah LAWRENCE on February 20, 1833.
Mary I. TOOLE married Joseph B. LITTLEJOHN, Jr., on January 11, 1838.
Susan Irwin TOOLE married Daniel HILL on November 5, 1835.
Mary A. TREVATHAN married Frederick DOZIER on May 16, 1848.
Sarah TUCKER married John J. KILPATRICK on September 8, 1826.
Martha TUNNELL married William R. DUPREE on January 29, 1840.
Addie TURNAGE married Parrot HARDY about October of 1858.
Margaret TURNER married Moses EDWARDS on or soon after January 11, 1844.
Susan TURNER married Bennet B. BELL on October 17, 1832.
Frances TYER married Elisha CHERRY on March 2, 1837.
Lycy TYLER married John F. WARD on August 26, 1858.
Ann E. TYRRELL married Francis M. COOK on February 16, 1859.
Mrs. Esther TYSON married John ATKINSON in December of 1831.

Mrs. Frances UNDERHILL married John M. BURGIS on January 29, 1829.

Louisa VANNOORDEN married William TAFT on February 15, 1844.
Martha Jane VAUGHAN married William Ely HOWELL on September 23, 1841.
Martha Ann VERELL married John A. HARRISON on October 27, 1849.
Susan VICK married Dr. John R. MERCER on November 18, 1849.
Emily VINES married Joshua K. BULLUCK on November 19, 1839.
Martha VINES married Jacob HORN on December 18, 1828.

Anne WALLER married James BILBRY on December 5, 1830.
Amanda WARD married James GROVES on August 19, 1855.
Margaret WARD married James WEDDELL on February 26, 1835.
Mary J. WARD married Lt. Solomon M. PENDER on January 28, 1864.
Elizabeth WARREN married Richard T. PHILIPS on March 2, 1857.
Mary Ann WARREN married John C. RICKS on February 29, 1857.
Mrs. Winnifred G. WARREN married Col. Joab P. PITT on March 2, 1843.
Caroline WATSON married William BELL on May 22, 1838.
Dolly B. WATSON married Levi HOWELL on July 24, 1827.
Sarah Ann WATTS married Maurice MOORE on November 1, 1832.
Emily WEAVER married Nathan PITT on October 21, 1841.
Emily WEAVER married John SKINNER on August 22, 1860.
Amanda WEEKS married Jos. J. N. MARKS on March 30, 1842.
Lizzie Ann WEEKS married Robert H. KING on February 27, 1855.
Martha WEEKS married John H. PRICE on November 10, 1859.
Martha J. WELLS married Robert H. KING on August 31, 1859.
Mrs. Priscilla WEST married John A. BENFORD on November 30, 1830.
Sarah WHARTON married Maj. Thomas J. GREEN on March 8, 1830.
Ann Maria WHITAKER married William H. WILLS on May 13, 1835.
Martha WHITAKER married Stephen BRADLEY on May 16, 1839.
Martha B. WHITAKER married Dr. Joseph J. W. POWELL on January 7, 1845.
Sarah WHITAKER married Robert AARON on February 14, 1828.

Mary E. WHITE married Jacob H. WHITEHEAD on December 16, 1845.

Charlotte WHITEHEAD married Ephraim DICKEN about November of 1832.

Mrs. Elizabeth WHITEHEAD married Canfield HARRIS about December of 1839.

Margaret S. WHITEHEAD married Isaac L. CUSHING on February 20, 1850.

Mary E. WHITEHEAD married Heshborn BISHOP on January 7, 1858.

Nancy WHITEHEAD married Thomas GRIMMER on August 10, 1830.

Rowena WHITEHEAD married Laertes M. PITTMAN on October 13, 1859.

Mrs. Temperance WHITEHEAD married Richard ARRINGTON on May 29, 1827.

Adelia WHITFIELD married William D. TISDEL on August 21, 1832.

Fannie J. WHITFIELD married George L. WIMBERLY on October 8, 1857.

Elizabeth WHITEHURST married Elisha CARNEY on March 21, 1850.

Sarah WHITING married Thomas SHIELDS, Jr., on June 27, 1827.

Ann WIGGINS married Robert SOREY on June 18, 1849.

Rozella WIGGINS married George A. SMITH on June 10, 1856.

Susan A. WILCOX married Thomas W. WATTS on September 6, 1831.

Caroline WILDER married Rufus W. EDMONDSON on October 16, 1845.

Jane WILKINS married William BARNES on December 3, 1833.

Mary WILKINS married S. W. BRANCH on December 25, 1827.

Susan WILKINS married Joseph John PORTER on February 16, 1837.

Eliza WILKINSON married Allen MAYO on March 10, 1841.

Elizabeth WILKINSON married Thomas TOMLINSON on May 25, 1856.

Mrs. Julia WILKINSON married George W. SCAY on November 16, 1859.

Melinda WILKINSON married William L. WILKINSON on January 9, 1837.

Sally WILKINSON married Willie ATKINSON on January 6, 1829.

Susan J. WILKINSON married Amariah B. COBB on May 12, 1857.

Adeline E. WILLIAMS married Rev. N. Collin HUGHES on October 17, 1848.

Amanda WILLIAMS married Louis B. DUPREE on February 15, 1842.

Caroline WILLIAMS married Maj. Robert R. FOREMAN on June 25, 1853.

Catharine H. WILLIAMS married David G. BAKER on January 26, 1834.

Charity D. WILLIAMS married W. W. ANTHONY on December 15, 1857.

Delha WILLIAMS married Dr. F. M. GARRETT on November 27, 1855.

Elvira E. K. WILLIAMS married Henry WILLIAMS on February 26, 1840.

Emily A. WILLIAMS married Dr. Noah JOYNER on April 28, 1841.

Margaret P. WILLIAMS married Robert NORFLEET on December 19, 1849.

Maria Louisa WILLIAMS married Josiah S. PENDER on January 25, 1842.

Martha A. WILLIAMS married Wilson CREDLE on February 12, 1861.

Martha Ann WILLIAMS married James M. SPRAGGINS on January 31, 1856.

Martha Ann WILLIAMS married Charles L. VINES on July 7, 1846.

Mary WILLIAMS married David C. BELL on February 10, 1839.

Mary WILLIAMS married Edward DAVIS on October 28, 1830.

Mary Catharine WILLIAMS married Rev. C. B. JANNETT on September 5, 1850.

Mary D. B. WILLIAMS married Whitmell KEARNEY on May 14, 1840.

Mrs. Mary L. C. WILLIAMS married Rev. Robert J. CARSON on March 25, 1840.

Mary O. WILLIAMS married William M. GAY on November 9, 1852.

Mary T. WILLIAMS married Sterling H. GEE on November 6, 1828.

Mary Richard WILLIAMS married John H. DRAKE on May 27, 1828.

Penelope WILLIAMS married William SLADE on October 13, 1829.

Temperance WILLIAMS married Thomas B. THOMPSON on August 1, 1832.

Elizabeth WILLIFORD married Stephen E. JAKWAY on July 27, 1847.

Lucinda WILLIFORD married Solomon SILLS on Marcy 28, 1844.

Mary Ann WILLIFORD married Samuel MOORE on March 5, 1837.

Julia Whitman WILLIS married Dr. Barron C. WATSON on February 26, 1852.

Mrs. Eliza WILSON married Rev. David ELLIS on November 11, 1830.

Mary Jane WILSON married Richard B. BASSETT on September 17, 1862.

Catherine Elizabeth WIMBERLEY married Archibald H. ARRINGTON on March 14, 1855.

Mrs. Creecy WIMBERLEY married Edwin DOYLE on February 18, 1832.

Mary Louisa WIMBERLEY married George W. WHITFIELD on December 13, 1849.

Gracy WINDHAM married William KENNEDY on April 12, 1837.

Sarah E. WOMBLE married Henderson POLING on December 23, 1855.

Mary Jane WOODARD married William H. EDWARDS on February 25, 1858.

Penelope WOODARD married James S. WOODARD on July 12, 1858.

Caroline WORSLEY married John PEOPLES on February 18, 1851.

Lezina WORSLEY married Capt. Jesse BULLUCK on August 13, 1847.

Harriet E. WORTHINGTON married Louis B. MYERS on June 30, 1831.

Sarah C. WORTHINGTON married Walter S. HANRAHAN on November 2, 1853.

Elizabeth WRIGHT married Theophilus CRISP on April 3, 1849.

Mrs. Harriet Eliza WRIGHT married Noel THOMPSON on October 18, 1838.

William Irena Jane WYNN married Harrison EASON on November 15, 1829.

Jeanette YOUNG married Baker STATON on December 20, 1827.